INTERPRETING DEVELOPMENT

Local Histories, Local Strategies

Maxine K. Weisgrau

University Press of America, Inc.
Lanham • New York • Oxford

Copyright © 1997 by
University Press of America,® Inc.
4720 Boston Way
Lanham, Maryland 20706

12 Hid's Copse Rd.
Cummor Hill, Oxford OX2 9JJ

All rights reserved
Printed in the United States of America
British Library Cataloguing in Publication Information Available

Library of Congress Cataloging-in-Publication Data

ISBN 0-7618-0655-5 (cloth: alk. ppr.)
ISBN 0-7618-0656-3 (pbk: alk. ppr.)

∞™ The paper used in this publication meets the minimum
requirements of American National Standard for information
Sciences—Permanence of Paper for Printed Library Materials,
ANSI Z39.48—1984

*To the memory of my father,
and for my families, in all their various forms,
in America and Rajasthan.*

Contents

List of Tables and Figures

Acknowledgments

The Issues and the Settings

    Chapter 1   **Issues and Identities**   1

    Chapter 2   **Fieldwork Landscapes:
Rural, Urban, Social and Otherwise**   18

    Chapter 3   **What Are Tribals? Who Are Bhils?**   57

Nongovernmental Organizations

    Chapter 4   **Local Strategies, Local Histories**   79

    Chapter 5   **The "G" in NGO: Global to Local
Politics in Development**   102

Intersections

Chapter 6	**Household and Family: Socio-economic and Ecological Constraints**	117
Chapter 7	**Comparing Programs and Strategies**	143
Chapter 8	**Women's Programs, Women's Voices**	157
Chapter 9	**Elections, Alliances, and NGOs**	174
Chapter 10	**Perspectives on Decision Making and Hierarchy**	186
Chapter 11	**Some Conclusions**	204

Appendices 211

References 223

Index 231

Tables and Figures

Figure 1 Map 1: Rajasthan	20

Figure 2
  Map 2: Chief Topographical Features of Rajasthan
  Map 3: Udaipur District
	21

Figure 3 Illustration of Rahat (Persian Wheel) Technology	25
Figure 4 Ford Foundation Grants by Type of Organization	211
Appendix 1 List of Scheduled Tribes of Rajasthan	212
Appendix 2 Population Tables:	
Table 1 Rajasthan Population 1991	213
Table 2 Rajasthan Population by Residence and Sex 1991	213
Table 3 Udaipur District, Gogunda Tehsil Population by Residence and Sex 1991	214
Table 4 All-India Population, Literacy Rates	214
Table 5 Rajasthan Literacy Rates 1991	215
Table 6 Rajasthan Literacy Rates 1981	216
Table 7 Scheduled Tribe Population 1981 Udaipur District	217
Table 8 Scheduled Tribe Educational Levels 1981 Udaipur District	218
Table 9 Scheduled Tribe Literacy Levels 1981 Udaipur District	219
Appendix 3 Bhil Social Reform Document	220

Acknowledgments

When I stepped out of the airport into hot, muggy, pre-dawn New Delhi in June 1989, all the uncertainties and anxieties of fieldwork were suddenly upon me. But as I drove toward the city I glanced out the window and saw an enormous full moon low over the horizon. I was calmed by its perfect roundness, which I took as an auspicious sign, and thought to myself, "This is all going to work out fine." And so it did. My work, friendships and experiences in Udaipur, kept current by a constant stream of correspondence and visits, are among my most cherished experiences.

I returned to India, Udaipur and Bagdunda for four months in 1995 to update this research and pursue another project on Bhil ritual and religion. Once again I took up residence in Bagdunda, this time in the home of Prabhu-bhai, my friend and guide. On my last night there, at about four in the morning, his aged mother started stirring, as usual, before everyone else. Most of her chores had now been taken over by younger women in the household, but the patterns of a lifetime still awoke her at that pre-dawn hour. I was half asleep, half awake, and felt her pull a quilt up over my shoulders, protecting me against the morning chill. I was choked by a flow of tangled sensations, this time generated not by fear, but of love and connection and the terrible prospect of having to say good-bye, again, to these families and friends whose kindness and generosity have made the completion of this project a reality.

This book would not have been possible without the support of many people and organizations in India and in America. The American Institute of Indian Studies (AIIS) and The John D. and Catherine T. MacArthur Foundation funded different aspects of fieldwork and dissertation research on which it is largely based; in addition AIIS granted a post-doctoral research fellowship which enabled me to return to Udaipur in 1995. For this financial support I am extremely grateful.

This study is about nongovernmental organizations and their village activities. My goal is neither to evaluate nor critique the work of organizations or individuals, but to place the phenomenon of development in the context of the social and historical forces that shape it in its local, contemporary form. Throughout various stages of this project I have discussed it at great length, and reviewed various versions of this manuscript, with several of the NGO participants discussed in this book. While our perspectives have differed at times those people have been my most selfless supporters.

My dissertation (Weisgrau 1993) identified only the district in which this research was conducted. When I returned in 1995 I discussed with many of the NGO people in Udaipur my decision to drop the anthropological convention of using pseudonyms throughout, and to identify organizations and villages. My strongest encouragement for this decision came from the NGO directors themselves. I am particularly grateful to Kishore Saint for his unequivocal advice that telling the truth as I see it can only be constructive.

Over the past several years I have observed the activities of scores of NGOs in Udaipur as well as other parts of Rajasthan and other states of India, and have conducted interviews with many of the people who work with them. A good deal of these interviews were "off the record" and were agreed to on the condition that the exact names of the individuals and locations of their organizations would not be used, a condition to which I agreed. As I have stated, this book is about history and process, not about individuals or organizations. The quotations here are attributed to the management of organizations when they were speaking with me "on the record" as representing their organizations or their own opinions.

It is with enormous gratitude that I extend to friends and colleagues in Udaipur my deepest and heartfelt thanks for their cooperation and support of this work. Particular thanks to the entire staff of Sewa Mandir, and to Chandra-ji, as she is known to all, Mrs. Chandra Bhandari, Ravi Bhandari, Mr. Kakari, Neelima Khetan, Ajay Mehta, whose office door was always open, Mr. Jagat Mehta, and Adithi Mehta. My friendship with the Mehta family, and the dialogue with Ajay that continues to span two continents, has illuminated every aspect of this research.

To the entire staff of Ubeshwar Vikas Mandal, my deepest thanks, particularly to the Prabhu-lal Meghwal, Sarpanche Kesu-ji; and Gulab-bhai. And to Har-ji and his family, and to all in Solaria and Morwa. To Sudesh Saint a special thanks, for being at my side from the first day I arrived in Udaipur on my first visit in 1988. To Kishore-bhai, it is impossible to describe all I have learned from our many conversations. To Bhatia, Roma and Vibha, my deepest thanks for being guides and companions on so many of the journeys described within.

Thanks also go to my cherished friends, assistants and translators Swati Patel and Tushida Lodha, and to Dr. Raj Bhanti, and Chris Deegan and Indu Deegan. And to the families of Gogunda House, Raj Niwas, and Chowda House who always extended a welcome and an exquisite meal, and most especially to my dear friend Gayatri Singh. And to the Das and Mahajan families in New Delhi, who on a moment's notice offered the same warm hospitality as well.

To Columbia University professors Ted Riccardi, Betsy Shalley-Jensen, Myron Cohen, Ainslee Embree, and the late Libbet Crandon, thanks for the comments and suggestions on various versions of the dissertation on which this book is based. Thanks to Joan Mencher for her advice at the very inception of this project ten years ago, and her cogent comments on this manuscript. And to Morton Klass, Bill Fisher, Abraham Rosman and Paula Rubel, for their continuous support of my research and teaching. To Carol Henderson, fellow *Rajasthaniwalli*, and my classmates at Columbia, my gratitude for boundless friendship and guidance.

To the memory of Leonard Schair, who always knew this day would come, even when I wavered. And to all the Palazzos, Weisgraus, Stempas, and Weilers, who kept me close in their hearts while I was away, and welcomed me so heartily when I returned.

Sara Blackburn, Jean Scandlyn, Miriam Sarzin, and Ron Palazzo have taken extraordinary care in editing and proofreading this manuscript, for which I am extremely grateful. But for any errors or misstatements, I alone am responsible.

Chapter 1

Issues and Identities

"Rajasthan has the least number of NGOs in India;
Udaipur has the most."

The Death and Life of Development
While theorists and academics write its obituary as a moribund intellectual concept, development is still a critical point of action for its practitioners and participants (Sachs 1992:1). Whatever its history and limitations, the idea of development has been integrated into and reinterpreted in thousands upon thousands of local landscapes around the world. As a career path, an institutional setting, and the hope for something better, development is vibrant and alive. Its resuscitation is being energized in part by donor and funding agencies which have channeled vast sums of money into the local programs of non-governmental organizations (NGOs) throughout the world.

The recent emergence of NGOs as a highly significant vehicle of local development is represented by NGOs themselves and the donors who fund them as a viable locally responsive alternative to the failures of large-scale, bureaucratically driven, inflexible governmental development. But rather than solving the problems of large-scale development, this trend shifts many of the unresolved questions and contradictions of development to the level of local program. Small-scale organizations and programs do not necessarily ensure consensus or even shared perceptions of the blurry concepts of development or progress.

This book examines how multiple and dynamic interpretations of these concepts are continually being re-formed, redefined, and renegotiated in local NGO activities and how this plays out in the interaction between NGOs and villagers over a decade in a district of northern India. It is therefore not about the vast subjects of development strategy, underdevelopment, or NGOs in India. It is about a particular location, Udaipur District in the state of Rajasthan, with a particular cultural, political, and development history. What actually happens on the ground, in the villages, and with the individuals deeply involved in this interactive process is profoundly influenced by this local socio-political history.

Village development is also profoundly influenced by complex variations in human behavior. This variation is one of the key issues in the local perception of development strategy. There are no "homogeneous" groups in any of this. People who share certain group characteristics vary in as many ways as they are categorized as being alike. The rural poor may share certain residential, economic, and social characteristics when grouped in demographic statistics, but the range of their alliances, skills, personalities, family and NGO connections, personal goals, and ideas about community cross-cut and undercut any generalizations or predictions about their perceptions of poverty, betterment, or "the good life."

To grasp the complexities of ideas about local development, one must continually tack between the local and the global, as well as between the past and the present. Always in the background of local interpretation is the presence of the national and international forces that impinge on and shape local interpretation. The construction of social and cultural categories of the past, reified by the administrative institutions and documentation processes of the British colonial period, organizes the experience and its effects. This construction, too, has a historical base, which plays an important part in its contemporary manifestation. So if we are to comprehend what has brought the players to the present, it is vital to examine the historical processes and categorical constructions of the past.

"The present" is also dynamic; development history continues to be constructed and reconstructed. Since this project began as dissertation research in the mid-1980s, many changes have taken place nationally and locally. The NGO sector, and the rural communities within which they operate, are the locus of complex events and forces with a global reach. Political events throughout India affect the outcome of local village elections. National economic policy and industrial liberalization come to bear on local rural markets and agricultural household decision making.

The NGO environment in Udaipur has also evolved, changed, and grown. There is nothing static or unchanging in the NGO culture of Udaipur nor in the cultures of the villages within which it operates.

Chapter One Issues and Identities   3

There is no "frozen moment in time" within which development or NGOs or rural communities can be identified and described. For example, rural villagers who a decade ago had their first introduction to NGO workers moving into their villages now have a sophisticated view of both the potential and the limitations NGOs represent for their lives. And the NGO strategies have evolved to respond to rising and influential local demands for programs and resources as defined by the communities themselves.

Despite these changes, shifts, and constantly evolving interpretations of development and progress, the important underlying themes that this study explores retain their relevance, primary among them the necessity for including pertinent history and culture in the evolution of local development strategy. As demonstrated throughout this book, the histories of group identity, representation, interaction, and access to strategic resources in precolonial, colonial, and post-Independence Rajasthan resonate in the local NGO-driven development strategies of the 1990s.

Why Another Book on Development?

Development, in all its social, economic, political, and intellectual forms, has generated an enormous amount of literature in the past decade. A recent computerized library search yielded more than 1,700 books and journals catalogued since the late 1980s with "development" in their titles. This book focuses on a central but little-examined issue: the complexities and contradictions of how development is interpreted and perceived by all its participants in a local setting. My goal is to illustrate how local social and historical forces shape and contribute to the complexities of this process; this book is therefore a multilayered view of these dynamics, presented in the context of people's daily lives.

My intention is neither to evaluate nor critique the work of specific organizations or individuals, but to make explicit some of the contradictions and conflicts that inhabit this interactive process. The emphasis here is on the interaction; local development strategies evolve in ways often unanticipated by the participants, who are all continually reinterpreting and reshaping strategies and responses.

Nongovernmental organizations are not new; what is noteworthy is "the scale and pace with which organizations of such nature have been multiplying and expanding during the last 10-15 years" (Cernea 1988: 2). And like any other rapidly expanding industry (subsequent chapters will show why the model of an industry, rather than that of a social movement, is more appropriate to this discussion), the forms it takes in its "second generation" of maturity in the 1990s deserve a more tempered and more nuanced analysis than its rhetoric of the 1970s and 1980s suggests (Annis 1988).

What Is Development?

To adequately define the concept of development on a local level, another question must be posed: development from whose perspective? Multiple perspectives on development are expressed in this book: NGO perspectives on development and organizational strategies; the local perspectives of villagers who participate in the programs and are employees of the organizations; and the author's perspectives as an observer. None of these perspectives is immutable or unchanging; depending upon differing circumstances (sometimes natural, such as drought or floods, and some of human origins, such as political electioneering periods) different ideas about appropriate strategy come to the fore. Nor are these perspectives monolithic or homogeneous; obviously not every villager shares with his or her neighbor the same concept of what will make their lives better, nor does every social worker or NGO organizer have the same organizational, theoretical, or strategic approach.

The term *NGO* is itself a catchword in development discourse that encapsulates an enormous range of structures, strategies, and organizational sizes. It is a term used rather loosely to refer to any organization that is not a direct division of a national government. It therefore is used to refer to a wide range of international private agencies, nationally situated organizations with international scope, as well as one or two local activists who decide they are an NGO. This lack of precision in terminology has implications beyond the academic's penchant for precise categories and typologies. Some of the managers and directors of the larger or longer-established NGOs in Udaipur have expressed concerns about the lack of accountability of ad hoc organizations to the communities in which they operate, as well as the relatively informal monitoring procedures of some donor organizations.

Small local NGOs very often do not have an explicit definition of development or a theoretical perspective underlying their strategic plans. Nonetheless, the following probably would be acceptable as a starting point to most members of the Udaipur development community: "Development is commonly defined, in its most elementary form, as a process of change mediated by some form of human intervention" (Carmen 1996: 5). On the whole, local strategies in the rural-operating NGOs employ a multipronged "basic needs" approach with an implicit concept of development as a reaction to a set of perceived needs. The problems these rural communities confront, as perceived by the various local organizations (and their international donors), are: deforestation, protection of existing common natural resources, agricultural water supply, illiteracy, gender discrimination, health and sanitation issues, political marginalization, and social discrimination. In this context,

Chapter One Issues and Identities 5

development involves a complex set of programs to tackle these serious and often devastating conditions, stressing community-based initiatives, local organization building, and mobilization of the social resources of the community. (See Chapter 4.)

Villagers prioritize and define their problems rather differently. For example, their concept of their own underdevelopment is defined almost exclusively in terms of household poverty and access to water, land, and other productive resources (discussed in detail in Chapter 6). From their perspective, development means obtaining greater household income and improved water supply for agricultural production. The very term *development* is a borrowed one; the Hindi word *vikas* (development in the sense of growth or evolution) is rarely used in informal conversation in Mewari, the dialect spoken throughout the district.

I have grappled with formulating for myself a relevant meaning of development from several different perspectives. By living with it locally and talking endless hours about it in the field, development has an individual, household by household, and highly localized meaning. This meaning is sometimes difficult to reconcile with my perspective as a teacher and academic, a perspective from which development is an idea created in the global political climate of the postcolonial and postwar years of the 1950s. This concept of development and its objectives, as well as the identification of population groups as targets, beneficiaries, or recipients (now more often referred to in the development discourse as "clients") is constructed largely on Western-derived standards and definitions of economic growth and modernization. These standards were transported to, then reinterpreted by, "underdeveloped" countries--a concept itself constructed by Western categories of growth and development (Escobar 1995). Nearly half a century of policy, strategy, hopes, and failures have demonstrated that development in the form in which it was conceived as a political strategy, cloaked in the goals of economic and technological change, has failed in its goal of improving the quality of life of the world's poor.

As the 20th century, synonymous in its first half with all that was hopeful, "modern," scientific, and possible, comes to a close, development as a theoretical and academic subject is now understood to be a process by which ideas about growth and progress are invented in a particular time and place with significant political and economic, as well as cultural, repercussions. The representation of the categories of development and underdevelopment, modernity, tradition, poverty, and culture, in the current discourse, is the result of processes that originated in the political capitals of the West and were reproduced, reevaluated and reinterpreted around the world.

The role of anthropology and anthropologists in both the construction of these categories and their subsequent deconstruction, has recently emerged as an important aspect of this evolving discourse. Escobar (1991), by drawing parallels between the anthropology and development and the colonial encounter, raises significant questions about the structuring of the anthropological engagement with development, and the underlying assumptions contained within this engagement. These observations on the role of anthropology and anthropologists, in what Escobar refers to as "the development encounter," are further enriched by the on-going critique of assumptions about positivistic anthropological knowledge or authority; as well as reflexive analysis of the (oxymoronic) undertaking of "participant-observation" and other forms of information-gathering. (See Chapter 2.)

When teaching students about these issues of anthropology and development, I find myself continuously challenged to reconcile the globally oriented intellectual issues with understanding or even inquiring into local systems of knowledge. To those who are trying to use their knowledge of development theory to help formulate local strategy that will help make peoples' lives better, this effort at reconciliation takes on a critical necessity. There are obviously no simple responses to these complex issues. I nevertheless believe that anthropologists have a potential contribution to make in exploring and clarifying the complexities of local knowledge and interpretation, if for no other reason than our inquiry begins with questions about local perceptions of local problems, and requires listening to local voices responding to those questions.

The Settings and Linkages: Rural and Urban Udaipur

The city of Udaipur, the district's capital, is located in the state of Rajasthan, in northwestern India. If known at all to foreigners it is as an exotic tourist destination. The Lake Palace Hotel, a magnificent white structure that seemingly floats in the middle of articially created Lake Pichola, was constructed during the 16th century reign of Maharana Udai Singh II, and it is one of the most photographed locations on the subcontinent for both Indian and foreign commercials and feature films. It is recognizable to Western film and television watchers as the fortress of James Bond's archenemy in the film *Octopussy* (a best-selling and widely advertised video rental in Udaipur to this day), and the palace of the fictional Maharana of Ranpur in *The Jewel and the Crown*, the televised adaptation of Paul Scott's *Raj Quartet*.

This city, like the other urban centers of Rajasthan, is growing rapidly, its growth fueled in part by the area's continual appeal to both

Chapter One Issues and Identities 7

domestic and international tourists, but more significantly by the profits of local industrialization, and particularly the development of new businesses with national and international reach. Its growing "middle class" (which in India generally refers to the top 10 percent of the total population in terms of household income and lifestyle, not the majority of the population in the middle ranges of income as in many Western countries) is composed of families whose members have college and university degrees, relatively high and stable incomes, and close family ties to Europe, the United States, and Canada.

The rural agricultural communities within which NGOs operate, some of them as close as 10 kilometers from the city, are a stark contrast to this globalized urbanization. The rural poor of this area are also for the most part (but not exclusively) members of caste groups now categorized by the Indian government as Scheduled Castes (SCs) and Scheduled Tribes (STs), a reference to the Government of India's extensive benefits program for low-status caste and tribal group members. The Bhils are the largest ST group in Udaipur District.

For most SC and ST families participating in NGO programs, agriculture is the primary economic undertaking. It is marginal and often unpredictable; household income is by necessity supplemented with day labor and other forms of nonagricultural employment, as well as by perpetual debt to local moneylenders. Small plots of land dominate the now-deforested landscape, which less than a century ago was dense with trees and wild game. Tractors are rare; even if the local agriculturists could afford them, such machinery would be impractical in the small discontinuous fields. Wells are replenished by unreliable monsoons; nonelectrified Persian wheel-type irrigation systems (*rahat*) deliver water to fields through hand-dug earthen channels. Frequent monsoon failures contribute to the fragility and unpredictability of agricultural production and household income.

But the contrast in demographics and technology between rural and urban Udaipur belies the connections and linkages. Daily activities of rural villagers are linked economically, politically, and socially to the urbanized centers of the state. Villagers are deeply affected by state policy, economic liberalization, and the increased availability of imported consumer goods. And global economic forces, as well as international sources of development funding, resonate in local individual decision-making.

SC and ST residents of the rural communities of Udaipur are citizens of India and of the state of Rajasthan. As such they are voters and taxpayers of the world's largest political democracy, but they participate in it to degrees that vary depending on their gender, literacy, and social status. Nor have villagers been entirely excluded from interactions with modern institutions of the state and nation. Limited access to television and widespread and enthusiastic access to radio and newspapers keep them very well informed on local and national events. Illiteracy, particularly among the Bhils, although widespread, does not equate with lack of access to information. Newspaper stories are regularly read aloud to assembled groups of men (and occasionally older women) by those men literate in Hindi or Mewari, the local Rajasthani dialect.

A global perspective is slowly being introduced into this local news coverage. CNN and Star TV are replacing the monopoly on television and radio coverage once enjoyed by the nationally owned and controlled media organization Doordarshan; satellite dishes and cable systems are now delivering international news and foreign-produced television and film programming to households throughout rural and urban India.

These villagers have vast knowledge of--and often bitter experience with--the programs of both governmental and private social welfare organizations, whose lofty goals and often tremendous budgets frequently are eroded by corruption and siphoning off of benefits before they reach their intended SC/ST beneficiaries.

Villagers also have extensive experience with local politicians, who during election campaigns court them with promises that more often than not remain unfulfilled after the elections. They have almost forty years of experience with the *panchayat raj,* the system of local governing bodies created in the early 1950s to bring representative democracy to the rural communities. Some villagers perceive the *panchayat* as reflecting the worst features of a corruption-laden political system. Yet in the last decade villagers and NGOs increasingly regard it as a potential vehicle by which SCs and STs can enter the arena of local government. Local panchayat elections in 1995 were marked by an unprecedented participation of ST and SC candidates (including women) in elections for these governing bodies, encouraged in part by a constitutional amendment and state-wide initiates in 1993 reaffirming the reservation quotas of candidacy slots.

Social Categories and Context

The social system within which rural life operates is powerfully influenced by caste affiliation. The highly communalized nature of national party politics in the 1990s throughout India has, according to villagers, renewed the local significance of traditional caste identity categories. Referred to locally as *jati* , the local endogamous caste grouping, this form of identity orders many of the social interactions of rural communities. Jati affiliation influences (but does not automatically and mechanically predetermine) residential patterns, daily social interaction, and most significantly in these rural communities, marriage alliances, as well as some of the more subtle norms of behavior between members of different groups.

Individual family strategies are drawn in part from the repertoire of rural caste-based social relationships. Economic survival, as it has in the past, often depends in part upon recognizing and utilizing patronage relationships, forming alliances with those who for any number of reasons-- caste ranking being only one of them--may have better access to economic or political resources not directly available to poorer or lower-status families. The pre-Independence ordering of these relationships was generally more directly correlated to caste status and hierarchy, reflecting the fact that patron groups such as the ruling caste of Rajputs, whose rural control was bolstered by the support of the British colonial administration, were likely to also control land, service employment, political power, and legal decision making. With the advent of post-Independence land reform and universal citizenship rights, the political and economic power of patron castes has diminished, but it has not disappeared.

India's caste system is probably one of the most written about and least understood social systems in the world. Many misconceptions abound about its manifestations and form. (See Chapter 2.) Recent scholarship on India is drawing attention to the overdetermination of caste in the representation of Indian culture and history by foreign historians and other social scientists who have relied almost exclusively on it to explain all forms of political, economic, and social phenomena in South Asia (Inden 1990).

Alliances and coalitions are mobilized, particularly during the time of elections, around a number of factors. Caste identity is only one of many themes underlying political process in contemporary India, both locally and at the highest levels of elected office. To those who followed India's mid-1996 elections in American newspapers, caste and religion would appear to have been the primary issues on which votes were decided. This conflation of complex issues in India with simplistic cultural explanations, as well as the tendency for reporting exclusively on oddities or disasters, is consistent with a general pattern of representing India in foreign English-language newspapers and magazines (Thomas 1993).

In Udaipur, the poverty of many rural agriculturalists is the result of a complicated process of social and political marginalization based on their limited access to educational and economic resources. Analyzing these complicated processes requires exploring broader issues, particularly the political, social, and historical contexts of the multiple terms for identity categories used in both national and local discourse.

Many poor, rural agriculturalists are classified as "Tribals;" a highly problematical term whose implications and analytic limitations will be described in detail in Chapter 3. Tribals are referred to in contemporary literature as *Adivasi*--a term that translates from the Hindi as "first, earliest dweller, inhabitant." The term *Adivasi* was coined in 1941 by the social worker A.V. Thakkar (Ghurye 1963: 147) in an effort to replace other more derogatory local terminologies. It, too, is laden with the stereotypical assumptions of pre-Hindu origins and isolation from mainstream political and economic process. The pan-Indian inclusive use of the term *Adivasi* belies the local nature of tribal identity, which is, as expressed by members of these groups, comparable to that of ethnicity. Members of these local groups share ideas about identity, conveyed through common ritual patterns and myths about their group history. This identity orders many of their social relationships and marriage patterns. Bhils, for example, express affiliation based on this local identity category; this affiliation is currently being crafted into a more inclusive district-wide rallying point for group mobilization efforts. But they do not spontaneously express connections or shared identity with other groups also categorized as Adivasi, except under some special circumstances, which will be described below. Nor do they express connections with Bhils in other regions or states of northern India.

Adivasis are also referred to as Scheduled Tribe members, or STs, a reference to the Government of India's schedule or list of approximately 450 tribes, several hundred castes and "Other Backward Classes" (OBCs), all of which comprise the government's complete list of "Backward Classes" (BCs). This system of categorization, which originates in the British colonial administration's census, was subsequently regularized by the Indian Constitution to provide special benefits and protection under the law to those groups identified as disadvantaged by virtue of caste status. These benefits include reserved positions for individuals who are members of groups so designated: government jobs; positions in schools, colleges and universities; and for elected office in areas with majority population percentages of these categories. This system of affirmative action, extended on a community-wide (or communal) basis rather than an individual one, has, since Independence, been a controversial and highly politicized aspect of social policy. As in the case of the American welfare system, modifications in its structure and benefits are often the anvil on which political alliances and campaign rhetoric are forged.

In 1990, then Prime Minister V. P. Singh announced his government's support of recommendations of the Mandal Commission, which proposed dramatic expansion of the list of OBCs that would receive benefits under the scheme of national reservations. According to some analysts of the Mandal Commission Report (named for its chairman when the report of the Backward Classes Commission was

Chapter One Issues and Identities

published in 1980), full adoption of the Commission's recommendations would have extended benefits to three-fourths of the total population of India, including Muslims and Christian converts, among others. When Singh's government announced that an additional 27 percent of government jobs and educational positions would be added to the existing 22.5 percent under SC/ST reservations, widespread and violent student-led protest took place throughout northern India (*New York Times* August 22, 1990). This issue eroded support for the government's fragile coalition, particularly among India's increasingly significant middle class, who perceive their own children's' future educational possibilities to be threatened by the expansion of the benefits system; this reaction contributed to the subsequent defeat of the Singh government in national elections in November 1990 (Dubey 1992).

In 1992, India's Supreme Court reaffirmed the principle that caste, not class, should be the criterion for identifying groups requiring benefits and aid, but made several additional recommendations: excluding the "creamy layer" among the BCs, those individual families with household income in excess of Rs.100,000 (the annual income of a top civil servant, military officer, or other "upper class" professional) from benefits; limiting access of the Backward Castes already well represented in government service; and application of the reservations only in appointments and not to promotions. The court also recommended that recruitment to technological posts in medicine, engineering, and the military should be made on the basis of merit only (Wood 1995: 37).

The so-called "Untouchable" castes or low-caste groups ranked at the bottom of the caste hierarchy by virtue of traditional "polluting" occupational status, were renamed by Mahatma Gandhi as *Harijans* or "Children of God"--a designation still in use but contested; it is rejected by some people as being patronizing to groups so designated. The term *Dalit* is widely recognized as an alternative term for Scheduled Caste groups throughout much of India. This term implies group members united for national political mobilization. "Literally, 'oppressed' or 'ground down,' [this] term for Scheduled Caste persons [is] preferred by militant and educated ex-untouchables and by many of those who sympathize with their aspirations" (Oldenburg 1995: 220). Dalit political coalitions have been successful in other parts of northern India, particularly Bihar and Uttar Pradesh; in rural Udaipur the term *Dalit* is not in widespread use either as a reference to imply political mobilization or a form of self-identification.

Bhils are the numerically dominant ST group in the section of Udaipur District in which I conducted my fieldwork. The term Bhil is as highly problematic, political, and contested as the terms already discussed above. I continue to use it because it is the preferred and explicit term of self-identification for the people so designated in the area in which I lived and worked. The term *Adivasi* is used locally only under very specific circumstances. It has special connotations and is used primarily in discourse around participation in political events; on banners in public demonstrations; in documents presented to political leaders; or in NGO-led political rhetoric. But it is not the term of self-identification used in response to questions put to individuals about their jati. And when I discussed these questions of self-terminology, as I did on several occasions in different contexts, Bhil was the term of self-identity spontaneously used.

The same reasoning applies for my use of the term *Meghwal* to name the group of Scheduled Caste members most often involved in local NGO activities in Udaipur District. *Meghwal* is also the local term of identity for this group, and is used as a surname by group members. As illustrated in subsequent chapters, it too has enormous significance in ordering a wide range of inter- and intra-group activities, such as marriage, residential patterns, and socio-economic patronage, as well as serving as a basis for group social mobilization and ritual reform.

Such group names and terms are continually negotiated and renegotiated on a local basis. State-based institutions, such as the Census and schedules of castes, tribes, and backward classes, play a significant role in this local process by reifying these terms and categories as they evolve locally, as well as rendering them economically significant in terms of the access to state-based resources they afford.

In the rural communities of Rajasthan, jati and tribal identity are one of many components of identity; they may structure an individual's life history but do not mechanically predict it. Yet in much the same way that false assumptions about the meaning of racial categories in America can be deconstructed and attacked on intellectual and scientific grounds, race still matters in our society. My conclusions about tribe and jati identity in the local rural context are, I believe, an accurate reflection of how people in these communities expressed how these identities matter in their lives.

Local Histories, Local Strategies: NGOs in Udaipur

In the past two or three decades Udaipur District and the city of Udaipur particularly have become a hub of NGO activity. One street on which several organizations have their offices is known throughout town as "NGO Row." Local NGOs are well known throughout India and in the international community of voluntary agencies, donor organizations, and academic development specialists. Among Euro-Americans conversant with the development industry in India, the district has become practically synonymous with NGO activity in northern India. The organizations, their founders, and their directors, are well known among the academic institutions, donor agencies and practitioners of development throughout the world, and receive a steady stream of foreign visitors.

The proliferation of NGOs in the area was humorously alluded to by the following, which was quoted to me by a man who had recently formed his own NGO after several years' employment with older, more established organizations: "Rajasthan has the least number of NGOs in India; Udaipur has the most."

Participants in the NGO sector have suggested that there are approximately 200 to 250 NGOs operating in and around Udaipur district; the exact number is difficult to determine, for only organizations that receive international funds are required to register with the central government. The unregistered organizations are eligible to receive money from Indian government or private sources; they are even occasionally funded with direct contributions from villagers or use the personal funds of the organizers. These are often small and spontaneously formed in a cluster of villages, and may have no connections to other NGOs or to any state-based or private donor institutions.

This is consistent with the general global perception of NGOs as localized, small-scale, and individually driven. But the reality is far more complex than a distinction between "local" and "transnational" organizations or those that do receive foreign funding and those that don't. The "local" founder of an NGO is rarely from the village within which it operates, and in those very few cases where the organization's founder is actually from the village, he or she brings extraordinary advantages, like college education, to the rural scene. And even the smallest of NGOs that do not directly receive overseas funding feel the impact of national and international linkages on their rural activities. For example, Earth Day and International Women's Day had no significance in the rural ritual cycle until a few years ago; now few villages with any kind of NGO presence fail to observe these global events.

Among these organizations, the NGO directors and some of their staff members are for the most part either from Rajasthan or have long-term affiliations with the area. They are often college educated, competent if not fluent in English as well as Mewari, and middle class, having been raised in an urban intellectual and economic environment in which caste was an issue of political and historical significance rather than a lifestyle determinant. Their families are geographically spread out, with ties to the major cities and overseas.

The vocabulary, the strategies, and the stated goals of their organizations reflect the general priorities of India for its citizens as expressed in its Constitution--economic and political equality in a secular state. The organizations tend to downplay the intricacies of intercaste relationships, and analyze them in the vocabulary of modern nation-state and economic system parlance. But underlying the rhetoric and the strategies are the constant reminders of hierarchy, status differentials, and assumptions about "appropriate" intergroup behavior.

The agenda and the vocabulary of these organizations is distinctly noncaste and nonhierarchical. The result is a paradox that in a sense duplicates the central government's struggle to reconcile secularity with communalism, by targeting specific jati groups for aid and support, specifically on the basis of group-wide affiliation, and not individual or household need.

Certainly there is potential for hierarchy and class-based divisions in any situation where one group has access to resources of development, particularly funding, information and connections, and another group does not. But the complexities of the social, economic and political relationships between the NGOs and the villagers are far more opaque than class and access to resources. Their separate social histories have forged the operational strategies of the NGOs, and these histories, to some extent define and delimit the nature of these strategies. Despite the apparent differences between the NGO community and local communities, they are not dichotomous or culturally oppositional. Rather, the NGO organizations and their workers share many of the subtle cultural norms with their rural counterparts. History and culture intersect in their relationships and in the resulting local development strategy; these issues will be discussed and illustrated throughout this book.

This observation is not to be interpreted as meaning that either group is "living in the past;" relationships and identities are continually being renegotiated. Neither group is in any sense isolated from broader national and international arenas of social, economic, and political events. Nor are the two groups discrete and unchanging. A villager who becomes an NGO employee rapidly evolves into a member of the NGO community and begins to share some of its values and goals.

Udaipur NGOs have come to be associated with a particular kind of development strategy, which focuses on the concept of slowly evolving local empowerment that develops through a gradual process of increased literacy, growing mainstream political participation, and protecting the natural resource base. It is a nonconfrontative strategy that complies with national government policy and regulation, and does not generally provoke open antagonism or violence.

This local strategy has its roots in the social and political history of Mewar, its British colonial relationships, and the post-Independence state of Rajasthan, discussed briefly in Chapter 2. It emanates particularly from the influential activities of a pioneering social activist in Udaipur, Mohan Singh Mehta, who during a remarkable career as a politician, diplomat, educator, and social welfare activist, founded many of the educational and social activist institutions that continue to thrive in Udaipur today. His life, activities, and social policies continue to influence the NGO sector in Udaipur a decade after his death. The policies and strategies he established have been reinterpreted by three or four subsequent "generations" of activists and organizations, but an analysis of their activities demonstrates the indelible stamp of his social strategy, as well as of Mewari culture and history, on the contemporary NGO scene. (See Chapter 4.)

There are exceptions to this generalization about strategy in Udaipur, as well as throughout India; the inclusion of historical and social traditions into the discussion of agendas for development and change does not mean that all the participants are automatically bound to duplicate the processes of the past. Far from it. Other organizations in the same region have adopted more radical and confrontative strategies, and will be discussed in detail. (See Chapter 5.) These noted exceptions do not, however, negate the conclusion that local NGO strategy, for the most part, reflects social and historical norms based on constructions of what constitutes appropriate, acceptable levels of confrontation and change.

The "G" in NGO

Another aspect of the multiple relationships examined here is the ambiguous status of NGOs in relation to state government. The operative word in "nongovernmental" is "government": the state policy that shapes the "nongovernmental" organizations' potential range of development strategies in the rural communities in which they operate. This is not unique to Rajasthan or India; the relationship of local NGOs to national government political and economic policy is a relatively unexplored aspect of the voluntary sector globally. (See Chapter 5.) Compliance with governmental rules and regulations may under some circumstances directly conflict with local NGO goals and strategies. This constraint became particularly apparent during national elections in India; local villages became a vivid landscape on which these forces were played out. This process is explored in Chapter 9, from the perspective of villagers who, during election periods, negotiated their multiple statuses of NGO employees, voters, political party members, and candidates.

Business or Calling?
The intergenerational organizational histories of local NGOs also has important ramifications for how they operate in Udaipur. Recruiting new personnel is an ongoing problem for those organizations that regard themselves as an institutional and continuing presence in the local communities, for recruitment and personnel development require a professionalization of the institution that is anathema to the philosophies of some of the practitioners.

In Udaipur the concept of development is closely linked in the minds of some of its local practitioners with principles of social upliftment embodied by the Indian Independence movement, and particularly by the social philosophies of Mahatma Gandhi. Many of my most stimulating discussions with NGO organizers in Udaipur emanated from this question of whether the sector can accurately be described as an industry; some took great exception to this characterization of what they perceive to be the humanistic mandate of social work. This perspective has obvious implications not only for the recruitment and training of personnel in these organizations, but also in the manner in which this industry will conceptualize itself as a profession and as an institutional and bureaucratic structure. Reconciling the "calling" of community work from a Gandhian perspective with the increasing visibility and professional mobility of a career in NGO-related activities is just one of the many intellectual and practical contradictions discussed and debated, observed and pondered, throughout NGO Row. This debate resonates in local activities and personnel practices, and is thus an important issue in local strategy.

Chapter Summary
Rajasthani Bhils are citizens of the world's largest democracy, but illiteracy coupled with grinding poverty result in their disenfranchisement and social marginalization. Local NGOs are attempting to elevate the standard of living of Bhils and other groups of the rural poor by, among other strategies, literacy training; political organization and activism; social and ritual reform; and the protection of natural resources. These organizations are increasing local awareness of social and political issues as well as encouraging participation in the local political process. But the potential for social change is offset in part by aspects of hierarchy and dependency in the relationship between NGO and rural community members.

The vocabulary, strategies, and goals of these organizations reflect the liberal rhetoric of casteless society. But underlying the rhetoric and strategies are local constructions of status differentials. The interaction between NGOs and villagers is therefore dynamic and potentially conflict-ridden. Each player in this interaction brings to it a set of beliefs, ideas, expectations, and strategies. Each has a social reality borne of experience and background. Each has an idea of what poverty is and what change should encompass. And each knows on some level that there is an inherent inequality in their interaction--that the bearer of development resources has more power in the interaction and in the relationship than does the client. This asymmetry is reenacted and renegotiated daily in local dynamics that are also being shaped by state and global forces.

Chapter 2

Fieldwork Landscapes: Rural, Urban, Social, and Otherwise

Going from India's capital city to rural Rajasthan, the traveler experiences two of the many extremes of modern India. The jet planes, skyscrapers, and traffic jams of New Delhi testify to all the benefits and costs of industrialization and economic growth. Evidence of the government's recent economic liberalization policy abounds: billboards advertising foreign manufactured products now dominate New Delhi's already congested and polluted environment.

Consumers in the cities of Rajasthan also have shared in the benefits of India's economically liberalized economy. But the economic rewards of Udaipur's increasingly prosperous urban middle class and the benefits of a steady stream of tourists to the city's major attractions elude many in rural villages. Even the most basic services--regularly supervised schools, electricity, potable water, or minimal health care--fail to reach many households.

Rajasthan's infrastructural underdevelopment is attributed in part by some observers to the conservative influence of Rajput ideology on social practices, an influence expressed through the state's contemporary political institutions. For example, the number of protesters who rallied against the rare and highly controversial act of *sati* (widow self-immolation) of Roop Kanwar near Jaipur in 1987, were far outnumbered by participants in political rallies supporting the right of her husband's family to allow the ritual to take place (*India Today* October 15, 1987). The organizers of these rallies, which according to

Chapter 2 Fieldwork Landscapes

some journalists attracted as many as 200,000 people, portrayed this controversial event as Rajput religious expression, and therefore protected by law (*India Today* October 31, 1987, Bumiller 1990).

Udaipur District is the locus of widely valued Rajput historical and cultural traditions, as well as a liberal social reform and educational movement that originated in the princely state of Mewar and has vital continuities in the local NGO setting. These two historic themes--the pre-Independence princely state and the nongovernmental development sector--intersect continuously in contemporary village settings, forming a rich and complicated arena in which development and group identity are continuously being reinterpreted and renegotiated by its participants.

Geography, Population, and Literacy

Despite the growth of its largest urban center of Jaipur, Jodhpur and Udaipur, Rajasthan remains one of the least developed states in India, based on its limited industrial infrastructure, petroleum-based agricultural technologies, rural electrification, paved roads, literacy, public health facilities, and levels of household income (Henderson 1993). When compared with other Indian states, Rajasthan has been consistently at or near the bottom of the national statistics on education and literacy generally, and female literacy particularly.

Urban population growth state-wide, with its corresponding demand for water, fuel, housing, building materials, and other local natural resources, is contributing to the crisis of Rajasthan's already fragile ecosystem. This crisis is most apparent in the now completely deforested Aravalli mountain system, which is linked to a larger regional ecosystem of forests, rivers, and desert. (See Figures 1 and 2.)

The Aravallis divide the state of Rajasthan roughly in half diagonally. Areas to their south and east are generally more fertile and more densely populated; the portion of the state to the north and west is considerably drier and less densely populated. Although the Aravallis are a natural watershed area containing many streams and rivers, these water sources are almost entirely seasonal, and they disappear a few months after the monsoon. The Thar desert, which begins at the easternmost ridge of the Aravallis, extends to the Pakistan border into the Indus River catchment area.

These geographic features have influenced Rajasthan's economic development and population distribution throughout its history: "The better climate and the proximity of the eastern districts to Delhi, the Moghul (and later the English and republican) capital combined to make the eastern section [of the state] more developed than the west, a situation which persists to this day" (Hadden 1974: 24).

Interpreting Development: Local Histories, Local Strategies

Figure 1

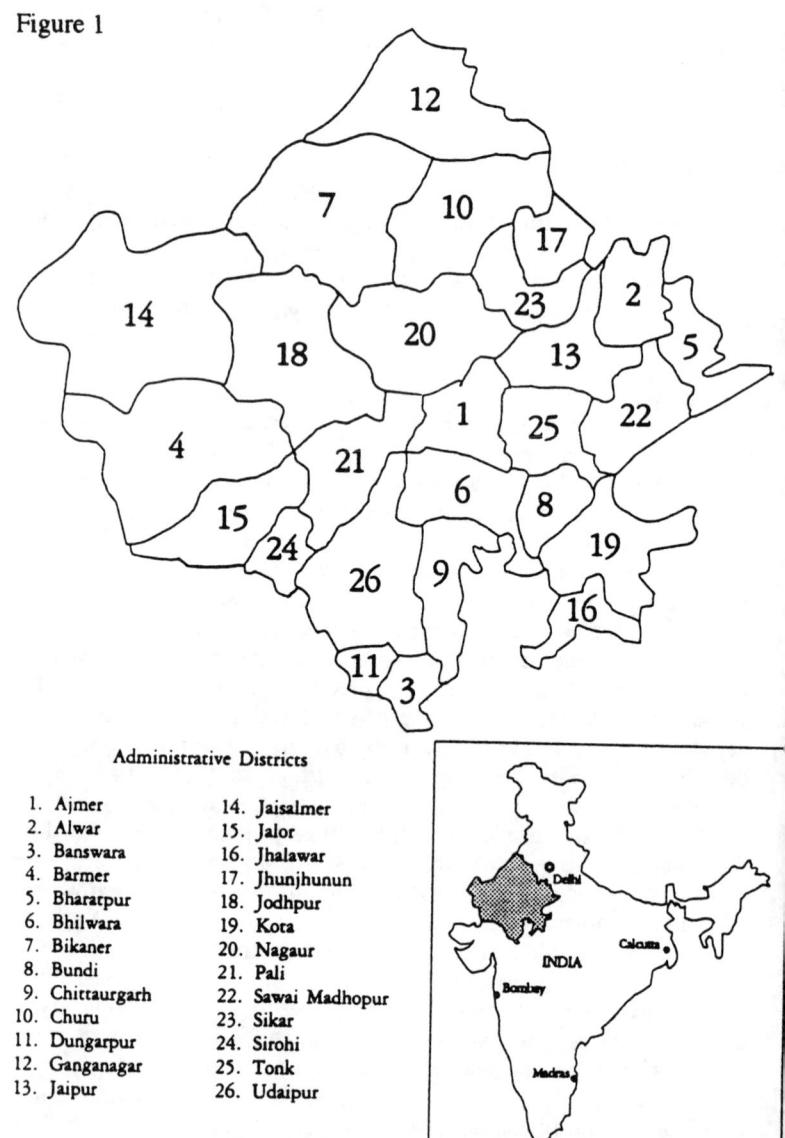

Administrative Districts

1. Ajmer
2. Alwar
3. Banswara
4. Barmer
5. Bharatpur
6. Bhilwara
7. Bikaner
8. Bundi
9. Chittaurgarh
10. Churu
11. Dungarpur
12. Ganganagar
13. Jaipur
14. Jaisalmer
15. Jalor
16. Jhalawar
17. Jhunjhunun
18. Jodhpur
19. Kota
20. Nagaur
21. Pali
22. Sawai Madhopur
23. Sikar
24. Sirohi
25. Tonk
26. Udaipur

Map 1. The State of Rajasthan

Maps 1 and 2: from Billig 1991. Reprinted with permission of the Association for Asian Studies Inc

Chapter 2 Fieldwork Landscapes

Figure 2

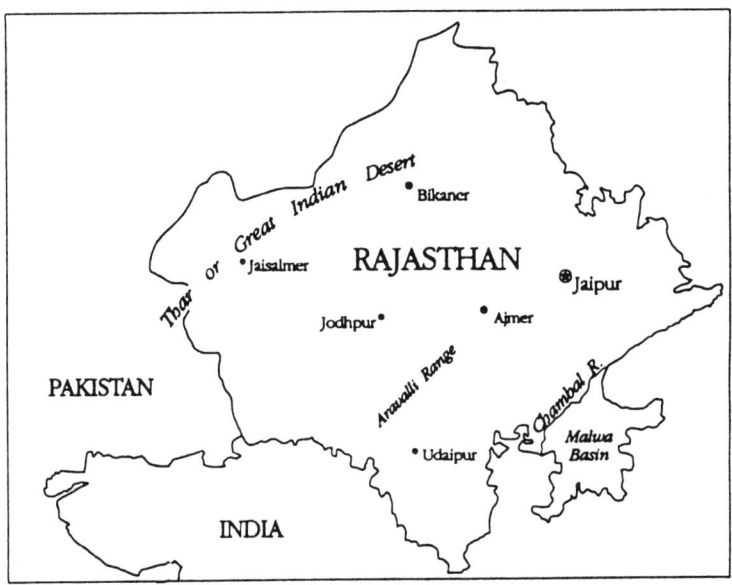

Map 2. Chief Topographic Features of Rajasthan

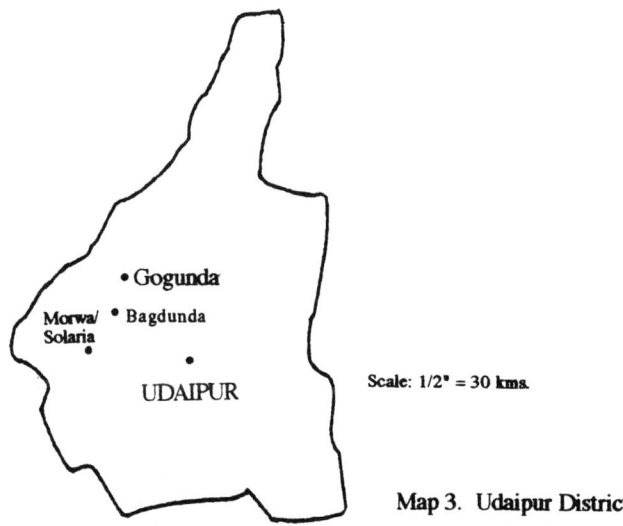

Map 3. Udaipur District

Udaipur District's capital city, according to the 1991 Census[1], has a population of about 308,000 and is the largest urban center in the southern Aravalli region of the state. To a native Manhattanite like myself it feels more like a town than a city, an impression reinforced within a few months of my arrival by the warm friendships I formed and the number of people I would recognize on my trips to Bapu Bazaar, the city's main market. Even in the city's high-trafficked banking and business sections, no buildings rise more than six or seven stories. Some retail stores, concentrated in market areas throughout town, are no more than small stalls, but despite their small size and lack of display space they contain a wide range of consumer products and electronic appliances, many bearing the names and logos of foreign companies. Fully electrified, free-standing glassed and mirrored shops, catering to tourists as well as the city's growing middle and business classes, are rapidly springing up throughout the city.

Udaipur's private entrepreneurial sector provides the most up-to-date products and services. Tiny shops throughout the city, fueled only in part by tourist demand, offer reliable overseas telephone and fax service. Other shops that a few years ago carried only manual typewriters for on-site use now offer a wide range of rapid printing, photocopying, and binding services. Satellite dishes and access to cable television, a rarity when I began visiting Udaipur in the 1980s, are commonplace features of most middle-class homes, along with VCRs and personal computers.

Despite the growth of the population of Udaipur city (nearly 80 percent in the past 20 years, and 3.5 times its population in 1951), 83 percent of the district's population lives in rural villages.[2] Scheduled Tribes make up a significant percentage of the rural population; over 34 percent of the total population of the district is comprised of Scheduled Tribes. In Gogunda *tehsil* (an administrative subdivision of a district) where my field study was concentrated, STs comprise about 40 percent of the population (ICI 1983a). There are twelve census-designated Scheduled Tribes in Udaipur District: among these Bhils are numerically dominant, comprising about 55 percent of the ST population. Minas comprise about 46 percent of the population state-wide, but are not significantly represented in Udaipur District. (See Appendix 1 and Table 7)

Literacy rates in the district show an urban/rural disparity as well as a marked gender bias. In Udaipur District's rural areas only 17.3 percent of the population is literate; only 3 percent of the females of rural areas of the state are literate. In Gogunda tehsil, which is entirely rural, a little over 15 percent of the total population is literate; only 3.5 percent of the women of the tehsil are literate. (Table 5)

When I discussed their perception of their lives with Bhil men they invariably named illiteracy as one of their primary problems. The extent of this problem is confirmed by census data: in 1981, almost 90 percent of all males and virtually 100 percent of all female Scheduled Tribe members in rural areas of Udaipur District were reported as illiterate. Education levels beyond the early grades of elementary school among rural STs in the district are so scant as to be unmeasurable in percentage points; fewer than 900 Scheduled Tribe males were reported to have attained a secondary level education; only 45 females are so reported. (Tables 8,9)

The Agricultural Cycle

The district's primary economic activity is agriculture: over 70 percent of the total population of the district reports its main economic activity as either "cultivator" or "agricultural laborer." (ICI 1983a: viii). There are two major crop seasons. *Kharif*, or rainy-season crops, are put in at the onset of monsoon, usually by the end of June. The primary kharif crop in Udaipur is maize, which is harvested in October. Recently ginger, a valued commodity crop, is being planted to either supplement or replace maize. While corn is occasionally roasted and picked off the cob as a snack, it is more important in the diet as a dry grain, ground into flour and made into *makhi ki roti* (corn flatbread) rolled into a large disc and cooked in an open rounded pan on the household *chula* (wood-fed cooking pit).

The chief *rabi*, or winter crop, is wheat. This is an irrigated crop that is planted in late October or early November and harvested in mid-April. Winter wheat is often intercropped with pulses or mustard, if sufficient water is available to support the intercropping. A third crop may be put in after the rabi harvest if water is available for irrigation-- usually sugar cane and sometimes tobacco. Because of water scarcity many arable plots lay fallow after the monsoon-fed harvest.

Wells, which are owned by families or groups of families, supply water for both irrigation and household use. Because of these family patterns of ownership there are also caste-based implications to well-water access. Only well owners are permitted access to their wells for irrigation use; local etiquette, however, allows anyone passing by to draw water out for drinking, provided intercaste hierarchical rules are maintained. Because of the intricacies of these rules and the sanctions for breaking them, people generally avoid using any wells other than their own.

Wells generally measure about 10 to 15 feet in diameter, with steps leading down into them to facilitate the removal of rubble during the building process and their future maintenance; steps are also used to descend into the well to collect drinking water.[3]

Water is removed from these wells by either a Persian wheel system (*rahat*) or, alternatively, a *charas* --a single leather bag attached to a pulley system. Both systems are activated by bovine animal traction. Wells are connected to the fields with hand-dug irrigation channels lined with mud, an inefficient water-transfer system that can result in as much as 30 percent water loss between the well and the field. (See Figure 3) Many local farmers, if they have access to the necessary capital for the improvement, construct cement channels to prevent this water loss.

Land holdings for rural SC/ST households are very small, on average in one Bhil *phala* (hamlet), approximately 1.25 $bigha^4$ per household, supporting about five people per household on average. The purchase of additional acreage is generally off-limits to most families because of the price of irrigated land, which was quoted by a local bank manager in 1990 at Rs. 20,000 per bigha. Land could be leased for about Rs. 400-800 per bigha per year, with the price dependent upon its access to water.

The U.S. dollar equivalents of these figures are meaningless; to contextualize them somewhat I will relate them to income and debt figures for the same year for the 32 households of Solaria, a Bhil phala. These figures were compiled by Mr. B. N. Bhatia, a "free lance" development worker in Solaria. The highest income reported of all the households was Rs. 7,500 in a household with five people; the lowest was Rs. 1,500 in a household of four. The average income in the 32 households was Rs. 3,800; average expenditures per household was Rs. 3,900; average debt per household was Rs. 2,500. (See Chapter 6 for further discussion of Bhil household economics.)

Extensive livestock loss was reported by villagers during the 1986-88 drought period; losses as high as 50 percent were reported in one cluster of villages around Bagdunda. The loss of any large animal has a particularly devastating effect on the agricultural productivity of small-scale agriculturalists. If a traction animal, usually a bullock, dies, the entire agricultural cycle for the household is curtailed. Although bullocks can occasionally be borrowed or rented for plowing once the monsoon begins, the window of opportunity for successful plowing and planting is small. Fields must be plowed and seeded during the first few days of rainfall; even a few day's delay may cause damage to the seeds or cause them to be washed away during subsequent rainfall. And even if animals can be borrowed for plowing, the problem of fertilizing the field remains unsolved.

In the study area, only the wealthiest farmers can afford to purchase chemical fertilizers; small-scale farmers rely exclusively on animal waste. Unless one owns animals, there is no access to the manure that serves as fertilizer, and also, when dried, is an important cooking fuel as

Chapter 2 Fieldwork Landscapes

Figure 3: Local Rahat (Persian Wheel) Technology

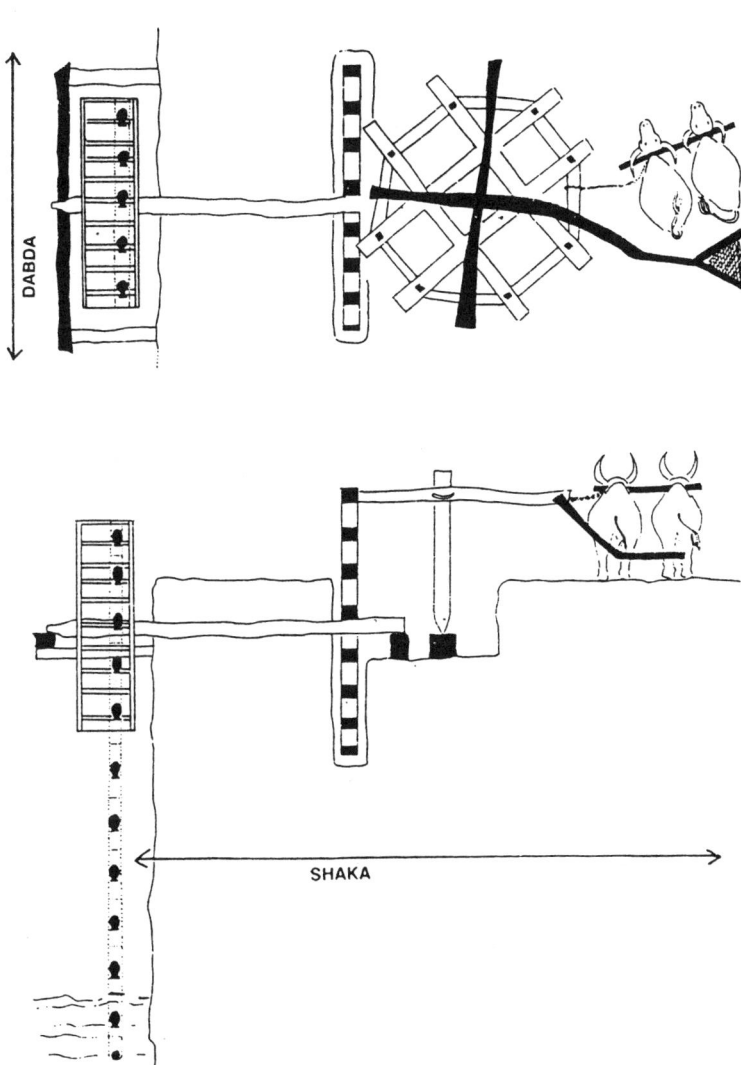

Illustration from Ubeshwar Vikas Mandal 1993:6. Used with permission.

well as a house-building and maintenance material. Because manure is such a valuable product, there is a recognized system for its collection and allocation. Manure belongs to the animal's owner; this is not problematic when the animal is in use on the owner's land or is tethered near the owner's home. When the animals are being grazed on public access lands or are in transit on roads, however, the droppings must be claimed and collected by the owners immediately; if not, anyone has the right to claim them if they are left unattended. A small rock placed on top of the droppings indicates that the manure has been claimed, and cannot be removed by anyone else. (See Harris 1966, Henderson Forthcoming for a theoretical discussion of cow usage and management in India.)

Supplemental Household Income and Debt

Few SC or ST families now can exist solely on income from agriculture. Animal husbandry, particularly the sale of young goats and cows, valuable for their breeding as well as milk production capabilities, supplements agricultural income. The purchase of a camel can be the start of a profitable local transport business. Other supplemental economic activities include sale or barter of milk derivatives and *ghee* (clarified butter), vegetables, and spices; and day labor on public or private construction projects. Out-migration of village men for employment is a growing and socially disruptive phenomenon; mines and construction projects throughout the district employ migrant male labor.

Household debt is endemic. Among Bhils, illiteracy and intergenerational social and economic ties to moneylenders complicate the debt relationship and obscure the details of payment and repayment. The moneylender, who is usually also a local dry goods shopkeeper, serves not only as a perpetual source of cash and credit, but also as a middleman in marketing agricultural products (Carrithers and Humphrey ed. 1991, Michie 1978). An important local link to urban markets, the moneylender may on occasion exploit their illiterate clients by undervaluing the crop sold and misrepresenting the market value of the grain. The Bhils are often powerless to challenge the details of the "contract" even when they know they are being cheated; they also know that the same moneylender will be there to extend more credit and cash for the future emergencies which are bound to arise.

Drought and Deforestation in Udaipur District

Udaipur District has been subjected to recurrent flood, drought, epidemic and famine throughout its history. Average rainfall in the district is 650 mm/year (about 26 inches), and almost all of this rain falls during the monsoon months, June to September. Failures of rains and accompanying drought conditions have been recorded throughout the history of Mewar, and continue to plague the local agricultural community. Deficient or partial rainfall resulted in widespread famine in 1662, 1764, 1883, 1888, and 1889. In 1900 a cholera epidemic wiped out five percent of Udaipur District's total population; it is estimated that from 25 to 30 percent of the district's Bhil population died that year (Rajasthan District Gazetteers 1979: 144). Floods in 1943 washed away 25 villages; in 1973 heavy rainfall, in some tehsils as much as three times more than the normal rate, caused extensive flooding resulting in 12 human deaths, the loss of 1,000 animals and the destruction of 1,500 houses (Ibid.: 141).

Systematic government relief measures, first instituted in 1963, have prevented the droughts from turning into widespread famine in the district, but the loss of livestock continues to be a major consequence. The district experienced scarcity conditions of varying degrees in 1963-64; 1966-67; 1968-69; and again in 1971-72 (Ibid.: 144); the rains failed in 1986, and were poor again in 1987.

Since 1988 rains have been reported at average levels, but even when good rains are reported throughout the state or district, localized areas can receive as little as half of the rain that falls in adjoining villages. A proverb well known throughout India says, "Monsoon rains can fall on one horn of a water buffalo, and not the other." And even under the best conditions of rain and irrigation, cultivable land in the Aravallis is limited; only half of the total land area of Gogunda tehsil is classified as "cultivable" according to census records, and only 12.5 percent is irrigated. The notoriously unreliable monsoons are the primary source of water for both domestic and agricultural use; underground aquifers are recharged only by the annual rainfall.

The effects of the unpredictability of monsoon and drought are even further exacerbated by rampant deforestation throughout the district. The ravages of deforestation are apparent everywhere in the Aravalli landscape. The hills are barren and naked; the ground cover completely gone. The landscape is dotted with hunting "blinds" built by the Maharanas and Rajput *thakurs* (local nobles) at various times prior to Independence. These blinds, once completely surrounded by thick forest growth, provided the necessary cover for hunting of tigers and panthers, which have all virtually disappeared along with the forests. These blinds, now totally visible on the denuded hills, are a poignant reminder of what was once the density of the forest cover and the variety of wild game it supported.

The deforestation crisis throughout the district has been observed for several decades, but is just recently being publicized and studied as a major economic and social problem. Deforestation in the Aravallis is now generally acknowledged by both scientists and government administrators to be the result of forest overuse by commercial logging and mining enterprises, increased population pressure, and local mismanagement of the forest resources.

There is, however, a general perception among Udaipur residents that the Adivasis are responsible for the destruction of the forests. This is partly due to the fact that, particularly during recent drought periods, Adivasi women in villages within a half-day's walk to Udaipur supplement their household income by carrying headloads of dried wood for sale in the city's lumber bazaars. These distinctively dressed women, carrying up to 25 kilos of wood on their heads, are by now a familiar sight walking along the roads leading into the city.

There is an equally wide-spread perception among the Bhils themselves that they are responsible for the current levels of deforestation. When I inquired in Bhil villages as to what happened to the trees in the Aravallis, the response was inevitably, "We cut down the trees." When I pursued this response further, people reported details about how rural women cut down trees for domestic use and sale, and how men were recruited to work on logging and mining teams, all activities involving destruction of forests.

Even a cursory examination of the extent of the deforestation reveals consumption of forest products far beyond the capacity of rural women to cause, either by domestic use or sale. And to attribute total forest loss to the Bhils cutting down the trees, while they were in the hire of Udaipur-based lumber brokers, or national and international logging and mining companies, is an equally incomplete explanation.

Prior to Independence in 1948, the Aravallis were densely forested, with 50-60 percent deep forest cover. Today it is estimated that less than 10 percent of the total forest cover remains, and what is left is dwindling rapidly. As a result, soil erosion is rampant. Forest cover and tree roots once protected the hillsides from erosion. They are now bare, and monsoon rains cause unrestrained topsoil runoff. Groundwater levels have been dropping significantly because the rapid runoff does not allow wells to recharge adequately. Some observers claim that rainfall intensity and frequency has dropped in direct correlation to the decrease in forest cover. Between 1957 and 1989, Rajasthan has experienced 19 years of drought conditions (Saint 1988); this same period has seen a dramatic decrease in the forest cover of the area.

Deforestation in the district has also been linked to increasing levels of desertification. The Aravallis form the eastern boundary of the Thar Desert; these hills have traditionally created a barrier to the eastward spread of this massive desert system. As a result of the deforestation some geologists have asserted that the Thar Desert is spreading eastward, unchecked by the now denuded forest boundary.

These environmental conditions form a significant prong of the NGO strategy in the district and are often the basis for the first point of entry into a village. The organizations' wide range of environmentally based interventions and social forestry programs will be described in subsequent chapters.

Identity Construction and Mobility

The contemporary rural social environment is strongly influenced by the history of the region. Rajput princes and land-owning nobles dominated the district politically and economically in the pre-Independence period. After Independence, land reform was instituted to break up large hereditary holdings. Many Rajput thakurs gradually sold off their rural land holdings and have moved into the city. They visit the villages once controlled by their families only occasionally; their local political and economic influence has eroded along with their control over land and agricultural resources. Many have converted their *havelis*, or city residences, into hotels and guest houses. Despite these changes in the local economic base, some of the ideals and models of social relationships of the pre-Independence sociopolitical structure continue to resonate in many contemporary rural institutions.

One manifestation is the emulation of Rajput behavior by lower-ranked caste groups in an effort to elevate their own group status. This is a variation of the process of Sanskritization, which according to the theorists who have proposed this model, generally emulates Brahmanical behavior as the touchstone for group mobility (Srinivas 1962, 1966). Although the Brahmans of Udaipur function as religious and ritual practitioners, this does not render them socially, economically, or politically dominant, as they are in other parts of India. The Rajputs, hereditary rulers and nobles, while hierarchically just below the priestly caste, set the ideals of behavior and established the standards and norms; thus the process by which other castes and tribes attempt to elevate their status within the local caste system is therefore more accurately referred to as "Rajputization."

These processes of mobility run counter to the general Euro-American perceptions of the Indian socio-religious system, which is generally used as the cultural example of a closed hereditary system of stratification "with social position locked in at birth with mechanisms of legal and social sanctions applied against those who seek to cross them" (e.g. Kottak 1994: 169). This widely held perception of the Indian caste system as synonymous with a rigid, immutable, and predetermined position in society certainly reflects some of the realities of caste position, particularly for those in the lowest categories (Mahar 1972). Nevertheless, it belies the equally important dynamic processes; the local construction of the social system includes mechanisms for both integrating outside population groups (Srinivas 1952, Woodcock 1962) as well as mechanisms of group mobility within the system.

This mobility "results only in *positional changes* in the system and does not lead to any *structural change*. That is, a caste moves up, above its neighbors, and another comes down, but all this takes place in an essentially stable hierarchical order. The system itself does not change" (Srinivas 1966: 7). Most of the early ethnographies on caste construction and mobility draw on data from village settings and stress the ritual and religious taboos associated with intercaste behavior (a classic and influential example in the anthropology of village India is Leach ed. 1971).[5]

As I observed this process unfold locally it became apparent that mobility by this avenue is not always welcomed by all jati (local caste grouping) members, nor is the outcome of the process guaranteed. Some Meghwals of Gogunda are attempting such a movement, spearheaded by the caste panchayat (jati council) leaders, a small group of wealthy men whose families have made comparatively large fortunes in the traditional occupation of scavenging and animal hide processing. These jati leaders are now urging all Meghwals to cease any occupation involving the handling of animal skins or the hauling of carcasses. Many of the Meghwal elites have moved to the city of Udaipur and are now successful shopkeepers; these city-dwellers have changed their surnames from Meghwal to other less readily identifiable ones.

The ban on handling leather or animal skins has not yet been entirely accepted in the villages. For example, one man who had recently begun a cobbler business refused to give up this new undertaking, which showed great financial promise. He said he would accept the sanction of outcasting (social isolation extended to both him and his immediately family members, which would include barring his children from jati-sanctioned marriages), but needed the shoemaking business to supplement the meager agricultural output from a small plot he owned. Other Meghwals in small villages grumbled among themselves that their rich kin in Gogunda could afford to abandon their leather businesses now that they had taken the money from it and invested it in purchasing real estate, operating retail shops, and other caste-neutral enterprises. Besides, they said, if the Meghwals don't do it, someone else would be hired and paid to do it. The dispute with the cobbler was settled when it was agreed that he could keep his cobbling business, but other Meghwals in the village were barred from hauling carcasses on threat of outcasting.

Others villagers complained that if they refused to remove carcasses this would create conflict with the upper-caste groups, particularly with the Rajputs. Violations of social norms between Meghwals and Rajputs still result in locally enforced sanctions. For example, about ten years ago, according to local informants, a Meghwal man during his *barat* (the premarriage procession of relatives from the groom's household to the bride's house where the wedding ceremony generally takes place) hired a horse, decorated it, and rode on it to his future wife's village. Although all groups, including Bhils, observe the ritual of the barat, the groom riding on a horse is a practice associated only with Rajputs and upper-caste groups. The Meghwal man was thrown from the horse and severely beaten by a group of Rajput men in punishment for his presumption in adopting a Rajput practice.

The goals of the movement are slowly being integrated into the jati panchayat discourse as issues of social and ritual reform. As most Meghwals already are small-scale agriculturalists the question of practicing "traditional" polluting occupations is slowly becoming moot. This movement is dominated by the issues of education and ritual reform. And in the case of the Meghwal attacked by the Rajput man during his marriage procession, the state judicial system was brought into the picture; the Meghwal brought criminal charges of assault against the Rajputs who organized the attack and, although it took several years to resolve the case, some of the perpetrators of the attack served a few months in jail.

The issues of Rajputization and mobility come to bear on tribal identity in general and Bhil identity specifically. The categories of tribe and caste, and their local meaning, are not oppositional or dichotomous; they are also fluid and constantly being re-negotiated, particularly in the local village setting (Deliege 1985). The identity of the Bhils in Udaipur District is formed by their history of relationships with the dominant Hindu caste-based society. While the category of Bhil has local significance in describing identity, what it means to be a Bhil in contemporary rural society has complex referents to Hindu and Sanskritized norms of behavior. (See Chapter 3 for further discussion of these issues.)

Rajasthan's History and Historiography

The representation of Rajput history and culture in eastern Rajasthan is often characterized by Western scholars by reference to themes of military ethos, martial traditions and sentimental adherence to the glories of its past (see for example Carstairs 1961, Gold 1988, Hitchcock 1958, Rudolph and Rudolph 1984). The written history of Rajasthan and of Udaipur District has been recorded in part by *charan*, official bards, and court historians from the perspective of its Rajput rulers, the Maharanas of Mewar. This bardic history was inherited by the British colonial administrators who were assigned to represent British interests in Rajputana and other parts of Central India.

James Tod, the British political agent for The Rajputana Agency from 1818-1822, was particularly captivated by this historiography, and drew on it extensively in his two-volume work on the history of the Rajputs, *Annals and Antiquities of Rajasthan* (Tod 1983(1829-32)). Tod is praised by some as being "the Herodotus of Hindustan" (Quanuco 1969: 103) although not all his contemporaries shared this appraisal. He was criticized by the British colonial administration for being "notoriously a partisan of the Rajput princes, particularly those of Mewar and Marwar ... who exaggerates their victories and minimizes their defeats" (Crooke 1920: xxxvi). Tod's partisanship with the ruling clans of Mewar led to unsubstantiated rumors of corruption during his service as the Mewar political agent (Ibid.: xxxviii). He retired from official service at the age of forty; ill health was claimed as the cause of his relatively early retirement. He left India in 1826 and died suddenly in London in 1835 (Ibid: xxxviii.). His diaries and extensive writings based on his travels around Mewar (Tod 1839) document the structure and mechanics of British influence over local law enforcement and the administration of princely states (see Inden 1990: 172-174).

An equally significant chronicler of the Mewar dynasties was Kaviraj Shymaldas (1836-1893) who was, like Tod, both historian and administrator. Shymaldas began his service to the Mewari court of Maharana Shambhu Singh, who in 1875 assigned him the task of writing a history of the Mewar kingdom. The Maharana put at his disposal a considerable budget and a team of scholars who translated texts from Sanskrit, English, Persian, and Arabic (G.N. Sharma 1992:59). Shymaldas was then pressed into administrative duties for the Maharana, including the gathering of local intelligence information in order to suppress an uprising of Bhils in Magri District in 1881 (Ibid.: 50). *Vir Vinod* (in Hindi) was completed and published in 1886 under the patronage of the next Maharana, Fateh Singh.

The works of these two historians are the sources from which most of the subsequent publications on Mewar and Rajasthani history and culture draw their references. Each produced a body of work significant not only for its content but also for the perspectives and assumptions each brings to these histories. Even more significant is their influence on subsequent generations of historians of Rajasthan. Tod's adulation of the Rajputs was framed in the Romantic vision of history that glorified feudal society. Tod was mostly self-educated, and was greatly influenced by the work of the historian Henry Hallam (Rudolph 1993), whose study of the feudal history of Europe, *View of the State of Europe during the Middle Ages*, was first published in 1818. Contrary to the prevailing negative view of early 19th-century historians, Hallam saw the European Middle Ages as "an era when honor, heroism and devotion inspired great deeds by great men" (Ibid.: 15).

Shymaldas, who was profoundly influenced by Tod's romantic vision of Mewari history, was also breaking new ground in historiography: "Shymaldass [sic] is positioned between the imaginative truth of Tod's romantic construction of Mewar history and the objective truth of the professional historians and Indologists of his time" (Ibid.: 17).

Soon after the death of Shymaldas, Fateh Singh ordered the contents of his monumental work sealed and placed under the personal supervision of the Maharana. *Vir Vinod* was officially "unsealed" in 1945; excerpts were published in book form (Sharma and Gupta eds. 1985). But the impression in Udaipur among those who know of the work is that access to it is still controlled by the royal family, as copies of the full text are available locally only in the palace library.

Some Historical Issues

The region of northwestern India that came to be known first as Rajputana by the British and later as the post-Independence state of Rajasthan, was originally comprised of 19 princely states,[6] ruled by hereditary Rajput Maharajas and Maharanas, the latter title used exclusively by the rulers of Mewar. Maharana Udai Singh II founded the city of Udaipur and made it the capital of the state in the mid-16th century. The contemporary district of Udaipur comprises about half of the former Mewar state. The descendants and kin of the Maharanas of Udaipur considered themselves to "rank first among the various royal households of Rajasthan" (Harlan 1992) because of their particularly heroic resistance to Muslim invasions during the reign of the Moghul kings, and their refusal, unique among the princes of the region, to arrange marriages for their daughters to the sons of the Mughal rulers.

Among the most noteworthy and often-quoted events in the history of Mewar's martial Rajput rulers was the battle of Chittaur. In 1303 the army of the Sultan of Delhi attacked Chittaur, the Mewari capital. The Maharana was killed during the first day of battle; resistance to the attack continued under the leadership of his successor. After a devastating day of futile battle, the remaining Rajput warriors, princesses, and concubines set fire to the royal castle, committing mass suicide rather than submitting to the humiliations of defeat. The women were led in this *jauhar* by the widowed Maharani Padmini. At the day's end, according to various versions of this story, 30,000 followers of the Maharana perished in the battle, and thousands more died by their own hand.

Despite claims by contemporary historians that challenge the authenticity of this story and the very existence of a Mewari Maharani Padmini (Qanungo 1969: 3-4), this and other legends continue to inform the dominant Rajput culture. Pride in their past and in their associations with the Maharanas is still widespread; Rajputs of all levels of society enthusiastically recount their connections with and service to the royal family.

Contemporary Rajputs of Udaipur are categorized into one of three major groups. Royal Rajputs are direct descendants of the Maharanas. Thakurs, or rajas, served the royal family and in exchange were granted estates, or *thikanas*, throughout the district. Nonaristocratic Rajputs are now farmers, tailors, teachers, and shopkeepers. The creation of this class of *chota bhai* ("little brother") Rajputs is attributed to the principle of primogeniture, as estates and titles were inherited in traditional Rajput society by the eldest son (Harlan 1992: 9).

The pre-Independence system of social, economic and political relationships was ordered around an agriculturally based land ownership pattern, with both political power and land controlled by the Rajput princes and their kin. Local thakurs were granted large tracts of land by the Maharanas and exercised near-total social, political, and economic control over all the inhabitants of their territories. An extensive system of service relationships bound all the various jati together into an agriculturally based socioeconomic system of patronage that granted to the local thakurs both rights and responsibilities towards those whose lives and livelihoods they controlled. This local control remained intact throughout the British colonial period.

British Rule in Mewar

It is apparent from the extensive written records and reports of British Political Agents (called Residents after 1881) that their primary role in the princely states was to promote the stability of their centralized dynastic rulers and protect this stability against both external and internal threats. The Mewar dynasty was greatly weakened by the beginning of the 19th century by dynastic quarrels with the rulers of Jaipur and Jodhpur as well as by invasions by the Marathas. When Tod was appointed the first Political Agent in 1818, Maharana Bhim Singh's government was bankrupt and its control over local thakurs as well as Bhil territories was nominal (Masters 1990).

The diffuse residential and political patterns of the Bhils were particularly threatening to the joint efforts of the British and Maharanas to consolidate state power through an Udaipur-based center. Bringing the Bhils under the Maharana's legal, political and social control was a strategic priority of Tod and other political agents of the early 19th century. This strategy becomes most fully realized in the British military support of Christian missionary activities among the Bhils, and through military response to tribal uprisings in Udaipur and surrounding districts at the beginning of the 20th century, both of which will be described subsequently.

Chapter 2 Fieldwork Landscapes

Mewar was subject to the terms of the treaties negotiated individually with the princely states; British control, in theory, extended only to external affairs. According to political scientists Lloyd and Suzanne Rudolph, the extent to which the British intervened in the domestic affairs of the princely state varied with the personalities and diplomatic skills of the Maharanas and the political agents.

> The British Government studiously avoided precision in defining paramountcy, the exercise of power over princely states....Paramountcy implied that the governor-general of India would exercise power in the field of foreign affairs, defense, communications, and coinage on behalf of the princely states. It left the states internally autonomous while guaranteeing the rulers protection against enemies foreign and domestic. The guarantee against domestic enemies brought with it unsystematic intervention in domestic affairs to insure that there would not be too many of them. [Rudolph and Rudolph 1984: 4]

The British agents and residents in Mewar saw themselves as instruments of law and order generally in Rajputana; this translated into support of the Rajput ruling structure, both in its center and in support of local thakurs. When charges against the Bhils were made, punishment was meted out quickly and without much official inquiry into the nature, cause, or guilty parties involved in the dispute.

Tod describes the punishment against a group of Bhils suspected of stealing from the British army cantonment at Neemuch:

> ...the step of plundering and retiring with their spoils to the jungles compelled me to apply to the Rana for his permission that our own troops might punish the offense. Armed with his authority, a party was equipped under command of Lieut. Hepburn, who conducted it with such caution, that he took the village completely by surprise, made prisoners of about thirty of the offenders, who were not only recognized by the parties aggrieved but whose huts furnished proofs of the plunder....Lieut. H [sic] conveyed his prisoners to the cantonment...Colonel Ludlow was instructed to select five or six of the ringleaders who were delivered over to a confidential officer of the Rana, by whom sentence of death was carried into execution by hanging them at different posts along the frontier...Five of them suffered, the sixth being respited by the Rana's officer on account of his youth and at my request pardoned. He was afterwards brought to thank me for his life, when he promised never more to join in such raids. [Tod 1837: 45]

A more systematic British attempt to deal with the "Bhil problem" throughout Central India by the British was the formation of the Bhil Corps. Established in 1825 by James Outram in Kandesh, the Corps by 1828 had more than 600 Bhil recruits. In addition, Outram opened a school for Bhils, and through the Bhil Corps recruits were encouraged to give up drinking and adopt settled agriculture; loans were advanced to Corps members for seeds and cash. Based on the success of the Kandesh Bhil Corps, a Mewar Bhil Corps was established in 1840 with headquarters at Kherwara, a town in the southern section of the district. Major K. D. Erskine, compiler of the Rajputana Gazeteer of 1908, describes the goal of this program as follows:

> The corps was raised between 1840 and 1844 with the object of weaning a semi-savage race from its predatory habits, giving it honourable employment, and assisting the Darbar in preserving order...Much good has been effected by the entertainment of these hill-men. Through the influence of those in the service and of the numerous pensioners, the entire Bhil population of these parts has been leavened with the germs of civilisation; forays into Gujarat and the neighbouring states are less frequent than they used to be, and there is greater security of life and property. [Erskine 1908: 79]

The Mewar Bhil Corps by 1908 had over 700 Bhil recruits, with all its officers British. Its jurisdiction included pursuing both political and criminal activities. In 1844 the corps was deployed at Dungarpur to suppress an attempt by the ex-Maharawal of the state to put a usurper into power; "many other Rajput chieftains would have been unable to retain their positions but for the authority of the Bhil Corps" (Carstairs 1960: 72).

Throughout the 1857 rebellion the Bhil Corps is described by its officers as having remained loyal to its British employers; their loyalty was demonstrated, according to Erskine, by slaughtering a squadron of mutinying cavalry: "At that time a squadron of Bengal Cavalry was stationed at Kherwara and left in a body for Nimach after endeavouring to persuade the Bhils to join it. The Bhils followed them up, killed every man and brought back their horses and accouterments" (Erskine 1908: 79).

Erskine described the Mewar Bhil Corp's program of "pacifying and reclaiming" the Bhils as a high point in Anglo-Indian rule. He cites as evidence of the success of this pacification program the loyalty of the Bhil companies during the Mutiny of 1857 and the number of Bhils who were recruited to serve as servants and household laborers, emulating the retired Bhil Corps members as "loyal and obedient soldiers" (1908: 230-31).

The Bhil Corps was closely associated with the missionary movement in the district. The Corps cantonment at Kherwara encouraged the presence of and activities of Christian missionaries among whom it was believed that mass conversions could be easily made among the Kherwara Bhils with the help of the Bhil Corps (Jain 1991: 67).

The claim of mass conversions seems to be somewhat of an exaggeration; A. W. T. Webb, the compiler of the 1941 Rajputana census, claims that in 1941 in all of Rajasthan the total number of tribal Christians was about 1,300 (Webb 1941). According to the 1981 Census in all of Udaipur district (where Kherwara is located) the total number of Christian tribals is reported to be 54 people; over 96 percent of the Christian tribals in the state of Rajasthan are in Banswara District, where Canadian missionaries had a stronghold. The Canadian Mission Society closed the last of its community health centers and schools in Banswara in 1974; remaining pastors of the faith are Bhils (Jain 1991: 78).

The legacy of the missionary period in Kherwara is not entirely a positive one in contemporary tribal society in that area, judging from some discussions I had there about the subject. During a field trip I made to that area, the first question I was asked when I appeared in a village was, "Are you a missionary?" Once I established that I was not, I was told stories of how the missionaries had tricked tribals into converting, or had threatened to withhold medicine or famine relief supplies if the tribals would not submit to conversion. One informant described a scene in which a missionary had arrived in a jeep; he secretly removed a part of the jeep's motor, and made a very public demonstration of how the motor would not start. He then performed a very vocal prayer, surreptitiously replaced the part, and attributed the miraculous restoration of the motor to the grace of the Christian God.

Among non-Christian tribals, the converted Christians are considered to be out-castes. The following comments were made by a woman in Kherwara concerning her sister, who married into a village that was subsequently converted.

> At [names a village] and other nearby places we have heard that the tribals have become Christian. My sister has turned into a Christian. Her whole family have become Christians. The Christian community people give them wheat and oil and turn them into Christians. I have seen that in about 25 houses in that village they now hang pictures of the Christian god. My family members have scolded my sister many times. If we go to meet her at her house we don't eat or drink there. For the last two years my sister was treated like an outcaste by my family members. We had boycotted them. My sister protested and told her husband not to follow this religion, to take the picture of Christ off the wall, but he didn't listen to her. We feel badly because they are getting free food. Then my sister's husband deserted her. Now she stays alone with her children. She has become a Hindu again and Shiva and Parvati are the gods she prays to.

Local Uprisings, British Intervention

Despite the institutional support of the British in the rural political infrastructure, a series of civil uprisings, characterized variously as "peasant rebellions" or "religious movements" depending upon the orientation of the observer, occurred in some districts where tribal populations represented, and continue to represent, close to 80 percent of the population. These movements were concentrated mostly in the districts of Dungarpur and Banswara to the south and the tribal districts of Gujarat. They and other uprisings provide considerable insight into the nature of Rajput-Bhil relations in the first half of the 20th century, the role of the British in local political affairs, and the relationship of these movements to the nascent Independence movement. The rhetoric of and issues contained within these movements bears close resemblance to those of more recent Bhil social reform efforts undertaken with NGOs. (See Appendix 3 for the text of one such document.)

Jain estimates that from 1778 to 1947 "nearly eighty cases of revolts among the Indian tribes" took place throughout India (1991: 30), and attributes this tribal unrest, particularly in Rajasthan, to the exploitive socio-economic relationships that characterized this region. A cluster of reform movements among the Bhils of Rajasthan and other sites in western India within the last century are attributed to famine, intensifying commercial interaction with other caste groups, and the Christian missionary movement in southern Rajasthan (Ibid.: 86). The activities of some reformers and self-proclaimed prophets are categorized in the relevant literature as the "Bhagat movement" (Mann 1983). While these movements are generally described as "religious" or "messianic" (Fuchs 1965) other scholars interpret them as being more political than religious in nature (Hardiman 1987 and 1989, Jain 1991 and B.K. Sharma 1990).

The oldest documented Bhagat movement among Rajasthani Bhils arose in what is now the districts of Banswara and Dungarpur. It was introduced over three centuries ago and died out without much impact soon after, but it re-emerged at the end of the 19th century. Its followers made pledges to refrain from eating meat and drinking liquor, accepting bride price, and engaging in widow remarriage (Mann 1983: 315), all of which were Bhil practices that contrasted with norms of Hindu caste behavior.

The Govindgiri Bhagat movement began in the same geographic area during the severe famine of 1900. Its founder Govindgiri, whose sect subsequently came to be known as Nath-panthi, was born into the Govalia Banjara caste, "a caste of semi-nomadic goods-carriers and, in former times, military camp followers" (Fuchs 1965: 241). After the deaths of his family members from famine he married the widow of his

Chapter 2 Fieldwork Landscapes

eldest brother and became a disciple of a Hindu monk, Rajgiri. He proclaimed himself to be the savior of the Bhils, and traveled widely throughout the Bhil regions of Southern Rajasthan and Gujarat:

> The new religious leader...preached devotion to Rama; he forbade inter-dining with outsiders, even Brahmins; he encouraged pious and virtuous living and the company of good people; his followers should always speak the truth, and abandon all kinds of falsehood; they should not steal, nor lust for another man's wife; they should abstain from meat and wine; they should bathe daily and wear clean clothes. [Fuchs 1965: 241]

Govindgiri's movement became increasingly political as it gained momentum and became focused on establishing a Bhil Raj. It held that the Bhils were the owners of the lands that were usurped by the Rajputs and as such were entitled to a "homeland." Govindgiri also urged his followers to give up liquor, which was a significant source of revenue for the government.

His activities attracted the attention of the British and the Maharanas of Dungarpur and Banswara; in a letter to the Governor General of Rajputana the Resident of Mewar complains that Govindgiri's preachings were "raising the social aspirations of the Bhils and thereby made them less amenable to unquestioning obedience of the orders of the Rajput Thakurs and officials, and tended to decrease the sale of liquor and thus affect the Abkari [liquor tax] revenue of the States in which the Bhils reside" (B.K. B.K. Sharma 1990: 25).

In November 1913, Govindgiri, accompanied by thousands of followers, proclaimed publicly his intention of forming a Bhil state. The British resident urged him to disperse his followers; on November 17 they were attacked by the Mewar Bhil Corps. Official reports state that "100 Bhils died and 900 were arrested" (Ibid.: 48) although Sharma states that it is likely that 3,000 Bhils died (1990: 110), and Jain states that 1,500 Bhils died in the confrontation (1991: 105). Govindgiri was subsequently arrested and sentenced to death; this sentence was commuted and later reduced to ten years' imprisonment. This movement prompted the British to advise the princely states of Gujarat, Central India and Rajasthan to pacify the Bhils with reforms; however "things remained at the level of correspondence only and nothing substantial was done" (B.K. Sharma 1990: 108).

Seven years later, in 1921, a movement in Udaipur district arose under the leadership of Moti Lal Tejawat, an Oswal Jain from the Jharol thikana, whose goals reflected those of several movements that had come before. His commercial dealings as a spice merchant brought him into contact with the Bhils throughout Udaipur district; he became sympathetic to their plight and began working for social reforms. His main preachings at the inception of his social reform movement were contained in the following manifesto to which followers pledged their support:

1. Liquor shall not be drunk.
2. A man shall not marry a brother's widow by force.
3. No woman whose husband is living shall marry another man.
4. Abduction of an unmarried woman shall be punishable by a heavy fine.
5. A widow can re-marry of her free will.
6. No money shall be taken on the occasion of the marriage of an unmarried woman.
7. A woman guilty of illicit intercourse with a man shall be excommunicated.
8. No Bhil shall eat the flesh of cattle.
9. No Bhil shall eat at the hands of a Muhammadan, Teli, etc.
10. No Bhil shall commit theft. [B.K. Sharma 1990: 108]

Strongly influenced by the national noncooperation movement, Moti Lal Tejawat urged the Bhils to join his *Eki* (Unity) movement. He urged his followers to refuse to pay land revenue taxes and to perform *begar*, or patronage-based forced labor (see below and Chapter 3). The Thakur of Jharol arrested Moti Lal in 1921, provoking a large demonstration of Bhils, which resulted in his release.

The British agents in Rajputana were well aware of the growing uprisings; their fears were exacerbated by references to the 1917 Russian Revolution alleged to have been made by the movement leaders. The following Rajputana Agency Report of 1921 by the Agent Wilkinson expresses the British concern:

Mewar is becoming a hotbed of lawlessness. Seditionist emissaries are teaching the people that all men are equal. The land belongs to the peasants and not to the State or landlords. It is significant that the people are being urged to use the vernacular equivalent of the world 'Comrade' instead of the customary styles of address. His Highness is said to have been threatened to be meted the fate of the czar. The movement is mainly anti-Maharana, but it might soon become anti-British and spread to adjoining British areas. [Wilkinson cited in B.K. Sharma 1990: 91]

The Bhils rejected concessions offered by both British and Udaipur officials and under Moti Lal's urgings they continued to defy the authorities. The military intervened, causing the deaths of several Bhils. Moti Lal Tejawat was arrested in 1929, effectively putting an end to this phase of his tribal rebellion.

Chapter 2 Fieldwork Landscapes 41

Although the organizers of the tribal and peasant uprisings in Rajasthan in the early 1920s drew inspiration from Mahatma Gandhi and the Indian National Congress, the INC goal of *swaraj* or self-rule for India did not yet extend to support for challenging the authority of the princely states. In 1920, during the Congress party convocation at which the policy of non-cooperation was adopted, a Rajasthani delegate failed to obtain INC support for the local movements against the abuses and excesses of Jagirdars (B.K. Sharma 1990: 87).

In 1938 the Mewar Rajya Prajamandal was formed by the INC as part of its efforts to involve the subjects of the princely states in the national independence movement. Founded with the sanction of the Maharana of Mewar, its activities were consequently limited by restrictions placed on it by the ruling family.

Famine in 1940 and floods in 1942-43 provided an opportunity for the Prajamandal workers to enter tribal areas unhampered to deliver much-needed relief supplies. They took the opportunity to also "support the cause of the down-trodden tribals more potently and to propagate the ideas more vigourously [sic]" (H. S. Sharma 1986: 18). Moti Lal Tejawat joined the effort as a Prajamandal worker and continued to preach his message of abstinence from liquor and beef-eating among the Bhils.

Sharma cautiously sums up the effects of the pre-Independence phase of rebellion and reform: "It may be said that during this decade (1938-48) the tribals may not have been awakened politically but the political organisations and the princely States had become conscious of the political necessity to awaken the tribals politically and socially so as to capture power in the changing political system which was in the offing" (Ibid.: 21). This caution is warranted; the continuation of some of the same themes in current Bhil reform movements indicates that these long-expressed goals of social equality have yet to be realized.

Jajmani, Land, and Labor

One of the themes of the various Bhil movements described above was the elimination of some of the excesses of the prevailing system of land, labor, and service allocation that connected Bhil agriculturalists to Rajput thakur landlords. This system, referred to as *jajmani*, has been described widely by historians and anthropologists as ordering the agricultural production system throughout northern India.

The village-level manifestations of this system have been the subject of a large body of historical, anthropological, and sociological literature (Baden-Powell 1957(1896); Elder 1970, Gould 1964, Kolenda 1963, Wiser 1963). The model of the village as a self-sufficient economic community dominates much of this literature; the analysis of the economic functions of the jajmani relationships reinforced this view of the village as a self-contained economic unit, within whose boundaries are found all of the productive and service resources necessary for its continuing function. Fuller (1989) has recently critiqued some of the historical and anthropological literature on jajmani for reducing and conflating a number of historically and regionally different village economies to a single uniform "system," as well as for reifying jajmani as the "traditional" village economy typology, in contradistinction to the "modern" market economy.

Classic descriptions of the jajmani relationship between patron (*jajman*) and worker (*purjan* or *kam karnewala*) assume it to be built on inequality of status and power, and domination of the productive resources of the system by land-owning castes. Along with payments of agricultural grain, the worker receives a series of concessions, among them free residence site, food, clothing, fodder, timber, dung, land, use of tools and animals and raw materials, credit facilities, and a funeral pyre plot (Wiser 1988: xxv). He is, along with his family, expected in return to supply the patron with service and labor when called, and other forms of manpower support when needed.

Most scholars who have recently analyzed the jajmani system point to change in the system on the village level since Indian independence. One significant change is noted in landowning patterns; throughout India, as several studies demonstrate, the traditional landowning castes have lost their pre-Independence monopoly on control of agricultural productive resources. As land has become available on the "open market," previously landless castes have acquired agricultural plots, shifting the economic dynamics of agricultural production and marketing (Bremen 1989).

Universal suffrage in post-Independence India has, according to some scholars, had a significant effect on the nature of interaction between castes. As Beteille (1965) describes for Tanjore, the vote of an Untouchable caste member is as numerically significant as that of a Brahman, and the electoral process puts caste groups into direct contact within this context on a presumptive basis of equality.

Technological changes in the post-Independence marketplace have also altered traditional socio-economic relationships. Factory-based employment and other forms of wage labor diminish the necessity for total economic reliance on jajmani relationships and further lessens the impact of village-level relationships through migration (Klass 1978). The introduction of hand-pumps and metal cooking utensils has to some degree eliminated caste categories of employment and service, such as water-carrier and potter (Wadley 1989).

The cash economy, coupled with increasing awareness (particularly on the part of lower-caste groups) of economic and social opportunities, has weakened the jajmani system's economic impact in rural Rajasthani communities (Michie 1981). In areas that are more remote, however, and where the opportunity for wage-related migration is limited, these relationships have not changed to the extent that they have in suburban villages. Ritual significance of jajmani "still remains intact to a considerable extent particularly in the exchange of services by low-caste groups and their patrons for life cycle ceremonies..." (Saxena 1989: 151). (The dynamics of the land-based service relationships between Bhils and Rajputs is discussed in historical perspectives in the following chapter.)

Contemporary Perspectives on Economic Mobility

In Bhil villages large landowners and merchants maintain their associations with ritual status in contemporary rural society; that ritual status is now reinforced by their status as privileged classes with economic and political influence. Bhils are not dependent upon Rajputs for subsistence or as nodal points of an agricultural production/distribution system. The local rural production and marketing system is far more complex than service-based agriculture, and cannot be reduced to a set of caste-based social and ritual obligations. It involves a combination of subsistence agriculture, local sale or barter of nonagricultural and dairy products, and commodities grown locally and marketed through a complex series of local and regional centers, some of which include overseas destinations.

The Bhils perceive their economic growth as a matter of increasing participation with the market system by the sale of both surplus and new commodity crops. Actualization of this growth process, however, is currently hampered by their socio-economic status and their current lack of some of the skills necessary to negotiate the processes of the market system. This is partly the result of widespread illiteracy and lack of education, serious impediments to full economic and political participation. And low household income and low levels of financial surplus constrain the ability to buy more productive land that would enable them to increase household income through increased commodity production. When household income is raised by agricultural commodity production and sale, an upward growth spiral beginning with investment in nonagricultural production (animal husbandry, transport animals, sugar cane production and other locally consumed goods and services like tailoring) further increases household income and has the potential of decreasing or eliminating debt.

Economic mobility is a reality of the village landscape, but the cultural and social dominance of the Rajputs continues to resonate in many aspects of local life. The eldest sons of some aristocratic Rajput families are still acknowledged as thakurs of the villages and towns in which their fathers and grandfathers once had almost total control, even though most of these families have sold off their land holdings and many are struggling financially under the burden of maintaining the large but decaying fortlike palaces in the villages their families once controlled. The royal family of Udaipur exerts strong influence over local politics and the social scene in Udaipur city; the role of the Maharana of Udaipur and other erstwhile rulers throughout Rajasthan in support of various candidates is cited by political analysts as a significant factor in the outcome of local and statewide elections (*Indian Express* October 19, 1989). And Rajput social norms continue to influence the ideals of behavior, particularly behavior for women of all castes and classes, urban and rural.

Women and Family: Urban Perspectives

Social norms manifest themselves particularly in practices that define appropriate and acceptable behavior for women (Harlan 1992). *Parda*, or restrictions on women's public activities (the Hindi word translates literally as "curtain," referring to the partition that traditionally divided the male-dominated from female-dominated spaces of large houses), is still observed, particularly by older women of the royal and noble classes. Its actual practice, while involving some house-bound activities particularly for older women, now consists more of modesty of dress, behavior, and appearance than of actual seclusion.

Many of Udaipur city's contemporary adult Rajput women, even of the aristocratic classes, are college educated and pursue professional careers or share the responsibilities of running hotels and guest houses with their husbands and other male kin. Even when parda is observed, it does not equate with isolation. Although the senior women of such households rarely leave their havelis, they are completely up-to-date on the news of the day; newspapers, television, radios, as well as a steady stream of relatives, servants and tradespeople provide all the news necessary to keep these women apprised of both local and global events.

I spent a good deal of time in the households of some of the major thakurs of the district. In one such household the senior woman was the actual head of the household, as her husband suffered from a debilitating illness. Her sons had a business in addition to supervising what was left of their lands in an adjacent tehsil. The sons were married, and their wives and families also resided in the haveli.

The younger women of the household did not work outside the home. They went out in company of other women for shopping trips or with their husbands in the family car, whose windows were screened. Although the senior woman of the house rarely left the haveli she was totally up to date on news and local events. Not formally educated, she is, however, literate in both Mewari and Hindi and read the Rajasthani newspaper every day. She has access to information from around town with amazing currency; she knew the details of events in the household of the Rajput family with whom I boarded (located about two miles away) practically as they unfolded. She is a valued confident and advisor to her sons, who discussed their business dealings with her in great detail and sought her counsel prior to undertaking any new ventures.

The three unrelated women in this household seemed to live in great harmony with each other. Pursuant with the Rajput *gotra* (patrilineage), exogamous, virilocal postmarital residence pattern, these three women were from three different families in different cities. Despite the ritual behavior of bowing, placing their forehead on the foot of their mother-in-law as a form of respectful greeting, and their brisk disappearance when senior men of the household appeared, the two daughters-in-law seemed to enjoy a personal dignity and contentment in the household. This family, like others of their class, is in the process of converting their haveli into a guest house. The women of the household are full participants in the supervision of this extensive construction project and are mediating their multiple roles and new statuses of hotel owners and construction supervisors with ease.

Misconceptions about parda and other aspects of Indian domestic and social life abound as fully in the Western imagination as do those about religion, caste and many other aspects of Indian culture. These misconceptions are fed in part by simplistic and stereotypical news coverage concerning crimes against women, such as dowry death (abuse of women in their in-laws' homes in an effort to increase dowry-related payments from the women's families, abuse that occasionally escalates to a level resulting in the death of the daughter-in-law).

Dowry death is a crime in India, as is domestic abuse in American contemporary society, and is slowly becoming recognized by the Indian legal and police systems as such. This serious issue has galvanized women's organizations throughout India to effectively lead a multipronged attack on some of the more socially conservative aspects of police and law enforcement, raising the awareness level of legal institutions to the criminality of domestic abuse generally in Indian society. Social activists in India, while addressing the serious matter of dowry death, point out that the number of dowry deaths reported in India in a year is about half the number of women's deaths resulting from domestic abuse in America, a country with one-fifth India's population.

Stereotypes of Western representation aside, the Indian social norms of arranged marriages and virilocal post-marital residence patterns do not automatically mean loveless marriages or a lifetime sentence of the tyranny at the hands of an abusive mother-in-law and elder sisters-in-law--an impression I often confront when discussing these issues with

American students. Such marriages can evolve into warm, loving and supportive relationships that bring into the marriage important social issues like intergenerational commitment to and financial, as well as social, support to a wide range of family members. Most of my Indian friends--both urban and rural--were horrified to learn that my widowed mother lives on her own. My explanations of the pride she takes in her health and independence, and her explicit preference for independent living, fell on deaf ears; most of the people with whom I talked about my family were shocked by what they saw as my lack of social responsibility to a parent.

Marriage and family norms in Udaipur still assume that a woman will be under the financial and emotional control of male family members throughout her lifetime. Divorce, even in cases of physical or emotional abuse, is rare and discouraged. Women must fight aggressively for access to inheritances from their fathers, despite civil law stipulations that are intended to ensure equal distribution of inheritance among sons and daughters. And if they do manage to inherit what is rightfully theirs under the law from their fathers' estates, women must then at times struggle legally and personally to protect that inheritance from their husbands' control.

The dowry system, despite legislative efforts to eliminate it, is still a significant issue in arranging marriages, and often places daughters at a distinct disadvantage to their brothers in negotiating marriages and protecting their rights after marriage. Dowry-related disputes after marriage are often the cause of dissension and conflict between the families of a married couple; dissatisfaction with dowry settlements often haunts a marriage for decades. The physical abuse of women by their husbands, when it occurs, is often traced to--and justified by--long-simmering resentments over disputed dowry or perceived failures of the wife's family to deliver promised dowry.

In a society so oriented to the extended family as the basic social unit, even when the actual residence structure is nuclear, traditions and norms emanating from the patrilineal, virilocal extended family unit order household relationships. In Udaipur city, it is very difficult for an unmarried woman, especially if she is without financial means, to find comfortable living arrangements outside of her family residence.

Many families express the belief that once a woman marries she is the concern of her husband's family, and no longer the responsibility of her parents or brother. After marriage brothers may refuse their sisters long-term or permanent residence in her natal home, out of fears of her claims on the paternal estate. The dowry she carries to her husband and his family at marriage is often seen as her "pre-mortem" inheritance settlement from her father, and as such is sometimes interpreted as the end of her natal family's financial, and sometimes social, responsibility for her.

Obviously the range of actual behaviors within these norms is wide and varied; some families actively intervene in cases of their daughters' or sisters' abuse; parents and brothers may welcome them back to their natal households in times of crisis. But emotional, residential and financial independence of women is still generally discouraged. The preferred strategy of resolving marriage disputes is for a third party--in the case of urban families this could be an attorney or employer--to negotiate a settlement by which it is agreed that physical violence stops and the marriage continues--but often without resolution of the emotional or financial issues.

Tourism and Identity Construction

The adulation and reputation of the Mewari rulers continues to this day, attested to by a steady stream of foreign and Indian tourists attracted to Udaipur for a glimpse of its royal forts and palaces, many of which are now luxury hotels. The lure of the Maharana's palaces in Udaipur, Jaipur and Jodhpur, as well as persistent promotion of the romanticized images of the deserts, hospitality, and the "exotica" of Rajasthan, all have contributed to a profitable tourist industry for the state. Tourist-related income accounts for nearly 15 percent of the state's income. This income therefore tends to benefit only the enterprises of and the entrepreneurial classes of the state's urban centers.

Two themes dominate the travel discourse and tend to perpetuate existing Western stereotypes about Indian culture: the luxury and romance of the Maharanas erstwhile palaces, now five-star hotels, and the exotica of Udaipur's "tribals." Periodic crafts fairs lure tourists and city dwellers into tribal product marketing centers, created specifically near Udaipur city for these events. Handicrafts created by various tribal craftsmen, consisting mostly of textiles, are sold in stalls. Dance and song performances attempt to recreate the tribal identity in this constructed setting or in hotels and restaurants.

Tourism-related literature published in India contributes to the stereotyping of the Bhils, perpetuating generalizations and categorizations that are contested in other forms of discourse. For example, the following description of the "hill tribes of Rajasthan" appears in a large-format English-language book on the folklore of Rajasthan that I bought in an Udaipur city bookstore that sells only English-language books and therefore caters in large part to foreign tourists:

> Most vivacious and zestful of the [ethnic groups of Rajasthan]...is the group of the ancient inhabitants, the forest and hill tribes called the Bhil, Girasia and Seharia inhabiting the region down south,

south-west and south-east of Rajasthan. *They are markedly short-lived but amorous and prolific, believing apparently at all times in the motto--a short life but a gay one.* They continue to live, as from the earliest times, a simple unspoiled life essentially on the products of the forests. Close to nature and deep in the jungles, one can find here and there, tucked away in a glade, a simple little home, very peaceful, solitary and inviting, with a happy smiling family sitting by its door and a toddler at play with his little bow. [Mathur 1986: 15, emphasis mine]

Attributing "markedly short-lived" life spans to the motto "a short life but a gay one" rather than to lack of access to a steady supply of clean water, food, rudimentary health care, and other subsistence resources obviously shifts the responsibility for that curtailed life span to the poor themselves as opposed to examining it from the perspective of the state's failure to provide minimal health and social welfare benefits.

India's tourist industry, which has generated over $1 billion annually for the past several years, has suffered several devastating blows recently. Hindu-Muslim conflict in Kashmir (a major international tourist attraction) has greatly reduced the flow of tourists from overseas; the assassination of Rajiv Gandhi in 1991 and the resulting civil unrest in major cities that followed further discouraged foreign visitors. The Gulf War also affected the flow of foreign visitors in 1991 and 1992. Widely publicized communal violence in 1993 and 1995 discouraged foreign tourists from visiting India in general and Rajasthan in particular. The tourist season, which reaches its height in Rajasthan in the autumn months of October and November, was devastated in 1994 by worldwide reports of pneumonic plague in northwestern Rajasthan, reports which some claim were both medically and demographically exaggerated.

Despite these continuous and unpredictable events, the Old City section of Udaipur is undergoing a building boom of small hotels and guest houses. Hundreds of new establishments, converted from old havelis and small buildings, are jostling for views of Lake Pichola, which is continually under assault by unenforced regulations the on dumping of waste and garbage into its once pristine waters. Many local environmentalists fear for the effects of this unabated building boom, which is accompanied by tremendous demand on the already fragile water table and on other natural resources of the area.

Rajasthan's success as a tourist destination is a good example of the "mixed blessing" of tourism in underdeveloped countries. The persistence of statewide underdevelopment despite the state's highly developed and profitable tourism infrastructure supports recent critiques of tourism as national development strategy (see, for example, deKadt

1976). While the benefits of tourism contribute generally to the state and national coffers, they rarely if ever trickle down into underdeveloped rural areas.

In Udaipur, tourists and their rupees rarely venture beyond the limits of the city, and when they do it is to travel back and forth in a single day's journey to tourist attractions outside it. The gap between rural services and tourist-oriented services is strikingly apparent; one has only to compare the quality of buses and roads that serve the tourist routes with those that service the outlying villages to see the stark difference in the quality of services and infrastructure. If tourists come into contact at all with people identified by local culture brokers, like tour guides or drivers, as Bhils or tribals, it is only at hotels or restaurants, or at handicraft expositions.

The disjuncture between tourist and local services was starkly illustrated to me while traveling in Rajasthan in 1988. The state was suffering from severe drought, the result of three consecutive years of monsoon failures; animal deaths were widespread, the agricultural output was severely curtailed, and water was in critically short supply. Despite this statewide devastation, the luxury hotel I stayed at in Jaipur advised guests, by way of a printed sign in the bathroom, to let their bath water run freely down the tub drain for ten minutes if it didn't come out hot enough for their taste.

Doing Fieldwork in Udaipur

Fieldwork for this study was conducted in and around Bagdunda, a multi-caste village located about 25 kilometers (15 miles) to the northwest of Udaipur city "as the crow flies" but reachable only by roads that double the length of the journey. Because intercaste interactions in relation to NGO activity is a central issue in this study, it was necessary for me to locate a multicaste village as a site for my research. I eventually selected Bagdunda as a primary field study site for several reasons, including the demographics of the village and the cooperation for this research project by the staff of the NGO Ubeshwar Vikas Mandal (UVM). UVM has been operating in Bagdunda and vicinity since 1985 and has a field office there. As do other NGOs in Udaipur, UVM focuses its activities among SC/ST participants. (See Map 3.)

Bagdunda has a primary school and a middle school. The village is electrified but many SC and ST homes are still without electricity. There is no primary health care facility in or near the village; people in need of medical care must travel either 15 kilometers north to Gogunda, where the pharmacist also supplies basic medical services, or from Gogunda to the district hospital in Udaipur, about 35 kilometers to the south, the nearest site where one can see a medical doctor.

A *pukka*, or all-weather paved, road connects the city of Udaipur with the town of Gogunda. To reach Bagdunda you change buses there for a private bus that continues the journey; the pukka road ends at Bagdunda. Beyond Bagdunda private buses traverse the dried river beds that serve as roads during the dry seasons; these become inaccessible at the first rains, and remain flooded until a few weeks after the monsoons, making foot travel the only way to reach many of the villages of the district during the rainy season.

Even during the dry season many prefer to walk from village to village rather than depend on the unreliable bus service. When buses do run they are crammed with people, livestock, and sacks of agricultural produce. These private buses are purchased by local entrepreneurs from the government transport system after years of use; they are then only nominally refurbished and put into service on the local roadways. A tragic bus accident in September 1995, when a private bus overturned into a gully on the road between Gogunda and Udaipur, resulted in 15 deaths and injuries to many more. Although it shocked everyone in Bagdunda, the accident was not a surprise; many had felt that it was only a matter of time until one of these unregulated crowded buses, with scores of people sitting on the roof, would be involved in a serious accident. For a day or two after the accident the local police checked private buses for inspection and registration certificates at the bus stand in Gogunda; those without the proper documentation merely circumvented the town and continued on their way. In October 1995 the state-owned bus system introduced twice-daily bus service direct from Bagdunda to Udaipur, much to the delight of local residents.

Bagdunda has a total population of approximately 1,500 people in 100 Rajput households; 30 Jain households; 12 Kumhar (potter) households; 17 Bhil households (plus another 17 Bhil families in Khera, the Bhil phala about a kilometer away from Bagdunda proper); 30 Meghwal households, and 2 Teli (oil processor) households. In addition, one house was identified as belonging to a Muslim, but it is unoccupied. A Brahman family lives on its own homestead half a kilometer from Bagdunda.

In addition I regularly visited Solaria, a Bhil phala, about 10 kilometers to the southwest of Bagdunda. Solaria is not a census entity; its population is 152 people in 32 households. The nearby multicaste village of Morwa, which is listed in the census, has a total population of about 500 people (including the residents of Solaria). Of these, 80 are Rajput and 200 are Bhils. There are also 3 Lohar (blacksmith) households, 10 Meghwal households and 2 Brahman households. The village of Morwa has a school building, although for many weeks at a time teachers failed to appear on a regular basis. It has no primary health center, and the only sources of water are family-owned nonelectrified wells or two hand pumps, subject to continuous breakdown.

Solaria is on the fringes of the geographic operating area of UVM and the organization has made some efforts at involving residents of Morwa and Solaria in its activities. Solaria Bhils have marital ties and social interaction with Bagdunda and surrounding phalas. They are familiar with UVM and other NGOs, and participate regularly in their meetings and gatherings.

My research also included long and fruitful discussions in the city of Udaipur with the directors and staffs of UVM, Sewa Mandir, Jan Jagran, Astha, and other local organizations on and near the street that is locally referred to as "NGO row" where many of the NGOs have offices and many of their staff members reside. The frequent flow of foreign and Indian visitors, including representatives of donor organizations, development specialists, students, volunteers, anthropologists and other concerned individuals, contributes to the cosmopolitan nature of this NGO community.

For an anthropologist, finding a field site that even approaches the expectations of one's dissertation proposal can be a chancy and difficult experience; expectations of cooperation or even finding people who will talk to you can often evaporate before the naive eyes of the first-time fieldworkers. To my good fortune, I have only read about these horrors of fieldwork. The people I met in Udaipur were generous and candid in sharing their work and lives with me.

I find it's impossible to discuss fieldwork without mentioning the emotional and human responses that are so much a part of this interactive research process. I have formed what will be lifelong friendships with many of the people I met, and as my work evolved my emotional connections became problematical. This analysis requires the attempt at stepping back and critiquing a complex landscape with some objectivity and distance. This objectivity that is not always easy to obtain when it involves the work of people whom I have come to admire for their dedication and personal commitment.

Fieldwork involves not only my perceptions of others, but also how others perceive me. Spending a year with the social workers and the village-level employees and members of these organizations obscured my position as an observer, and I had to confront the perception of village informants of my being part of these organizations. This perception had both positive and negative effects. At times, especially at the beginning of fieldwork, I am sure that information was shared cautiously with me; but as time progressed and I became a regular fixture in the villages, people approached me more openly. My alliances and friendships were well known to all; when my friends had arguments or conflicts they shared this information with me.

I have no delusions, however, about having been perceived as either neutral and unaligned. I was clearly not one of "them"--either social worker or villager. Although I spent most of my time in the villages, it was clearly known to everyone that I had a room in Udaipur complete with the plumbing fixtures -- and high rent -- befitting my foreign status, and that I had the financial resources to pay for it, as well as to come to and go from the villages as I pleased. (After the bus accident I came and went several times in a hired car--a luxury by any standards in Bagdunda.) Even more significantly from the village perspective, I had easy access to the top levels of management of the organizations that many villagers' livelihoods were dependent upon. These were all forms of social and economic capital that clearly set me apart from my friends and colleagues in the villages.

How did they perceive me? Aspects of my identity which I pride myself on disappear in this context. The Ph.D. which consumed so much of my efforts and energy for a decade means nothing to people in Bagdunda and Solaria. It's a humbling and important reminder that what I am in this context is defined virtually entirely in terms of the people I am associated with--the NGO workers and organizers and social workers. I am an outsider--not an American, but an outsider. When I traveled with, and attended NGO functions and meetings with, two female social workers employed by UVM who lived and worked in Bagdunda, all three of us were perceived, particularly by Bhil women with whom we spent much of our time, as of a very similar category. The local women knew they both came from Delhi and I from America, but that was not terribly significant to them as the concept of America as a foreign entity across the ocean was unknown to them. We were all from "outside." We were all links to resources outside of the villages. And all of us could help them, from their perspectives, in ways that were often at odds with the strategy of the organization and inconsistent with our personal ideas about how best to aid individuals and communities.

Despite my desire to become an unnoticed part of the social landscape, this was an unrealistic fantasy of fieldwork in a rural community. I was continuously and always an outsider. There were moments, occasionally, late at night, just before dropping off to sleep, or surrounded by local family members or large groups of women at special gatherings, when I felt truly connected and part of the community as an individual, and not as a representative of any other group. But in reality these were fleeting sensations; I was always and will remain an outsider no matter what my intentions. I entered this rural setting with access to resources my friends there could not envision. I was there by choice and could leave by choice.

This is not to imply that close human bonds weren't formed. Spending extended periods of time with families over the past eight years has sealed friendships throughout this area. In this time children have been born, marriages made, illness, accidents and deaths taken place--all events that I've shared and participated in, sometimes over the years only through letters and with private tears.

Many people in the villages have told me that they will always hold me in their thoughts for a simple reason--I return. Even though five years passed between my last two visits, the fact that I came back to their villages is regarded as enormously significant. Unfortunately, this is a poignant reminder of the constant visits and unfulfilled promises of representatives of local institutions, political parties, and organizations who do not return.

My presence, constant questions, endless tape recording of conversations and meetings, was not always regarded as positive. Some people saw it as exploitive--as an unfair taking away of something from their community without remuneration. When I returned to Bagdunda and Solaria in 1995, I was recording stories about *gavri*, a local ritual cycle performed by the Bhils of this district. One man, who was in his fifties, was referred to me because of his encyclopedic knowledge of the stories and legends associated with this ritual cycle, which he shared with me. But he made it clear that he expected remuneration for his time--the first occasion on which I had been directly confronted with this request. I agreed to his request; however, my field notes for that and subsequent weeks are filled with voluminous ramblings about this issue from all possible perspectives. But my decision came down to a simple fact: I had a grant that was paying for my time. Why should he sit and talk to me for hours at a time, providing me with invaluable information, and not receive remuneration? Was his time so different from my time? Did I stop and consider the ramifications of paying a doctor who spent time giving me information about my health problems? Obviously not. Did this exchange of money for information compromise the value of the information on gavri and local mythology? I think not.

Another aspect of this issue for me was whether to make cash donations to organizations. I have made a personal commitment to help both individuals and communities in the area as best I can by donating money and time where I think it can best be used, and is most needed. Upon my return from Rajasthan in 1990 I helped establish a relationship between Bhatia and Trickle Up, an organization in New York that makes $100 grants for income-generating projects throughout the underdeveloped world, grants that are supervised and coordinated through local NGOs or responsible individuals. Bhatia has reported great individual successes with these grants; in Solaria $100 goes very far in training a young man and setting up a tailor shop, buying the equipment to process and market *gur* (a widely used sweetener made from boiled sugar cane juice) or organize a family plot and workers to plant ginger, a very profitable commodity crop. I have also donated money directly to some organizations in Udaipur that I believed had the need for individual donations and could best channel the funds according to community-established priorities.

With all these typically messy and complex human emotions, perceptions, and misunderstandings surrounding fieldwork and research, what can anthropological investigation contribute to a body of discourse on development? I think the primary potential contribution lies in the methodology: in being there; in being forced by necessity to listen to multiple voices, multiple perspectives. In starting first with questions, and then paying attention to every word of every speaker in every setting. In being forced by human and intellectual necessity to go beyond expectation and stereotype, label, and mechanistic device, and hear the words, listen to the conflict, see people in their multiple roles as parents, workers, employees, farmers, laborers, men, women, political party members, brothers, sisters, Bhils, Rajputs, husbands, wives--all of which contribute to the meaning of an event or a particular interaction on a particular day.

Hearing these multiple voices makes the comfortable dichotomies and categories disappear. There's no such thing as "traditional" or "modern" in this complex context. And there's no such thing as "them"--as in the comment I so often heard from middle-class Udaipur residents when I said I was working with and living with Bhils: "Why don't you do-gooders just leave them alone? They're so happy as they are--dancing, drinking--why don't you just leave them alone?"

Finally, intellectually dealing with the ideas of development, people's participation, organization, strategy, constantly talking about development while trying to configure it within a broader complex of phenomena--with the ever-present warning that talking about it makes it an *it*, gives it reality beyond what is being constructed for it by this constant discourse.

Chapter Summary

The history and variety of NGO activities has created a distinct NGO "culture" in Udaipur district; the proliferation of these organizations and the frequent flow of foreign and Indian observers to them both contribute to the dynamism of this complex community. The structures within these organizations, as well as the interaction between them, are significant factors in the rural development landscape; the evolution of the strategies of interorganizational competition as well as cooperation has therefore resonated on the village level.

Chapter 2 Fieldwork Landscapes

These organizations are just one aspect of the complex rural cultural landscape, a landscape shaped in part by contemporary national and global forces, and in part by social and political history. To understand the complexities of how the strategies and policies of NGOs are interpreted by, and subsequently translated into action in, rural communities, one must consider all these aspects of local and national histories. And one must address how these histories, which include the construction of categories of group identity, have been recorded, interpreted, and reinterpreted within various colonial period, as well as contemporary, political, anthropological, and developmental paradigms.

---

[1] A decennial Census was conducted in 1981 and 1991. At the time of the final editing of this book only some of the figures and tables for Rajasthan were available from the 1991 census; these later figures are used wherever possible.

[2] By way of comparison and explanation of census categories, Jaipur is Rajasthan's most populous city, with over 1.5 million people. Its population has grown about five times since the 1951 census, and it is the 13th most populous city in India; Udaipur is the 6th largest city in Rajasthan, and its all-India ranking is 91. Urban areas in the census include Census Towns, defined as having a minimum population of 5,000 with at least 75 percent of the male main working population engaged in nonagricultural activity.

[3] Step wells were identified by health specialists as a primary source for transmitting guinea-worm disease. See Chapter 7 for a discussion of the extensive communitiy health program designed to eliminate this devastating endemic disease.

[4] A bigha is approximately two thirds of an acre; one bigha is equivalent to about 0.135 hectares or slightly under one fifth of a hectare. A bigha is a locally defined unit and its area varies from region to region. It is the unit all local people use in describing the size of their land holdings; "outsiders" like engineers or land survey professionals compute land holdings by hectare.

[5] One of the first anthropologists to fully document the political and economic, as well as religious significance, of caste group mobilization in a complex urban setting was Lynch (1969), a study of the mobilization and eventual conversion to Buddhism of the Jatav caste of Agra . A more detailed discussion of the anthropological issues in the study of intercaste relationships is outside the parameters of this study. For a review of recent literature on the anthropology of caste see Inden 1990 and Raheja 1988b.

[6]The 19 "Native States" administered under the British Rajputana Agency were Abu, Sirohi, Jodhpur, Kherwara, Partabargh, Udaipur, Jhalawar, Kotah, Deoli, Shahpura, Jaipur, Karanli, Dholpur, Bharatpur, Alwar, Bikaner, Tonk, Bundi and Kishangargh. These 19 states were divided into the following administrative units: Mewar Residency, Western Rajputana States, Jaipur Residency, Eastern Rajputana States, Haroti and Tonk, Alwar Agency, Kota Agency, and Bikaner Agency.

The Mewar Residency encompassed Udaipur, Pratabgarh, Dungarpur, Banswara, Khewara, and Kotra. The Western Rajputana States Administration encompassed Marwar, Sirohi, and Jaisalmer. The Jaipur Residency included Jaipur and Kishangar. The Eastern Rajputana Agency included Bharatpur, Karauli, and Dholpur. Haraoti and Tonk Administrative Agency included Deoli, Bundi, Tonk and Shahpura. The Alwar Agency included Alwar and Nimrana. The Kota Agency included Kota, and Jhalawar. The Bikaner Agency included only Bikaner.

Chapter 3

What Are Tribals? Who Are Bhils?

> How can people who have no unity, no language of their own, no specific occupation, no pure racial features, no distinctive culture and above all no identity, be considered as a tribe? (Deliege 1985: 15)

The terms *tribe* and *tribal* have slipped into both anthropological literature and general usage undefined and critically unexamined. As Morton Fried lamented thirty years ago, *tribe* figures high up on the list of ambiguous terms in the vocabulary of anthropology:

> If I had to select one word in the vocabulary of anthropology as the single most egregious case of meaninglessness, I would have to pass over 'tribe' in favor of 'race.' I am sure, however, that 'tribe' figures prominently on the list of putative technical terms ranked in order of degree of ambiguity as reflected in multifarious definitions. [1966: 528]

As Fried implies, the issues of tribe very often conflate with those of race; although he was not addressing tribalism in India specifically in the work in which this quote appears, this ambiguity remains a characteristic of this discourse throughout its history, and in contemporary policy that emanates from it.

The fascination of the British in India with tribals in general and Bhils in particular has created an enormous body of literature that reflects an almost obsessive search for racial divisions and their respective physiological diagnostic markers. British observers, ethnologists, and colonial administrators (often one and the same person) combined their civil, political, and military authority with control over the intellectual discourse on caste and tribe to codify the system of categorization of social groups as "races." The histories of groups of people designated as Adivasi in contemporary India are being reevaluated by contemporary scholars, particularly in light of the role played by British colonial institutions and intellectual traditions in their representation.

The immense body of literature on the Bhils is marked by assumptions made by "under-informed 19th century administrators" which are still repeated in contemporary ethnographies to this day. Many ethnographies still refer to the Bhils as belonging to the Dravidian "race"--the "oldest inhabitants" or "earliest settlers" of Rajputana. "Anthropologists have done little more than reify through repetition these assumptions without any empirical evidence at all. The confusion between 'tribe' and 'primitive', 'archaic', 'backward' or 'savage' has led most of the writers to accept any hypothesis as truth...But in the last analysis what anthropologists have been repeating is nothing else than traditional clichés about tribals..." (Deliege 1985: 13-16).

Contemporary representation of the Bhils combines Sanskritic, ethnographic, anthropometric, and historical "evidence" with racial theory of the 19th century. Underlying this representation is the assumed difference between caste and tribe; a division believed to have its origins in the replacement of indigenous, "Dravidian" peoples by the "invading" Indo-Europeans, who brought with them to India the social system of caste divisions.

These assumptions and stereotypes were then reified through a series of British census and ethnological documents, eventually integrated into the Constitution of India. The stigmas and cultural generalizations asserted with this system of "tribal" categorization also influenced social science literature, as well as general attitudes that informed policy and prejudice. These are critical issues that have a significant impact on the contemporary representation of the Bhils of Udaipur and other tribal groups in India today.

The Construction of Bhil Identity: A Brief History

Contemporary study of the Bhils is still strongly influenced by translations of Sanskritic literature into English by British colonial period philologists, wherein tribals in general and Bhils in particular are referred to as *dasyu* which is variously (and inconsistently) translated as savage, barbarian, and robber. They are also referred to as *Nishada*, "the general term [in epic literature] for the non-Aryan tribes who were not under Aryan control, as the Sudras were" (Law 1973: 99).

Ktesias (alt. Ctesias), a Greek writer to whom several historical works dated around 400 BC are attributed, described "a race of Pygmie people" in Central India. His reports of monstrously deformed humans,

Chapter 3 What Are Tribals? Who Are Bhils?

once taken as falsehood or his own invention, were rehabilitated in light of 18th- and 19th-century translations of the Sanskrit epics.

> He [Ktesias] writes that in the middle of India are found the swarthy men called Pygmies who speak the same language as the other Indians. They are very diminutive, the tallest of them being but two cuts in height, while the majority are only one and a half. They let their hair grow very long--down to their knees, and even lower. They have the largest beards anywhere to be seen, and when these have grown sufficiently long and copious, they no longer wear clothing, but, instead, let the hair of the head fall down their backs far below the knee, while in front are their beards trailing down to their very feet. When their hair has thus thickly enveloped their whole body, they bind it round them with a zone, and so make it serve for a garment. Their privates are thick, and so large that they depend [sic] even to their ancles [sic]. They are moreover snubnosed, and otherwise ill-favoured. [McCrindle (1973(1882): 15-16]

These fantastical creatures described by Ktesias, and in later works attributed to Ptolemy, were explicitly linked by British colonial documents to the Bhils. For example, the entry on the Bhils in the *Imperial Gazettteer* of 1908 states that: "The Bhils seem to be the 'Pygmies' of Ctesias (400 BC.) and the *Poulindai* and *Phyllitae* of Ptolemy (AD. 150)... The typical Bhil is small, dark, broad-nosed, and ugly, but well built and active" (Imperial Gazetteer 1908: 101).

Sir Herbert H. Risley (1851-1911), the major British architect of race theory in India, established a system of physical characteristics associated with the different "races of the Indian Empire." The physical variables included stature, complexion, facial hair, eye color, head shape and nasal shape and length (Risley 1969(1915): 370). His views and theories were widely distributed in documents subsequent to the publication of the Census of 1901, for which he was Census Commissioner. The multivolume *Imperial Gazetteers*, published and updated with census data, included detailed ethnographic descriptions of tribes and castes of India, and drew heavily on data compiled for this Census (Inden 1990: 58).

Based on data on 200 "Rajputana Bhils," Risley concluded that they definitely belonged to the "Dravidian" type (1969: 370). Other British observers were less inclined to follow the conventions of racial categorization, and included in their discussions observations of differentiation, environmental constraint and the processes of intermarriage. For example, R. E. Enthoven, Superintendent of Ethnography, Bombay Presidency, in a 1920 survey of the castes and tribes of that region, noted wide variation in the appearance of Bhils throughout Central India:

> Bhils differ much in appearance. As a rule the Gujarat Bhil is small, light-limbed and active, some having handsome though irregular features. The typical Kandesh Bhil, the wild woodman of the Satpuras, is dark, well-made, active and hardy, with high cheek bones, wide nostrils and in some cases coarse almost African features. These are no doubt stunted and degraded by want and ill-health, and perhaps by intermarriage with still older and lower tribes. Among the southern and western tribes, who probably more nearly represent the original type of Bhil, are many well-built and even some tall handsome men with regular features and waving hair. The plain Bhils are scarcely to be distinguished from local Kunbis (agricultural castes). [Enthoven 1920: 154]

Despite the observation of physical diversity within these so-called racial groups, the model of the Bhils as belonging to a Dravidian race persisted. Implicit in this racial model for the identity of the Bhils is the belief that they once spoke a non-Indo-European, Dravidian language. The absence of any evidence of this language by the 1800s was problematical to followers of this theory, but this absence was explained as being evidence of its complete replacement by the speakers of Indo-European languages, an explanation readily taken up by 20th-century anthropologists.

Koppers and Jungblut, for example, state that the absence of a Bhil language is evidence that it has been lost: "On finding that the present language of the Bhils is an Aryan one whereas they themselves are certainly pre-Aryan, we cannot but conclude that they have lost their own language" (Koppers and Jungblut 1976: 33), conclusions that were echoed by the anthropologist Morris Carstairs (1954).

All documentation of the languages spoken by various geographically located groups of Bhils indicates that they are local dialects influenced solely by neighboring Indo-European-language speakers. Grierson's 1907 Linguistic Survey of India, one of the definitive works on linguistic variation in India, states that: "Bhils speak the cognate dialects of Gujarati, Marathi, Rangdi, Mevadi, Hindi, Rajputani, etc., in accordance with the proximity of the larger languages. These dialects vary much in corruption from the source from which they are borrowed..." (in Enthoven 1920: 154).

In summarizing the linguistic evidence analyzing the languages and dialects spoken by the Bhils of Rajasthan and Gujarat, Deliege concludes: "Ancestors of the present day Bhils may well have spoken non-Indo-European languages but we have nothing to prove it" (Deliege 1985: 28).

Bhil "Egalitarianism" and "Isolation" Reexamined

Another prevailing assumption about the tribals in general and Bhils in particular is that their communities had little or no internal political

Chapter 3 What Are Tribals? Who Are Bhils?   61

or social stratification. However, observers have noted factors of social and economic differentiation for over the past two centuries. Based on his observations in the 1820s, Sir John Malcolm, political and military administrator of Central India from 1818 to 1822, noted that the Bhils were divided into three "distinct classes":

> ...which may be denominated the village, the cultivating and the wild or mountain Bheel. The first consists of a few, who from ancient residence or chance have become inhabitants of villages on the plain (though usually near the hills), of which they are the watchmen, and are incorporated as a portion of the community; the cultivating Bheels are those who have continued in their peaceable occupations after their leaders were destroyed or driven by invaders to become desperate freebooters; and the wild, or mountain Bheel, comprises all that part of the tribe, who, preferring savage freedom and indolence to submission and industry, have continued to subsist by plunder. [Malcolm 1970(1823)): 520-21]

Elsewhere Malcolm makes reference to "pure Bhills [sic]" and their "impure" counterparts, the former having given up meateating and in so doing raising their status to the point of commensality with Rajputs (Malcolm 1827: 80).

The hypothesized political and social egalitarianism cited in typologies of tribal life was maintained by separation or isolation of tribal groups from caste Hindus. The actual extent of tribal "isolation" is challenged, for example, by Hardiman in his work on the Adivasis of Surat district in Gujarat: "The isolation of the adivasis has...been overemphasized. Their economic contact with the outside world was not, in many cases, confined to trivial barter. Even before the coming of the British, merchants and moneylenders were plying their trade in many adivasi villages, advancing loans and selling in urban markets considerable quantities of the crops grown by the adivasis" (Hardiman 1989: 12).

The extent of this economic dependency was noted by a colonial administrator, A. F. Bellasis, who observed in the 1850s:

> The very seed [the Adivasi] sows is often not his own, but borrowed at an interest so exorbitant that the lender claims the produce, when it is repeated, leaving to the wretched cultivator a bare subsistence of the coarsest grain. He cannot read or write. He often does not know the rental of his land, and cannot tell you the amount of his yearly increasing debt. [cited in Ibid.: 86]

Bhil-Rajput Relations

Tod enumerates many instances, particularly during the wars with the Moghuls, when the Bhils came to the aid of the Rajput rulers as military allies, making significant contributions during the ongoing conflict. The recognition of Bhils as military allies is evident on the royal seal of the ruling house of Mewar, which to this day consists of a Bhil bowman and a Rajput soldier of equal size. This pictorial representation is often interpreted as symbolizing historical political equality between Bhils and Rajputs and implying an alliance between equals. Other forms of representation, however, illustrate a more ambivalent and asymmetrical relationship.

This relationship is illustrated in the legend of Guha (alt. Goha), the mythological founder of the ruling clan of the Sisodia Rajputs from whom the Maharanas claim descent. This well-known and often-quoted story provides belies the image of the Bhils as independent allies to the ruling Rajputs. In this story they are easily fooled by an orphaned Rajput prince in the ninth century; Guja is befriended and protected by the Bhils but later takes advantage of their kindness by tricking them into giving up their territory to him. This story is significant for a number of reasons. Through trickery the Rajput Goha easily establishes the kingdom of Mewar by stealing the realm of the Bhils. In addition it makes reference to the participation of a Bhil in the coronation of a Rajput king by the application of a *tika* (also referred to as *tilak*–a ceremonial mark) on the Maharana's forehead.

Deliege interprets the many instances of the tilak mentioned by Tod as evidence of a contractual transfer of power from the Bhils to the Rajput princes, and not as an acknowledgment of Bhil power by the Mewari Rajputs. This transfer is not absolute, notes Deliege, and "the attempts to regain the power after a while testify to the political capability of the Bhils" (1985: 58). He also notes that the application of the tilak is a widespread phenomenon; Bhils themselves apply the tilak on many occasions of social life, particularly at weddings, another example of a contractual relationship solemnized with ritual.

Malcolm states that the ceremony was in decline by the early 1820s (1970: 69). When I talked with a contemporary thakur family about this practice of a Bhil applying the tilak to the forehead of the new Maharana, they insisted that I was misinformed. They said they had no knowledge of it and vehemently denied that it ever occurred.

Economic Relations Between Bhils and Rajputs

Under the land tenure system of pre-Independence Rajasthan, sole ownership of land belonged to the hereditary princes, who had the authority to reapportion it after certain periods or at the death of the original owner. They also had the right to confiscate land or transfer it from one cultivator to another (G.N. Sharma 1968: 288). Land taxes, rents, and related transit and customs duties were the main source of revenue to the princes (Imperial Gazetteer of India 1908: 146). Land was divided into two general categories: *khalsa* (also referred to as *khalisa*) which was under the direct management of the crown; and land

Chapter 3 What Are Tribals? Who Are Bhils?

held by various grantees. Khalsa lands were owned outright by the ruler, but in actual practice the grantee had complete control over the land including the right to sell and mortgage it as long as rent on it was paid to the Maharana.

Land grants were awarded for a number of different reasons; the land category name reflected the type of service. Jagirs were granted to jagirdars, who received the property in return for military, civil, or political service. Rajput jagirdars paid a fixed annual tribute to the Darbar of one-sixth the income of their estates, as well as owing manpower service annually. Non-Rajput jagirdars, either Mahajans (bankers or moneylenders usually of the Jain religion) or Kayasths (a caste of official record keepers) were required to pay tribute on the occasion of a coronation and to provide regular services to the Darbar, but were not required to pay annual tribute based on estate income.

Rao relates the formation of three distinct classes of the Bhils to the Rajput state land tenure system. He notes that the Bhils who migrated to or settled near khalsa villages fared far better than those in jagir villages: "The Bhils in khalsa villages got opportunities to have contact with the state level officials. This provided them an opportunity for some liberal treatment. They were subjected to lesser atrocities and oppression. The Bhils who were in khalsa villages took to skilled agriculture. They had opportunities to learn from the caste Hindu cultivators" (Rao 1988: 28). In contrast, Bhils living in Jagir villages were under the total control of the jagirdar, who "intervened in all aspects of social and cultural life of the people...The Bhils in the Jagir were required to submit to all the command of the Jagirdar, any time at the pleasure of the latter" (Ibid.: 28).

Among those commands was forced labor, or *begar* (also referred to locally as *lag-bag*). Under the begar system all caste groups, with the exception of Rajputs and Brahmans (Jain 1991: 39), were required to perform services for the jagirdar on behalf of the Maharana. Jagirdars were free to charge whatever rate they wished, "...without giving any rational explanation. Thus one-third to two-thirds of produce was taken away as land revenue and what remained was paid by way of lag-bag. The cultivator was left with negligible means for his existence...If there was deficit in the budget of the thikana, it was made good from the tenants. In fact, the Jagirdar and his personnel threw the burden of their expenses upon the tenants" (Ibid.: 41). The burden of service placed upon the Bhils was particularly onerous.

> The Bhils were required to carry the luggage of officials from one place to another during their tour, and arrange for their lodging and boarding--all without any payments. The laws of Begar empowered the various categories of officials to extract Begar from the Bhils.

> These officials also had the privilege to realise a fixed quantity of foodstuffs from them.
>
> The institution of Begar had a profound influence on the life of the members of this tribe. It could be enforced at any time and for any length of period, rendering their living and working programmes uncertain. It could be enforced during the sowing and harvesting seasons, which was most detrimental to their own economic pursuits. [Doshi 1971: 18]

Rajput political domination brought with it increasingly significant contact with commercial castes, traders, and moneylenders. The role of Banias, or merchant-moneylenders, in rural Rajasthan has been documented in several studies (e.g. Breman 1974, Jones 1991, Michie 1978, and McCurdy 1971). These studies elucidate the commercial and economic dynamics of Bhil life historically, and have also corrected previous assumptions about Bhil cultural and economic isolation. They also detail the process by which indebtedness has become a distinguishing and enduring feature of contemporary Bhil existence.

The *sagri* system is the local manifestation of the debt-based labor relationships between Bhils and (primarily) upper-caste moneylenders in Rajasthan. (Bhils, however, are not the only caste group to suffer from constant indebtedness, nor is moneylending activity limited only to upper-caste groups.) Sagri requires labor by the debtor that is applied only against repaying interest on the loan; the principal remains due in cash. The obligation of the sagri (debtor) to work for the lender remains in force until the cash principal is repaid. If the debtor dies before the loan principal is fully repaid, the obligation is passed on to the next generation. The institution of sagri is as much cultural as it is economic; it is described as being structurally similar to the jajmani relationship because it involves both mutual protection and obligation that is transmitted from one generation to the next (Vyas 1980).

Sagri and other forms of forced or bonded labor were banned by Article 23 of the Indian Constitution, which prohibits forced labor; other central government legislation outlawed moneylending and debt-slavery. Rajasthan's State Sagri Abolition Act was passed in 1961. A study of sagri in Dungarpur District in the 1960s concluded, however, that this legislation had little impact on the condition of existing sagris. The authors stated that the primary reason Bhils go into debt is to finance ritual and other nonproductive expenses, such as *dapa* (bride price); marriage expenditure; death feast; or repayment of old debt. The interest rate they pay on these loans increases the size of the initial debt seven-fold in three years (Vyas and Chaudhary 1968).

This study concludes by observing that the binding force of the sagri relationship has recently been weakened, and that debt relationships are currently more based on agricultural labor than domestic service. The hold of traditional moneylenders in Dungarpur District has been somewhat weakened by government wage labor projects, famine relief programs, and labor opportunities for migrant workers in Gujarat and Madhya Pradesh.

Who Are the Bhils?--Alternative Models and Explanations

Considering the weakness of racial, linguistic, biological, and historical representations of Bhil identity, the identity of contemporary Bhils can best be described in terms of social process. Deliege, for example, concludes that the Bhils are people who: "...escaped the influence of Brahmanic culture [and] found a way of living, a social organization and practices which were more suitable to their environment. Occasional fugitives, banished peoples, defeated soldiers, mixed with these people of the Hills and tinged their culture with Hindu elements. The constant reference to the 'degraded character' of the tribals as well as their myths of origin would make sense within that context" (Deliege 1985: 34).

Deliege argues that Bhils had contact with plains groups from time to time (particularly during times of siege, as when Muslim invasions caused Rajput rulers to seek refuge in the mountains), but he states that "it is difficult to infer from these occasional contacts a complete loss of a ghostly culture and language" (Ibid.: 35). Rather than subscribing to the conventional theory of their having been chased into the hills by plains people, Deliege concludes that the Bhils were "always hill people," a hypothesis he acknowledges is "conjectural and not based on empirical evidence" (Ibid.: 36).

Y.V.S. Nath, who studied the Bhils of Ratanmal (located on the southeastern border of Panchamahals District of Gujarat) reached similar conclusions:

> In retrospect, there is plenty of evidence to believe that not all the people known today as Bhils constitute a single tribe. On the contrary, one is inclined to believe that a congeries of tribes living in adjacent areas and bearing only a superficial resemblance in their general way of life in the eyes of plains men, were probably lumped together under a blanket term....The terms like Gond, Koli and-- today Raniparaj, are well-known instances. [Nath 1960: 21]

The most recent scholarship on the tribal communities analyzes the category of tribe in terms of colonial and precolonial political economy, and challenges the structural framework that stresses the existence of "tribe" in relation to its presumed opposite, "caste" society. These studies of tribal societies in contemporary India link tribal agriculturalists to the prevailing economic system in precolonial and colonial India, and the "creation" of tribal designations in relatively recent history.

Unnithan (1991), for example, in analyzing the Girasia of south Rajasthan (who identity themselves as Girahya) states that categories "such as caste and tribe were not representative of the divisions arising from the day to day interactions of the various groups and individuals in southern Rajasthan" (1991: 28). She argues that the category of "tribal" is a permeable and ambiguous one, in much the same way as is "Rajput," which is "historically more permeable than other castes in accommodating the heroic and the wealthy, landed gentry" and hypothesizes a process by which this "tribal" category was imposed onto marginal, petty landholders (Ibid: 30).

The Census and "Tribal Diversity"

When "tribal name" distinctions are considered in light of the weaknesses of various racial and linguistic theories, the fluidity of these categories becomes apparent. The historical, political, and economic relations between the Bhils and Rajput state, and the evolution of the patron-client relationship and its economic and social functions provide sufficient data to account for the processes of tribal category creation, stratification, and subsequent marginalization, without resorting to racial theory or mythical typologies for explanation of the "origins" of these groups.

The proliferation of tribal group categories in Udaipur and surrounding districts (see Appendix 1) is evidence of the process by which individual groups adopt a new name or modify the form of an existing group name in an effort to elevate their status and distinguish themselves from other lower-status tribal groups. Many of the census category terms for tribal groups therefore reflect an attempt on the part of a particular group to disassociate itself from the general term Bhil, which has traditionally implied participation in non-Hindu practices of ritual and diet, and is therefore rejected as a derogatory term.

A. W. T. Webb, political agent of the Bombay Presidency who supervised compilation of the Rajputana Census of 1941, reports that when gathering data for that census few respondents in areas known to be populated with Bhils identified themselves as such. Webb describes the following conversation with a local woman, who explained the ambiguity of self-identification to the census takers:

> 'And can you explain why nearly every Bhil one meets calls himself a Mina?' She smiled knowingly. 'That's easy to answer,' she replied. 'Ever since the Bhils have become government servants in the Bhil Corps they've started to give themselves airs, and to call themselves by the name Mina, which they regard as denoting a better caste than Bhil.' She paused then and added: 'I'm a Bhil myself, and proud of it, but you will realize that it's a bit sickening always to be called 'Salar [a clan designation of a local tree] Bhil.' [Webb 1941: 191]

Chapter 3 What Are Tribals? Who Are Bhils?

The only characteristic shared by Bhils, Minas, and other "tribes" of India today is that they have been so designated by the Government of India. This is the culmination of a process that began during the British period by which social categories, based on arbitrary characteristics and ill-defined processes, were perpetuated through the publication of a census every ten years (Beteille 1987: 77).

Tribal as a Government/Administrative Category

The unresolved issues of definition of tribe and tribals were "more or less settled definitively by the Constitution of India" (Fuchs 1973: 23) through various articles and provisions that provided special safeguards and protection to the population groups categorized as "Scheduled Tribes," along with "Scheduled Castes" and "Other Backward Classes." The constitution did not state explicitly how a "tribe" is to be recognized or identified nor how it is to be distinguished from a caste (Ibid.: 24), but did establish by schedule or list what population groups officially belong to the government of India's category of Tribes. This list of Scheduled Castes and Scheduled Tribes became the basis for the Government of India's reservation system, a controversial series of educational and financial incentives and reserved seats for so-designated caste and tribe groups throughout the government's extensive educational and employment system.

This policy of compensatory discrimination arose primarily out of the national government's effort to reduce the stigma of Untouchability by legislation; the Indian government was committed to "reduce invidious distinctions among groups, coupled with a conviction that it was permissible and perhaps necessary to employ these discredited caste notions to effectuate the equalizing policies...." (Galanter 1984: 40). The framers of the Indian Constitution originally envisioned this benefits scheme as a temporary one; it was to have expired ten years after its initial phase of operations in 1959. It continues to be a recurrent divisive political issue as well as a source of increasingly bureaucratically laden inequities.

Bhils throughout Udaipur District are well aware that the government has a system of benefits for which they are eligible. Actualizing their access to these benefits, however, has been constrained by local political and social inequities. Some have cited the corruption of the local governing bodies responsible for establishing eligibility. For example, one man told me that being placed on the local schedules, by name, as a Bhil ST by the local record-keepers required payment of an enormous bribe. Others reported that people of noneligible categories paid bribes to have themselves listed as SCs or STs in order to take advantage of the benefits.

Another aspect of local disenchantment with the benefits program was the low regard that some people hold for SC/ST individuals who had somehow managed to "work" the system. These people are generally perceived as taking unfair advantage of the system at the expense of those less politically skilled or financially welloff. (See Rajora 1987 for a discussion of tribal elites and utilization of ST benefits in Rajasthan.)

The poor educational levels attained by ST members eligible for educational benefits and reservations indicates the failure of the administration of this system to reach its intended beneficiaries. STs are eligible for nationally financed benefits for higher education if they reach the level of higher secondary or 12th-level pass; according to the 1981 census 500 individuals among all Scheduled Tribes in Udaipur District (total ST population approximately 800,000) have reached that educational level; 166 ST individuals have graduated from college or university.

Tribe to Caste: Bhil Religion

Contemporary anthropological and sociological literature on Adivasis in India describes the changes in tribal life that have resulted from contact with caste Hindus. Data for these studies is drawn from local-level observation of tribal institutions and how these institutions have been modified and changed over time as a result of contact with Hindu caste groups.

This transition is one of gradual and subtle changes in lifestyle and behavior. "There is no absolute cultural or social distinction between all tribal and all caste peoples, but rather a range of variation between tribal and caste traits. At the middle of the range there may be very little difference between a group that considers itself a tribe and one that claims to be a jati" (Mandelbaum 1970: 574).

The distinction between "Bhil religion" and "caste Hindu religion" is vague and indistinct; equally problematic is the distinction between "religion" and other aspects of Bhil life and ideology (see Mann 1984 for a complete discussion of these issues). A concern with the supernatural forces of the universe imbues an enormous range of human and environmental interactions. Virtually every activity or undertaking is preceded by invoking spirits and deities, either at household prayer niches, outdoor altars scattered throughout the village, or in the temple, a separate structure found in almost every Bhil phala.

The Bhil deity Mahadev is often equated with Bhagwan and Siva. Mahadev's image is always present among ancestor stones and in temples. Parvati is his consort. Ramdev is also usually represented within temples, and is depicted as riding on a horse. A Ganesh figure is also usually depicted in the temple in stone, although all these images are now available in printed form as well, in town markets and at the market around Ekalinji Temple. Smaller versions of pictures, particularly of Ganesh and Hanuman, are generally found in small niches within people's homes; larger versions are placed in the temples. For special occasions, such as the inauguration of a new temple, a statue will be commissioned from a stone carver from Udaipur or Nathdwara.

Bhil temples are generally constructed along the same pattern as houses, with a large inner rectangular room and outside verandah running the length of the building. It is usually the first building completed when a new phala is settled. It is the central meeting place for the community; all gatherings of any purpose are held there. Even the most secular of discussions on politics or development issues are held on the temple verandah or grounds. These discussions usually begin and end with *bhajins*, religious songs. Public statements made during these sessions are, according to informants, sanctified and held to as pledges to the community and the spirit world.

Outside the temple a row of ancestor stones commemorates the deceased; both male and female patrilineal ancestors are commemorated. The ancestor stones are 1 to 3 feet high, and about 8 to 10 inches wide. The erection of a stone, which involves a great expense, may be delayed for many years because of financial constraints. Until the stone is constructed and installed, it is believed that the spirit of the deceased will be restless and uneasy, and may cause difficulties for family members.

As McCurdy indicates, ancestor spirit worship is ideologically in contradiction to the principles of reincarnation, which is also part of the Bhil belief system. This contradiction was not noted by the residents of "Ratakote," his field site in Udaipur. "Most villagers believe both in the real existence of their ancestors and in rebirth and see no contradiction between the two" (1964: 217).

Ancestor spirits, as well as deities, communicate with the living through possession. Anyone can be possessed by either ancestor spirits or other nature spirits; during the course of rituals and worship both men and women may become possessed. It is believed that the possessed individual is in direct communication with the spirit, who takes over both the body and mind. The recipient falls into a trance state; the words of the person in the trance state are believed to be the direct communication of the spirit, who is delivering messages to the assembled audience. Trance is generally preceded by participation in rhythmic drumming, fasting, or excessive smoking.

Although any adult can be possessed, the temple *bhopa*, a male part-time religious specialist, is possessed on a regular basis. The bhopa also engages in agricultural or other secular work. He does not have any religious authority, although he is viewed as an expert in religious ritual matters, such as the timing and preparation for festivals--information he receives directly from the spirit realm. His "authority" is based on his tendency to become possessed by various types of spirits and his ability to speak for the spirit world during possession. When in a spirit-induced trance the bhopa dispenses advice which is invariably followed and is also believed to have curative powers. But bhopas do not have the ability to control the spirit world, nor are they seen as having powers unique to them as individuals or as a class of individuals.

Bhils as Caste Hindus

So-called traditional Bhil practices, such as ancestor worship and belief in spirit possession, continue alongside what is described by scholars as the Sanskritized practices of vegetarianism and abstaining from alcohol. As previously described, social reform movements are part of the on-going process by which Bhils emulate caste Hindu practices. McCurdy associates these revitalization movements with the power and authority of the Rajput jagirdars during princely state rule: "Rajput jagirdars were known to execute Bhils caught killing cattle and to put increased pressure on them to conform to Sanskritic Hindu norms" (McCurdy 1964: 265). McCurdy also observed that in the 1960s the secular institutions of the government were weakening the effects of Hinduism generally and particularly amongst the Bhils (Ibid.: 266). Thirty years later, socio-political developments have actually reinforced caste-based religious norms and values.

Beginning with the elections of 1989-90, when the coalition party toppled the Congress party from state and national majority for the first time since Independence, the Bharatiya Janata Party (BJP) in Rajasthan communicated to the Bhils a heavily Sanskritized political rhetoric. Many Bhil men told me that they were being courted by the BJP "as Hindus" and were advised that they should vote for the BJP because it was the Hindu party. (For further discussion see Chapter 9.)

Bhils consider themselves ritually superior to Meghwals, the SC community with which they most frequently interact in rural Udaipur. They will generally not eat in a Meghwal home, nor will they accept food cooked by a Meghwal. Their own ritual position in relation to the Rajputs is also acknowledged. Bhils do not generally enter a Rajput home; they may receive *chach* (the thin watery liquid that separates from heavier creamy components of milk) or *chapatti* (another name for *roti*, or flat bread), but they bring their own *thalis* (plates) and food is placed on them. If they are served on a utensil from the Rajput home, it will be in a disposable clay cup or a leaf plate.

Although the Bhils observe these and other caste-based rituals in public behavior, discussions about this issues and observations suggest that they are not deeply concerned with the subtleties of purity and pollution or with reconciling ideological issues. Hindu norms are woven seamlessly into the fabric of daily life. Most believe in an afterlife and speak about destiny being linked to good deeds and honesty-

Chapter 3 What Are Tribals? Who Are Bhils?

good deeds defined by the values of trustworthiness, loyalty, and hard work.

Bhil-Rajput Relations: Contemporary Perspectives

In response to my questions about their land access and use patterns, Bhil villagers related that the lands they now farm represent the culmination of a long process of migration, settlement, and subsequent fragmentation of their land holdings as the result of many generations of inheritance coupled with the inability to purchase more land. Their lives could be interpreted, over the last several generations, as representing rural "downward mobility." They describe a process by which they became settled agriculturalists during the mid-1800s and practiced a form of slash and burn agriculture. Access to forest land at that time was generally unrestricted: they cleared a small area of forest and burned the remaining scrub and vegetation. Seeds were cast onto the fertile surface at the onset of the rainy season. Their agricultural production was supplemented by collecting minor forest produce, fruits, and small game from the forests. Gradually, according to local informants, in emulation of Rajput agricultural practices and because of their own decreasing access to new land, they adopted plow agriculture.

People speak of the past nostalgically as a time when, as opposed to the present, resources were relatively abundant. Without idealizing or romanticizing the past, it is possible to locate some objective factors that have greatly impacted on Bhil agriculturalists and their quality of life.

First and foremost is the Forestry Department's enclosure of what used to be dense forests to which the Bhils and others had unlimited access. Coupled with the commoditization of land and regularization of land ownership, expansion or migration to another geographic area in which a family could realistically expect to start up farming without a large capital investment is part of the past. Restricted access to forest lands has also curtailed the income-producing potential of nonagricultural, forestry related marketing. Deforestation has set off a chain of ecological crises, including, according to some, subsequent monsoon irregularities. Today it is difficult, if not impossible, for an average-sized household to exist exclusively on income derived from agricultural production because their output is so unpredictable.

The history of Bhil settlement patterns reflects the asymmetrical power relationship between Bhils and Rajputs; disputes with the Rajputs, which the Bhils inevitably lost, compelled migration to another area. As access to forest land was generally unrestricted, finding a new settlement area could be accomplished relatively easily. For example, the history of the village of Solaria was reported by one current resident as follows:

> Our forefathers used to say that originally we lived in [names an area approximately 50 kilometers north-north east]. There we had a fight with the Rajputs and from that village those people came here. First they came to Morwa but the Rajputs threw us out. From there we came to Solaria.
>
> When we first were in Morwa there were no Rajputs there. One of them came and said to us that we are alone, please help us and we will stay here. Our forefathers gave clothes to them and made the Rajput's wife their sister. But after some time, when the Rajput family started expanding and they became powerful, they threw us out. They forgot the relation we were to them. Then we came here.
>
> Earlier when we had to pay tax to the ruler they used to give sixteen [in Hindi *solah*, thus the name of the phala] measures of grain. The Delwara in-charge used to collect the tax, that was once a year. The tax was less then. The tax has increased after the Congress government came. The measure was then called *payali* which was equal to three-quarters of a kilo so totally we used to give 12 kilos of crops as tax.
>
> Earlier there was more land. We first made the temple. It was set up by our grandfather.

During my recording of the actual genealogies of these families, it emerged that the great-great-grandfather of the speaker lived in Morwa. His three sons, the speaker's great- grandfather and his two brothers, made the settlement of Solaria. When I asked how many generations had passed since the founding of other Bhil phalas, I generally received the response: "five or seven," which is the phrase used to refer to several or a long time ago. When urged to report how long ago something happened in the distant past, invariably people would say "five or seven generations ago."

The histories of the founding of the Bhil phalas generally reflected the same pattern of migration from another area, usually by members of one nuclear family. Residents generally trace their descent to brothers who formed the phala. In some of the more remote areas, village histories include a second wave of migration into the Bhil phala by members of a different *gotra* (lineage group) by invitation of the first. In this region, when asked about what prompted the initial migration, informants usually replied that they needed more land and could not get it where they were residing. Just as often they cited conflicts with other caste groups, particularly Rajputs, as the reason.

Some of the men in Solaria who are now in their fifties, although they have severed their obligatory relationships with the Rajputs, still vividly remember their families' service. One man described the relationship of his family with their patron Rajput family, whose

Chapter 3 What Are Tribals? Who Are Bhils?

household and lands were located approximately one kilometer away. The speaker continually spoke about this relationship with this paritcular Rajput family with reference to the respect they command and the fear they can provoke; Rajput influence over the local bureaucracy, police, and other state institutions is still local reality.

People also cited demographic variation that correlates to the level of compulsion and service to Rajput families. Where the population of Rajputs is as numerous as that of Bhils, and the area is remote and isolated, the bonded labor relationships continue. In areas in which Rajput settlements were never made, or where the Rajputs left, the Bhils are independent and unafraid. According to one Bhil man strangers rarely enter these areas because of fear of thievery and violence.

Another variable that seems to be relevant in the case of Solaria was exposure, in the 1960s, to a Marxist political candidate who came regularly to this area. The speaker quoted below recalled this man's intensity and his messages. In another interview the same speaker referred to the influence this man had on his awareness of the injustices inherent in the traditional service relationships. The impact of this political message may have contributed to the severing of service relationships by the speaker and his four brothers. "Pal Singh" is a pseudonym; the surname Singh is common to all Rajputs.

> My grandfather and his family worked for the family of a Rajput Pal Singh. Whenever Singh desired, my grandfather and his family used to go to work at his household. My grandfather and his children worked on his fields, tended to his animals (about 15 in number), accompanied family members whenever they visited kin in other villages, and worked as laborers. The women of my grandfather's family fetched water, cleaned cattle stables of cow dung and collected firewood from nearby forests.
>
> In return for this work my grandfather was given roti [bread] for his entire family. They were given food only on those days they were called to work. When not called to work they were given nothing.

At another interview this speaker indicated that they would be called for service at most only six months out of a year, and even during that period not every day, so they therefore could not rely on a daily supply of roti.

> When they were not called they were given nothing. No Bhil was permitted to enter the kitchen of Pal Singh and touch their family utensils. The rotis that were given to my grandfather and his family were prepared by Pal Singh's wife.

My grandfather was required to work 10-15 days at a stretch whenever *nukta* [death feast] or marriages were performed and hundreds of guests were invited from near and far. My grandfather would go to all the villages delivering the message and invitation. He could not refuse any work assigned to him. In exchange he was assured that he and his family would not go hungry. His family depended on Pal Singh because in years of drought/famine, there was no support available for survival and only Pal Singh could protect them from hunger.

Pal Singh made full use of my grandfather's family to get any job done, like deepening of wells, repairing the *rahat* [Persian wheel] or plows, and so on. Therefore the good will of Pal Pal Singh was very important. All Rajputs were addressed as *Data*---provider of food and everything.

My grandfather had no other income, and no knowledge about farming or animals although he did have some land he called his own. This was 40 or 50 years ago. When my grandfather died he was followed by his son [the speaker's father] and he did the bidding of Pal Singh. My father had five sons, and when they came of age, they refused to accompany him and work as bonded laborers and wanted to strike out on their own.

The relationship with the family of Pal Singh ended about 30 years ago when I was about 15 years old. This was a time when we started having goats and buffaloes and thought of taking to the plow. My uncles and father also became laborers, doing odd jobs for other Rajputs, not attached to one family, and they worked only if they were paid regular wages [usually in measures of grain]. They dug wells but had to stop when they struck hard stone--water would accumulate during the rainy season.

Today none in my family or my brothers' family would go and work for Rajputs, even if it means starving. There are still two or three individuals in Solaria who are maintaining old contacts with Rajput masters but this relationship is now only to be available at a Rajput residence to attend to his guests on an important occasion. Or to help them smoke tobacco through the *chillum* [pipe] and to show respect. They get food in return. Nowadays no woman from Solaria goes to work for Rajput families. Young men demand Rs. 25/day to work on Rajput farms or repair their wells. [The official daily minimum wage at the time of this conversation in 1990, then equivalent to less than US$2.]

Nowadays Rajputs come to Solaria on religious festivals to perform *puja* in front of deities in our temples. Even on such visits Rajputs do not drink water or eat food served by us, although some addicts do not mind sharing alcohol.

Chapter 3 What Are Tribals? Who Are Bhils?

> All the assets of Rajputs have been built with our sweat who could not give it back to them [in kind] for fear of Rajputs withdrawing the support our family was used to. Fear still exists in our minds and we would not like to be on the wrong side of Rajputs, because law and police favor them and we can be harassed for no reason.

In another village located about 7 kilometers from Solaria, there are approximately 150 Rajput families and the same number of Bhil families. Of this village informants in Solaria said: "Even today these Bhil families dare not raise their heads--they cannot even cast their votes unless approved by their Rajput masters. The Bhil lands have been mortgaged to Rajputs which is against the law and Bhils plow the land for benefit of Rajputs. In this village Bhils work as slaves to Rajputs, who get away with it because it is located in a distant remote area."

Another village located approximately 4 kilometers from Solaria over the hills, with no access road, was settled entirely by Bhils; there are no Rajputs in the vicinity of the village. An informant said of this village, "Rajputs never created settlements here and never got any attention from Bhils. If a Rajput enters this area and creates any problem he pays with his life."

Many factors influence the way in which Bhils conceptualize their relationships to others. My friendships with people in Solaria and ongoing contact with news of this village gives some insights into how an individual's perception of himself in relation to others shifts over time. One man, whose family I am particularly close with, has undergone dramatic changes in his life and his presentation of himself. When I first met him in 1989 we often discussed local issues as well as their connections with national politics. He was and continues to be extremely well informed about historical and contemporary political issues. When discussing political changes in India over the past thirty or forty years in one of our early discussions, he said of Bhils of his area, "We have no knowledge of Independence. Even today we do not know what it means." And in another interview in 1990 he said in a very subdued voice, "Even with all the changes recently, I still can't raise my eyes in front of a Rajput."

When I returned to his village in 1995 and re-acquainted myself with his family, we discussed several significant changes in his life. He was still suffering emotionally from the sudden death of his wife the year before, and struggling with the new responsibilities of raising four sons alone, two of whom are still very young. He has benefitted greatly from a Trickle Up grant, which helped form a ginger-growing cooperative of which he is a member. His household income has tripled since 1990, and he has, he said, totally eliminated his debt.

Equally significant is the confidence with which he makes decisions about how he conceptualizes his own future. He is a close friend and local ally of Bhatia, the free-lance development worker, who serves as a critical link for people in Solaria to outside capital resources. While still respectful of and deferential to Bhatia in public, this man has, over the past few years, made several decisions about his own use of household resources that put him into direct conflict with what Bhatia saw as more appropriate strategy. Bhatia and I discussed at great length the level of confidence behind this confrontation with his primary "patron" in the 1980s, a level that neither of us could have imagined possible when all first met in 1988.

Self-Identity Terminology

The multiplicity of names for tribal groups can routinely include up to four different names for group and self-designation: what they call themselves amongst themselves; what outsiders call them; a derogatory, slang name used by outsiders; and the name they use for themselves to talk about themselves to outsiders. This multiplicity is particularly pertinent in discussing how Bhils are referred to and in what contexts group names are evoked. Even more significant to this discussion is the terminology used when they refer to themselves.

In my experience, in conversation people use the term "jati" generally as the category of either caste or tribal group; to determine a person's self-identification I would ask, "What is your jati?" If someone responded "Bhil," I inquired further about this term. People often said that there were some tribals in the area who don't use the name; that they refer to themselves as Mina, but they are also, most assuredly, Bhils.

The Bhils of Solaria occasionally identify themselves additionally as Gameti or Gameti Bhil, reflecting the local tendency to use this term, which denotes Bhil phala political leadership, as one of group identity. When I asked if they are Adivasi, they would respond, "Yes, we are Adivasi people," but this was never used as a a spontaneous response to a question about individual identity. This term is almost exclusively used in the context of political movements or other forms of mobilization. For example, in October 1995 I observed a political rally in the city of Udaipur in which many people I recognized as Bhils gathered under the organizational umbrella of a local NGO. About 500 people marched through the city and rallied in front of the residence of the District Collector. The banners they carried, written in Hindi and therefore understandable only to a very small percentage of the rural participants, proclaimed them to be "Adivasis" rallying for their rights to access to enclosed lands.

In Bagdunda most of the Bhil workers on the staff of UVM were followers of a local guru who preached vegetarianism and abstinence

Chapter 3 What Are Tribals? Who Are Bhils?   77

from liquor. All gatherings and meetings started with the singing of *bhajns* (hymns) referring to "Ram" and "Sita." This local movement is evidence of the "Sanskritization" of the Bhils and their integration into the local caste system.

Their sense of unity or connection with Bhils of other areas, or Adivasis as a whole, is very limited. The only time it was expressed was at the prompting of outsiders (like NGO workers) when discussing issues of identity, poverty, or when attempting to generate a sense of group cohesion. The cultivation of this pan-tribal identity, as well as the production of a counter-discourse by Bhils, will be described in greater detail in Chapter Seven.

Chapter Summary

The history of the representation of Bhil identity is an example of how assumption, supposition, myth, and legend have been absorbed by contemporary social science. The establishment of these categories belie the fluidity of the boundaries between them, and have until very recently discouraged inquiry into the nature of these boundaries and categories.

Tribal and caste group names and designations are, despite the general impression of the Indian social system, fluid and flexible. Tribal groups have multiple and changing designations of self-identity, designations that become integrated into the administrative system and census categories of the central government. What people call themselves may differ from what others call them.

Among villagers in the section of Udaipur District where I conducted my research, the term Bhil is the preferred term of self-designation. I had long conversations with villagers about this terminology; they acknowledged that many people in other parts of the district call themselves Mina. But, they stated, they are Bhils, "as we are," and they all share some important social and cultural characteristics. In addition to this emphatic usage of the term Bhil as self-designation, Bhil is also the term used historically by scholars of the region. To avoid the possibility of inventing a term that may have some scholarly justification but no local or historical referents, I therefore continue to use the term Bhil.

On a village-level, the scant amount of information available on the historic processes of Bhil settlement indicates a pattern marked by family migration motivated generally by conflict with local Rajput elites. Once settled, Bhil communities established patronage relationships that provided minimal protection and support and in return compelled disproportionate levels of service and labor.

The level of compulsion attached to the rural patron-client relationships has weakened somewhat over the past few decades. Bhils and other low-caste groups have become more assertive in demanding payment for their services, particularly if payment is withheld or is not consistent with what is considered adequate or appropriate.

The Bhils of Rajasthan, according to the census and other demographic data, still have the lowest standard of living of any group in the state and the highest rates of illiteracy.

But disadvantaged and illiterate does not mean passive, nor does it mean unaware or unable to cope with the complexities of the local sociopolitical system. Quite the contrary, survival in this environment requires constant and ongoing analysis of and strategic reaction to the local centers of power and influence. An individual's and family's ability to "work the system"--or more accurately, the multiple systems of caste-based, state-based and NGO-based resource allocation--is a necessity for tapping into whatever resources are available and for utilizing whatever form those resources take. One of the results of the presence of NGOs as a source of development resources is the growing sophistication of the villagers in terms of their relationship with the organizations. Neither the organizations nor the local villagers are passive agents in the NGO landscape; a dynamic process of analysis and decision making in terms of which organization will be allied with is now taking place. These and other issues related to the crowded local NGO landscape are described in the next chapter.

Chapter 4

Local Strategies, Local Histories

I mentioned at the beginning of Chapter 1 an oft-repeated humorous reference to the proliferation of NGOs in Udaipur District. The extent of the NGO "traffic" in this local landscape was illustrated in Bagdunda in 1990. Two organizers, who were then members of the Ubeshwar Vikas Mandal staff, planned to hold a meeting as part of their beginning effort to organize the Bhil women of the area into *Mahila Mandals,* or women's groups. They decided on the following day for the meeting and began to spread the word. Each woman we spoke to gave us information that caused the meeting to be rescheduled; Sewa Mandir had scheduled a meeting for women the following day at which payments were to be dispensed for work performed. And the day after that SWACH, the community health program was holding a meeting. The day after that a meeting of UVM's male organizers was scheduled, so some of the men who were to participate with the women's groups could not attend. We therefore had to wait four days for the "traffic" to subside before the women's meeting could be held.

This proliferation of NGO activities, while particularly intense in Udaipur District, is not unique to this district, or to India. NGOs have existed globally for as long as there have been missionaries and private-sector welfare organizations. But it is only within the past two decades or so that they have emerged, particularly in Asia and Africa, as such permanent and visible fixtures within the global development scene.

What Is an NGO?

Any attempt to define and categorize NGOs according to their activities must first confront their diversity. Giant organizations with international reach, such as Save the Children, Oxfam, or CARE, occupy one end of the spectrum, and at the opposite end, one or two social activists working in a local village. All these, as well as large organizations formed and operating within one country, are categorized under the single rubric of "non-governmental organizations."

The generally accepted definition of an NGO is an organization engaged in development work that is not established by the government. Cernea makes the distinction between service-oriented and production-related organizations; the latter are also referred to as economic NGOs in that they support people's productive activities and include credit and consumer cooperatives, dairy coops, tree-growing associations, etc. (1988: 14).

The primary strength of NGOs as development agents is their potential ability to reach the rural poor in remote areas to promote local-level participation in programs presumably addressing locally identified and defined priorities. NGOs organize and work in specific local areas, fostering ongoing relationships with a beneficiary community. They are generally involved in low-technology projects, and work on small budgets. Because these organizations are generally small--in many cases in Udaipur consisting of only one or two organizers--they are theoretically able to react quickly to local conditions and changes, and theoretically can be responsive to a community's shifting priorities.

Their impact, although it can be substantial in the local area, is often limited to a small number of people or a particular localized area. These characteristics may represent both strength and weakness: "Nongovernmental grassroots organizations are so frequently lost in self-admiration that they fail to see that the strengths for which they are acclaimed can also be serious weaknesses. In the face of pervasive poverty, for example, 'small scale' can mean merely 'insignificant.' Politically independent' can mean 'powerless' or 'disconnected.' Low-cost' can mean 'under financed' or 'poor quality'. 'Innovative' can mean simply 'temporary' or 'unsustainable'" (Annis 1988: 209).

NGOs are generally formed as the result of the commitment of a small group of people, sometimes even one highly motivated individual. These individuals may have a high level of dedication but low level of technical or managerial skills resulting in a "seat of the pants" management style and technical contribution.

The majority of NGOs arise out of local communities and conditions, and their activities are conducted on a local scale. They tend to focus their activities and attention on the needs of people without access to an array of resources or power bases. They generally work independently from other organizations or government institutions, although they may join together for specific activities or movements, even forming extra-national linkages to generate publicity and international support for their causes. One such coalition mobilized NGO-based resistance to a massive dam project along the Narmada River in three states of northern India, and is discussed in Chapter 5.

There is an inherent contradiction in the idea of "large-scale small-scale development," that is, small-scale, grassroots organizations being a permanent, structural component of the development strategy of a nation: "Can a species of development flourish that maintains the virtues of smallness but at the same time reaches large numbers of people, transfers genuine political power to the poor, and provides high quality social services that are delivered by permanent, adequately financed institutions?" (Annis 1988: 209). And despite the smallness of local organizations, the global financial implications of NGOs are anything but small: the financial significance of nongovernmental organizations to development assistance worldwide was estimated at US$4 billion by 1985, up from $1.4 billion in 1975 (Ibid.:6).

NGOs in India: Typologies and Implications

During British colonial rule foreign missionary organizations played a non-governmental role in education and social reform. The independence movement, and particularly the impact of the philosophy of Mahatma Gandhi, strengthened the voluntary movement in the 1920s and '30s: "This was seen in [Gandhi's] call for constructive work and in the inspiration he gave to thousands of young women and men to work among the rural poor, the scheduled castes and the deprived in areas of education, health, employment, income-generation....volunteers sacrificed their lives to the cause of the socio-economic upliftment of the poor and the weak on the one hand, and the cause of freedom from foreign rule, on the other" (Tandon 1988: 17).

During the 1950s several voluntary organizations were formed in response to specific environmental disasters. These groups primarily provided relief and rehabilitation to large numbers of people affected by flood, drought, and famine. A number of philanthropic, charity oriented voluntary organizations also arose to implement educational, health, and nutritional programs among the poor. During the 1970s, voluntary organizations experimented with community health programs, drinking water programs and nonformal education, as well as political and economic activism. "Though few in number, such voluntary agencies began to demonstrate, through their practice, the ineffectiveness of the prevalent model of development which had continued to believe in the trickle down theory. They also threw up some alternative principles and ideas for people-based, localized, people-controlled popular development strategies" (Tandon 1988: 17).

Simultaneously, a new type of voluntary organization emerged in India, currently referred to as Social Action Groups (SAGs); their general characteristics are described by Unia as the following:

> --A shared analysis of the causes of poverty and underdevelopment, and a shared belief in the necessity for social change through a process of empowerment of the poor.
> --A shared methodology of theory, practice, action, reflection.
> --Emphasis on creating awareness and building people's organisations: village committees, women's committees and youth clubs.
> --Typically the SAG consists of a 'core' group of between 5 and 20 people. They also employ a number of animators from the local community. In theory at least, the SAGS are non-hierarchical and democratic in their functioning.
> --The range of activities includes non-formal education/conscientisation, street theatre, leadership training, para-legal training and informal meetings.
> --The activities are centered around putting forward demands through the committees for such things as street lighting, drinking water, bus services, bank loans, as well as initiating struggles over wages, tenancy rights, access to land, etc. [Unia 1991: 89]

In Udaipur many of the organizations that refer to themselves as NGOs follow some of the strategies and philosophies consistent with the description of SAGs, although I never heard the term used by workers or participants, who described their own organizations as NGOs--a phrase that has become part of the local language and is used regularly by Mewari and Hindi speakers.

The concept of "social movement" is often attached to NGO activity in its own discourse. In the case of Udaipur NGOs I believe this would be an inaccurate categorization, as it implies a shared set of values, ideals, and goals with a strategy of organized collective action to evoke change from state-based political institutions. The well-known ecological activism of Himalayan peasant women, widely identified in global discourse as the "Chipko Movement," is a good example of this concept, as is the Jharkhand Movement, which in 1996 obtained recognition from the Government of India for some of its claims of territorial autonomy on behalf of its peasant and Adivasi mobilizers (see Omvedt 1989 and 1993).

The concept of the new social movement would probably resonate as a form of identity with local NGOs; this more diffuse concept emates from post-modernist discourse challenging the "metanarratives" of social action and social transformation.

Chapter 4   Local Strategies, Local Histories

> New social movements were associations within the subaltern classes where (embryonic) processes took place concerning the creation of new, non-commoditive values, new lines of horizontal communication--in short the creation of a new identity...an identity, contrary to the universality of the modernity project, with its own localised goals of emancipation, which did not lead to a bid for political power, but was based in local movements with multiple identities located in civil society, stressing new ways of social communication (solidarity and mutual understanding) and a new harmonic relationship with nature. [Schuurman 1993: 189]

These various types of organizations now generally referred to as NGOs have existed in India and throughout Asia for several decades, their number has grown enormously in India over the past 30 years (Franda 1983: 15). Quantifying the NGO segment is difficult because of the transitory nature of some of these organizations, as well as the ambiguity of the term itself.

> No one knows how many voluntary associations there are in India, and much depends on how one defines the category. If cooperatives and credit societies are included...the numbers soar into the hundreds of thousands. If caste, religious, educational, linguistic, regional, and communal organizations count, then there might be as many as a million or more. If the term is restricted to only those organizations external to the village that have as their explicit goal the attempt to promote economic development in rural areas, then the numbers would come down to a few thousand. In any event, what surprises most observers is the vast numbers of active voluntary associations and the way people at most levels of Indian society share a rich associational life. [Ibid.: 12]

According to documents produced by the Ford Foundation, which has targeted the NGO segment in India for development through their grants,

> ...the number of NGOs registered as private societies with the government is now approximately 100,000. About 18,000 of these are development groups, ranging in size from such well-established groups as SEWA [Self Employed Women's Association, Ahmedabad], which now counts 50,000 members across India, to two or three people working as activists in a village or an urban slum." [Staples 1992: 29]

The Ford Foundation's increasing commitment to NGO activity is reflected in its allocations funding the activities of non-governmental organizations, which grew from less than 1 percent of its total grants in

India in 1960 to almost half of its total grant allocations in India in 1990, with a corresponding decline in grants to governmental organizations (Ibid:: 79). Sewa Mandir has been the recipient of several grants directly from the Ford Foundation; other Ford Foundation grants have reached Udaipur's NGOs through the Foundation's support of intermediary funding, research and advisory sources. (See Figure 4.)

NGOs in Udaipur: History and Strategy

The NGOs of Udaipur District reflect the range of organizational size and strategic approaches encapsulated in the term for the rest of India and globally. Their activities include projects in adult literacy, health care and education, environmental protection, local political organizing, women's groups, and income generating projects. With the notable exception of the SWACH program, a five-year health project jointly undertaken by the government of Rajasthan and UNICEF and facilitated in part by local NGOs, they generally do not engage in high capital undertakings. Their primary goals are to provide educational and organizational input, and to facilitate development of community based initiatives. Their strategies, with few exceptions, are generally non-confrontational, in that they do not directly or violently confront the individuals or institutions of power.

Another aspect of the NGO scene is the role of "free lancers." During the course of fieldwork I encountered several retired businessmen who were independently undertaking development and social welfare work in the district. They had loose affiliations with other NGOs, but worked independently. The activities of the independent organizer Mr. B. N. Bhatia as mentioned previously, are particularly significant in the Bagdunda-Solaria area. His continuing presence and evolving operations, as well as interactions with other organizations, provide contrasts with and insights into other organizational and operational strategies.

After a chance meeting on a train with Kishore Saint, founder of UVM, Bhatia moved to Bagdunda and lived there for six months, talking to the villagers and learning the Mewari language. He had an affiliation with UVM that he officially severed after a conflict over policy in 1989. From his home in Jaipur, he continues to travel to Bagdunda and nearby villages each month for about ten days and is therefore now an integral part of the complex local development scene. His explicit policy of development as income generation led him to enthusiastically embrace the Trickle Up program, which has not been the policy of other organizations in the area. Locally run informal educational centers, his first programs in the area, have been less successful, and most of them have been disbanded.

Chapter 4 Local Strategies, Local Histories

The organizational structure and strategies of the NGO segment in Udaipur continue to reflect the liberal spirit of the man who is generally acknowledged to be its founder, Dr. Mohan Sinha Mehta. Dr. Mehta, who died in 1985 at the age of 90, was the founder of many of the educational institutions that continue to thrive and shape local development in Udaipur, as well as of Sewa Mandir, the largest of the local NGOs. His career, which continued actively until his death, also paralleled the major social and political events of Rajasthan in the 20th century, and he was an active participant in many of them.

Dr. Mehta's career is most closely associated with the philosophical traditions of liberal reform, and was strongly influenced by his exposure to and participation in British liberal educational and reform movements, as well as by his family's association with the Mewari court and his own employment by it.

Born in 1895 in Bhilwara, into a family of highly placed advisors and ministers in the Mewar state administration, Dr. Mehta was educated in Ajmer, the only district in Rajaputana under direct British administration. (This tradition of upper class Udaipur residents educating their children in the private English-medium schools of Ajmer continues to this day.)

He continued his education in Agra, and returned to Ajmer as a Lecturer in Economics in 1919. While in Agra he was introduced to the Boy Scouts movement by an English Army officer; his association with the Scouts movement in India continued throughout his lifetime. This association not only shaped his educational and development philosophies, but also provided the network from which teachers and students were recruited to the staffs of the various educational and welfare institutions he subsequently founded. This was particularly the case for Vidhya Bhavan, founded in 1931, the first coeducational nondenominational educational institution open to all school-aged children in Udaipur (Jones n.d.: 6).

According to Jones, the Scout movement of pre-Independence India "occupied a somewhat dichotomous position, encapsulating a fundamental nationalism with imperialistic connotations. The Scout association...engendered three crucial ideas; the consciousness of nationalism, the idea of service and an interest in rural life" (Ibid.: 6). But as is apparent from Dr. Mehta's career, the philosophic traditions of national identity and independence often conflicted with his family obligations, and, by extension, his obligations to the Mewari state government. As a student he attended Congress party meetings and was a lifelong admirer of Gandhi's philosophical and educational principles, although as a Mewari administrator he retreated from political organizing and devoted himself to the business of government. He served as District Officer of Kumbhalgarth, and Revenue Officer in

Udaipur, and simultaneously established Boy Scout troops in Udaipur and other towns of the state.

Following the untimely death of his wife in 1925, Mehta traveled to England, where he studied law while attending the London School of Economics, as well as continuing his association with the Scout movement there. While in London he visited several of the settlements established in the East End of the city by the social reformers and social workers who were living and working among the urban poor, as well as visiting a number of progressive schools throughout England.

He returned to Mewar in 1928, a barrister with a doctorate in philosophy, steeped in the legal as well as liberal educational philosophies of Great Britain of the 1920s. With the cooperation of friends and associates of the Scouting movement, he formed Vidya Bhawan in Udaipur in 1931, an educational institution that has subsequently grown from its origins as a progressive primary school to include an undergraduate and postgraduate level Rural Development Institute, Teacher's College, and Rural Engineering School.

At the same time Dr. Mehta continued to work as a Mewar state official, serving as Revenue and Finance Minister before his retirement from state service in 1948. He was then appointed by the new Indian national government as Ambassador to The Netherlands; he continued his career in the Indian Foreign Service with terms as Indian High Commissioner in Pakistan, and Indian Ambassador to Switzerland, Austria, and the Vatican. He retired from the Foreign Service in 1958, at the age of 63. In 1959 he was appointed a member of the Indian Delegation to the United Nations General Assembly, and served as Vice Chancellor of Rajasthan University from 1960 to 1966.

In his late sixties Dr. Mehta turned his attention to a goal he had begun formulating in the early 1930s: establishing a private social service organization he named Sewa Mandir (literally, service temple). The cornerstone of the building that was eventually to house the organization was laid in 1931, but it did not actually come into existence until Dr. Mehta's retirement from Rajasthan University three decades later.

Sewa Mandir's primary activities in the early 1970s focused on rural adult literacy and were funded in their initial stages by Dr. Mehta's own personal assets. He later received grants from World Literacy of Canada. Because some of Dr. Mehta's associates in the organization's early years were his contemporaries from the Scouting movement and from Vidya Bhavan, he found it necessary to recruit a new "generation" of managerial staff members whose activities in and around Udaipur continued his liberal reform and educational traditions. Among the early recruits were (self-identified) Marxists and other radical political

Chapter 4 Local Strategies, Local Histories

organizers who eventually left the organization to pursue more confrontational organizing strategies.

Sewa Mandir's recruitment of new professionals into the administration of the organization in the early 1970s also reflected the increasingly transnational globalization of local development. Among the new recruits were specialists in adult literacy and education whose own education and careers broadened the local perspective on development issues, as well as laying the groundwork for future proliferation of NGOs in Udaipur.

Om Shrivastava and Ginny Dobson Srivastava joined Sewa Mandir in the early 1970s. Following postgraduate studies in Toronto, Om Srivastava, a graduate of the University of Rajasthan, returned to Udaipur in 1970 and worked on the literacy and organizational programs of Sewa Mandir. Ginny Dobson Srivastava, also the holder of the postgraduate degree from the University of Toronto, began working at Sewa Mandir in 1970. They both were tireless local workers who established the structures and methods of local field organization. Ginny Srivastava is particularly admired by rural women for her commitment to local issues; when I visited Kherwara tehsil in 1990, where she worked with Sewa Mandir, village women who had not had any contact with her for over five years asked me if I knew her and recollected fondly her frequent trips to the region.

During the early to mid-1980s, in a period marked by organizational upheaval at Sewa Mandir, Ginny Srivastava and Om Srivastava both left and, along with several other former Sewa Mandir employees, formed Astha Sansthan, which began operations in 1986 in and around the Kotra tehsil of Udaipur District, a region whose population comprises over 85 percent tribal groups. Astha's primary strategy has been since its inception, and continues to be, local community organization, with the organization acting as facilitator and trainer of local men and women to assume leadership of these organizations.

Educators Kishore Saint and Sudesh Saint were also recruited in the early 1970s by Dr. Mehta, while working at the Friends World College in New York. Both were associated with Vidya Bhawan from 1972 to 1975. Kishore Saint joined Sewa Mandir in 1975 and Sudesh Saint focused her career in Udaipur in progressive education and issues of women's development and human rights. In 1983 Kishore Saint left Sewa Mandir and formed Ubeshwar Vikas Mandal, an NGO concentrating on ecological and environmental issues within the local socioeconomic context, issues to which Saint is still passionately devoted.

UVM began its operations in Dhar village in 1983, and about three years later opened its field office in Bagdunda. Compared to Sewa Mandir it is a relatively small organization, with at varying periods of time since its inception in 1983, approximately 30-40 employees, and activities in approximately 50 rural communities.

Sewa Mandir continues to be the "node" of NGO activities in Udaipur. The largest organization of its kind in Udaipur, it currently employs approximately 200 full time employees, and over 700 part-time employees and volunteer associates, and has a presence in over 400 villages in throughout Udaipur District.

It also serves officially as the "nodal" NGO for the administration and supervision of a variety of governmental grants to smaller and newer organizations in Udaipur. Because of its long and ongoing relationship with major Indian universities and charitable trusts, as well as international donor and educational institutions abroad, it also serves as a magnet attracting young academics, volunteers, and scholars from around the world.

Within Udaipur's development community Sewa Mandir also serves as the training ground for NGO workers, a growing industry in the area. And the fissioning process that began in the 1980s, with the branching off of Sewa Mandir senior personnel to form two new organizations, continues as a local pattern of organizational development. The vast majority of development workers in Udaipur who have formed their own independent organizations or have become staff members of other groups have had some association with Sewa Mandir or have been employed by it.

The implications of this organizational phenomenon go beyond tracking who has worked for whom at what point in their careers as NGO workers and organizers. Certain continuous threads of strategy and philosophy run through many of Udaipur's NGOs. Although their development focus may vary--from environmental protection to literacy to health-based programs to organizing women to include, as most NGOs now do, mainstream political activity--all the programs are within the liberal reform tradition exemplified by Dr. Mohan Singh Mehta and perpetuated through subsequent "generations" of NGO workers and organizations. This tradition translates into a strategy of an ongoing NGO presence in the local community in the form of educational and organizational programs. These strategies tend to originate from the organization and not from the community. The strategy is political in the sense that it includes active and growing political participation in the mainstream political process by the client community, but does not include support of violent confrontation or illegal activities, such as land seizures or illegal encroachment.

Local Funding Sources

One NGO manager reported to me that in 1990 there were 160 registered NGOs in Udaipur District, and only a small percentage of

Chapter 4 Local Strategies, Local Histories

them were actually receiving funding that originates overseas. According to this informant, this figure included organizations consisting of one or two individuals working in a small cluster of villages; such smaller organizations are sometimes funded in some instances by the rural beneficiaries themselves, these funds being supplemented with specific project funds from CAPART, a governmental funding agency (see below), by local private donations, and, in some rare instances, with foreign-originated funds that are dispersed by local donor organizations.

One source of financing for local income-generating projects is the Government of India's Council for Advancement of People's Action and Rural Technology (CAPART). CAPART was formed in 1986 by the merging of two existing organizations: Council for the Advancement of Rural Training (CART) and People's Action for Development India (PADI). The organization funds rural development projects that are designed to raise the income of participants, to generate employment opportunities, or increase productive resources. Their intended beneficiaries are "small and marginal farmers, rural women, landless agricultural laborers, village artisans, fisherfolk, forest dwellers, freed bonded laborers" (CAPART 1986: np). Health and education projects in rural communities are also funded where there is an urgent and pressing need for them due to the lack of other facilities. Projects that involve building expenses or the purchase of equipment are not funded by CAPART. Maximum funding for any project is Rs. 5 *lakhs* (1 lakh= 100,000; 500,000 rupees was the equivalent of approximately US$25,000 at the 1990-91 exchange rate of 20 rupees per US$).

CAPART dispensed funds amounting to Rs. 30-40 *crores* in 1986-87 (1 crore=10 million); 50 crores in 1988-89; and were authorized to dispense up to 100 crores (approximately US$ 5 million) in 1990. CAPART's assistant director in 1990 reported to me that only about half the annual budget is actually dispensed. Projects are funded by submission of proposals, approximately 50 percent of which are accepted. The balance are rejected primarily because they do not fit the precise profile for CAPART-funded projects--income-generating rural-based projects--or because the applicants have not provided the proper documentation for the proposal. Projects are evaluated by and funds dispensed through "nodal" NGOs (relatively well-established organizations in the area in which the project is proposed) who receive a fee of Rs. 1,000 (in 1990) for implementation.

Among the goals of CAPART funding is "to increase the level of awareness of the target groups in regard to the programme content and facilities provided under such programmes as IRDP, NREP, RLEGP, TRYSEM, DWCRA, etc." (Ibid.: np). One can only imagine the reaction of a Hindi-speaking local development worker to this array of administrative bureaucracies and unfathomable English-language acronyms.

A knowledge of English is a distinct advantage for NGO workers, particularly if they are interested in starting their own organizations; representatives of overseas funding agencies generally do not speak Hindi and certainly don't speak Mewari. Even Delhi-ites occasionally are not comfortable conversing in Hindi. The language of interaction between foreign and sometimes even Indian funding agency representatives and the NGO, when these representatives make their brief visits to the organizations, is therefore English.

Two organizers who had formed their own NGO in a district outside of Udaipur agreed to discuss CAPART with me. Neither could read or write in English. Both, prior to striking out on their own, worked for Sewa Mandir, which acts as the nodal agency for CAPART in Udaipur. Both described their difficulty and frustrations in meeting CAPART guidelines in preparing their proposals. They submitted them handwritten in Hindi, which, despite official acceptance of this format by CAPART, they said, they knew put them at a disadvantage. They also expressed dissatisfaction with the control over their proposed project exerted by a larger and more powerful nodal organization whose priorities, they felt, may not be the same as those expressed in the proposal.

Issues, Strategies, and Cultural Conflict

NGO activity in the study area at the present time can be broadly categorized as environmental protection, income generation, and education. Very often the NGO is the only contact point that the poor, marginalized agricultural villagers have with any social services or resources emanating from outside their village.

NGO activity generally takes the form of information, literacy and social reform training, or under some circumstances, capital expenditure projects, such as the installation of hand pumps or the establishment of seedling plantations. Small dams, reservoirs, and most recently, lift-pumping systems have been installed in selected villages by Sewa Mandir and Ubeshwar Vikas Mandal.

All of the NGOs studied had programs specifically aimed at women: "self-help" groups and savings/credit schemes controlled by the village women had been attempted, with varying degrees of success and continuity, in all of the communities under study. Among the major issues discussed at regular women's meetings were social conditions of women, literacy, status issues, domestic abuse, male alcoholism, ritual practices and expenses, and women's rights .

Most NGOs educate their beneficiaries in the necessity for self-reliance, self-initiative, and community independence. They all

Chapter 4 Local Strategies, Local Histories   91

undertake discussions of political institutions and local power structures. The causes of poverty and caste- or class-based exploitation are discussed in varying degrees, depending upon the political orientation of the organizers.

Deforestation is a critical aspect of both the Sewa Mandir and UVM programs; social forestry and reforestation programs are a major thrust in their strategies for economic and social development of the tribal area. Sewa Mandir has been particularly active in the past five years in implementing Rajasthan's Joint Forest Management policy, which gives local communities the right to participate with the Forestry Department in developing and implementing policy and access on lands previously controlled exclusively by the state. Other programs involve "conscientization," nonformal education for both children and adults, plantation work, social forestry and water management, and, for some organizations, techniques of political organizing and activism. Most of the local NGOs have at one time or another participated in rallies in support of the national coalitions addressing environmental and ecological issues. Some of the organizations have also lent their support to a small organization attempting to stop a local dam project that would result in forced relocation of villagers.

The stated mission of all the NGOs is to improve the social and economic conditions of the communities within which they work. Certain structural constraints, noted previously, potentially undercut the realization of these goals. The NGO, through its bureaucratic organization and staff, controls resources, specifically money; has power, by virtue of its access to bureaucratic, political, and governmental institutions; and can easily interact with other institutions of power by virtue of its members' educational level, political and social contacts, and fluency in English. The beneficiary communities share none of this access to the district, state, or national bureaucracy. They are dependent on the NGOs for wages and access. During the severe droughts in eastern Rajasthan in 1985, 1986, and 1987, these communiites relied on NGOs, which were a distribution node for emergency relief, for these state-derived benefits.

With good monsoons in 1988, 1989, and 1990, the cessation of famine and drought-relief programs created problems between NGOs and beneficiary communities that brought into focus a deeper rift in the philosophical and theoretical perceptions of the role of the NGO in the community and illuminated the absence of a shared ideology of development.

The issue of dependence is hotly debated between NGOs and their beneficiaries and among and between NGO executives and workers. The contradictions--and effects--of attempting to build local independence and self-sufficiency by supplying strategy, money, and materials from outside the community is continually discussed. Different organizations have developed different strategies to address this question. The result is a regionally fragmented approach, with each NGO in the study area applying a separate strategy in its own geographic territories.

Structure and Conflict

NGOs inevitably share some structural characteristics with traditional elites in their relationship to their beneficiary communities. This has been noted by Chowdhary in a study of NGO activity in Bangladesh:

> The most striking contradiction in activities are, while trying to work in development work with the rural poor, NGOs tend to become a substitute for traditional patron-client relationships; a new type of dependence emerges between the self-help initiators and the target groups who tend to become 'recipients' of development while the NGOs themselves take over the functions of government and politicians and work only for the grassroots. They tend to antagonize the traditionally established elites and this creates tensions among these groups which may adversely affect programme implementation. [Chowdhary 1989: 26]

These tensions, which Chowdhary notes, have complicated underlying causes that go deeper than competition over resources. NGO activity within villages can contribute to intercaste conflict. This conflict results from the alliance of the NGO with the Adivasi or other low-caste groups in the village, to the actual or perceived detriment of upper-caste groups. In a few isolated cases, local organizations orchestrated more direct forms of confrontation by promoting the political candidacy of Bhils, and actively organizing the subsequent political campaigns. In one case in another district, the NGO organizer spearheaded the seizure of lands claimed by Adivasis to have been unfairly taken as settlement of outstanding debt, resulting in a bloody confrontation between Bhils and the local police. (This incident will be described in greater detail in Chapter 5.)

More often, however, intercaste conflict occurs not as the result of the presence of the NGO, but rather from the deepening of already-existing rifts in the community; the NGO's activity merely exacerbates these rifts, or contributes to the issues being debated. Nevertheless, one NGO director with whom I discussed these issues in 1990 told me:

> We may unconsciously create caste conflict. We're so interested in the poor we don't pay attention to the others, to the rural realities. For the sake of one's own interests all groups have to be considered within the community....We [NGOs] should pull out after three years. There is going to be dependency no matter what. If there is a

dependency, make it a fruitful dependency. Don't just go in there, create tension, then leave. Fortunately, we're not that effective... It's easy to say 'we make you aware, now claim your rights.' We will never replace these organic relationships or the indigenous types of dependency. The local-level worker will not replace the thakur. The NGO sector won't replace anyone. The system will continue. The NGO won't change the system.

Territorial Franchise, Operational Hierarchy

In the 1980s, during the fissioning period associated with the proliferation of smaller organizations in Udaipur, various geographic areas in the district were for the most part informally allocated to each of the organizations functioning there. Although some overlap occurred, with two organizations occasionally operating in one area, the general consensus was that the geographic integrity of the respective NGO's "territories" would be observed.

This concept of territoriality has been modified significantly for a number of reasons. Both the NGOs and the local communities are becoming increasingly sophisticated in their experiences with each other. Sewa Mandir, the largest of the local organizations, perceives itself and its services now as being consumer driven rather than organizationally driven, and is attempting to reach across these constructs of territory and encouraging participation in services that are more tailored and responsive to people in a wider variety of settings. Sewa Mandir is unique however in its size, structure, and "reach" throughout the district, and the wide range of services, with institutional support, it potentially offers to communities.

As noted earlier, each of the many smaller organizations in the district has a different perspective, strategy, and set of goals. They variously stress local organization and literacy; social forestry and environmental reclamation; income-generation programs; or political organizing in a cluster of villages. Each of these organizations makes a localized contribution to the development of its particular area, or more accurately, to those households that choose to participate. But no unified, coordinated, replicable strategy for the district is emerging from these localized efforts.

The one strategic element that almost all the local NGOs share is their ongoing presence in the villages. They envision themselves as becoming a permanent part of the social landscape, and establishing a permanent bureaucratic and institutional presence. This strategy has significant implications for understanding how the NGO perceives itself in relationship to the local community. They intend their services and their structures to be integrated into the social and political fabric of the village, and from this perspective they begin to offer a wide variety of programs from their "menu" of existing and newly developed services. This allows for meeting local needs, as perceived by the NGO, but it has other results as well.

Rarely if ever is a termination plan articulated as part of the organizational strategy. None of the NGOs sets itself a specific set of goals that will be implemented, and results measured, so that when the goals are reached to the satisfaction of the local community, the organization can terminate its activities or turn them over entirely to local participants. Indeed, the concept of results is somewhat vague, as is quantitative measurement of effect.

The concepts of goals and results are themselves highly contested ones. Over the years NGO workers and organizers have expressed varying and heated opinions about the concept of "results" and "measurability" of "success" of NGO programs in this context. Some energetically questioned the idea that their goals of social and political awareness could be measured, and that the concept of "results" has any place in this intensely people-oriented strategy. "How can you measure the growing awareness of a village woman to her political and social rights?" I was once challenged to explain during a discussion of these issues with an NGO worker. "How can you measure her standing up to her husband or her mother-in-law and demanding the right to go to school or to vote? How do you measure the stages by which her consciousness emerges?"

The structural organization of the NGOs also contributes to the perpetuation of territoriality and the nature of this type of development process. During the time of my study I encountered no groups started by, staffed by, and directed by villagers themselves. Most of the organizations, no matter what their size, had offices in Udaipur, and these were organized and staffed by well educated educated, literate people with varying levels of ties to the rural communities. The organizational hierarchy of these organizations can be broadly divided into four levels:

1. founders/directors: primarily nonrural residents whose activities are concentrated in Udaipur offices.

2. division/operational managers, including social workers, other professionals: non-rural residents whose activities are concentrated in Udaipur offices with frequent daily trips to the field areas.

3. local-based workers and supervisors: field office employees who live and work in the local areas and are generally not from the villages in which these offices are located.

4. village level workers--paid and voluntary workers: villagers

Often the founders/directors of the organizations are well-educated, English-speaking people who have close ties to Europe and America, either by virtue of having traveled or lived abroad. Their knowledge of

Chapter 4 Local Strategies, Local Histories

overseas funding organizations and academic institutions and their ties to them have created a sophisticated, cosmopolitan rhetoric. They are as comfortable speaking with the representatives of government and foreign donor organizations as they are with their local staffs and village workers. Policy and strategy are established at this level, and it is also at this level that all decisions regarding the local allocation of project funding are made.

The second level of managers have varying backgrounds. Some come from outside Udaipur, and outside India, as previously mentioned, and have been drawn there because of the many development organizations in the area. Others are from Udaipur and its environs, and have been attracted to the NGO segment.

The field office staffs expressed dedication to the organizations and concepts of development espoused by the various organizations, but on occasion they privately grumbled about working conditions, low salaries, lack of input at the organizational level, and lack of upward mobility potential. Another widely heard staff complaint is that the directors and managers from the city don't stay in the villages; they come and go on a "commuter" basis and do not live for any period of time under the same conditions as their local employees and volunteers.

The directors and founders expressed dramatically different perspectives on NGO work and workers. Two distinct opinions were expressed, representing two very different attitudes towards development work and social work. One position echoed Gandhian and socialist principles that social work and development work were a special calling, and that social workers and development workers should receive only the barest minimum of salary to meet their daily needs. The work itself--the service to community--is the most significant aspect of the career.

Another NGO director had a far more pragmatic attitude towards social workers, development workers, and the NGO segment in general. He discussed the class difference between the NGO organizers/workers and their village-level beneficiaries and employees, and said on several occasions that his and other NGOs are "middle-class organizations that exist because of the poor."

In speaking of the NGO segment as a professional career path, this man stated that many people come to his and other organizations because "they cannot get better jobs in the government sector. Some of them have matured into great workers. Some become excellent managers. Some who originally began as grassroots workers become good managers." These jobs, however, do not share the status or the salary of other professionals with whom the NGO workers come into contact (such as engineers, doctors, computer specialists or management specialists). And, he said, this often results in conflict between these two groups of professionals: NGO workers and better trained, higher status and better compensated specialized professionals like health care specialists and engineers. The latter group "often doesn't share the humanistic values of the social workers" but does have skills that are critical to executing NGO projects. "If we don't pay these professionals more [than the social workers] we will not get their necessary services."

He cited the example of an engineer who had been hired to design and build small dams in rural communities. The engineer did not share the humanistic commitment to his work others within the organization had; he spoke disparagingly of the rural poor and did not relate to local village residents or workers. He did, however, design and build dams efficiently, effectively, within budget, and on time. In Udaipur, which has a limited professional pool from which to select job candidates, a pool that is limited even further by the relatively low salaries NGOs offer, the organization had to balance the engineer's professional skills against his humanistic deficiencies when making a personnel decision.

In another conversation the NGO director spoke of the necessity of organizations to grow beyond rhetoric to become more effective professionally. "If we ourselves don't grow, we will become ineffective, like many Gandhians. They just haven't grown beyond the rhetoric and strategies of two generations past. The challenge of our organization is to create motivation among its workers, even if the worker came here for a reason other than a desire to perform public service."

Philosophical differences between NGOs, coupled with the effects of some organizations having being founded around a particularly charismatic or influential individual, further contribute to difficulties in recruiting and maintaining a middle-level staff. The drive and commitment of the founders may not be equaled by staff members, who see their work as a means of individual and professional mobility and not necessarily as a "calling to service". This has created what could be interpreted as "intergenerational" divisions within these organizations. The charismatic "fathers" and "grandfathers" who established these organizations are subject to criticism from their "offspring" and employees--opinions that are not always welcome.

I do not use this analogy of the family lightly. The concept of the father and the respect due to him and other elder, particularly male, family members, is a clearly articulated principal of household relationships that still abides in Udaipur. The respect and honor due to elder senior males in the family was often articulated in different social settings, ranging from the modern houses of upper-middle-class English speaking households to the rural communities of Udaipur District. The analogy of the family was used by local workers themselves, even those who had left better-established NGOs to form their own organizations, often under acrimonious circumstances. Despite this acrimony and often emphatic criticism of the directors of the organizations that had previously employed them, the younger generation of workers always expressed in our discussions gratitude, respect and honor to those generations of NGO founders who came before them. One man who had left an Udaipur NGO to start his own organization in Gogunda said of the organization he left that he will always honor the founder as a father. He made the move he did because of a desire for personal upward mobility and greater control over his financial security. Although he criticized the strategies of his previous organization, he continually acknowledged the work of his "fathers and grandfathers" in Udaipur, whom he credits with his training and introduction into the field.

The family analogy within organizations affects the nature of staff-line interaction. While encouraged theoretically in the rhetoric of these organizations, an open and candid nonhierarchical interchange in establishing policy and strategy has yet to be translated into operational reality. Decision making tends to be firmly centered at the upper levels of management. The effect of the organization structural hierarchy is not limited to employer-employee relations; it also shapes to a degree the range of communications between the organizations and their rural clients and the nature of that relationship.

"People's Participation" as Rhetoric and Strategy

The emergence of the NGO sector globally coincides with the disenchantment with large-scale government and bilateral programs of the 1950s and 1960s and the strategy of decentralization. Simultaneously, the discourse of development shifted, to be dominated by the language and concepts of "participation" and "grassroots"-- implying a bottoms-up restructuring of development, and change designed and executed on the local level.

Consistent with this global development trend, the NGOs in Udaipur invariably describe themselves as implementing strategy based on "people's participation" and "bottoms-up management." This theoretical approach is elusive in its actual practice, in Udaipur as well as throughout the world, and seems to be one of the universal structural contradictions inherent in nongovernmental organizations. As Cernea noted: "Upon inspection, many NGO projects turn out not to be participatory despite their rhetoric, and involve 'enlightened' top-down control by the NGOs themselves, sometimes along with control of decisions by local elites" (Cernea 1988:20).

The promise of the rhetoric has failed to materialize for a number of structural reasons (see, for example, Rahnema 1992). One of these has to do with the design and execution of a "grassroots" project. A local program or a grassroots program is in itself an ill-defined and ill-conceived concept; this fuzzy analytical category is created at the highest level of conception, the donor agency or the funding source, and its fuzziness is perpetuated all the way down the line of program design and execution.

What is a local participant in a grassroots program? What is an "outsider?" Many donor agencies design their funding structures to eliminate the direct participation of "foreigners" in the design and execution of local programs; instead, local NGOs are funded to execute them, presumably because they are better able to assess local needs and communicate goals and strategies. But is being an Indian national, or a speaker of the local language, or long-term resident of the state or region in which the program is executed sufficient credentials to be a rural "insider"?

Common sense tells us that a college-educated, English-speaking urbanite is hardly of the same class, background, caste, socioeconomic status, or shared experience as a rural villager. But the dynamics of local class divisions and hierarchy, along with common sense, are often obscured in the enthusiasm of conscientization rhetoric. Often, but not always. Very often the clearest and most explicit statements of common sense are made by the villagers participating in the meetings and gatherings called by and led by the representatives of local NGOs.

In the summer of 1988, while conducting preliminary field research in India I attended a meeting held in the western section of Rajasthan sponsored by a state-supported women's development organization. The meeting was one of several held each year and attended by rural village women who were participating in the program. The program's ideological and strategic thrust was feminist-oriented consciousness-raising. Social workers were training local women in the formation of village-based women's groups that would focus their activities on priorities identified by the rural women, such as access to well water, electrification, getting a school or primary child care center built, and so forth.

The meeting I attended was part of an intensive, two-day training session for the village women who were local organizers within their own communities. The meeting was organized and led by city-based, college educated social workers, many of whom were fluent in English as well as Hindi and the local dialect. Approximately fifty village women and five social workers were present.

The social workers who led the discussion were articulating a feminist-oriented analysis of rural women's problems. They talked about the exploitation of women and the burden of double and triple days and their multiple responsibilities of income generation, child care, and household responsibilities. They defined these problems as being common to all women, and being linked to their gender. The

Chapter 4 Local Strategies, Local Histories   99

social workers reiterated that domestic, household, and ritually-enforced gender inequalities were the causes of the problems of rural women, and stressed these issues as they spoke.

The social worker who was leading the discussion talked about her own life. A college-educated, upper-middle-class woman, she had married into and resided in the particularly conservative household of her Rajput husband, a household dominated by her widower father-in-law. She talked about the indignities of having to cover her face when in the presence of her husband's father, and the constant necessity of avoiding his presence. She articulated her anger at this situation, and contrasted her behavior and status at home with her activities outside, in which she pursued an active and very visible career as a social worker. She said that because of her experiences within her own household she understood the exploitation faced by the village women.

At one point during this lecture a village woman spoke out. She said that her problems were not caused by being a woman. She said that her husband didn't exploit her, nor did other men in her village. Her exploitation, she said, was from "your Rajput cousins"--the landowners in her village. Her poverty, she said, was her primary problem, not being a woman. Although she was indicating specific caste groups as the exploiters, she was not attributing the exploitation to ideology. It was by virtue of their being landlords and money lenders, not because of ideologically or ritually imposed hierarchy. At one point during her impromptu speech she said that "God doesn't make inequality; people make inequality."

Her comments were a pointed critique of the social worker's exposition on the purported cross-class unity of gender-based discrimination; she was clearly countering that message with her own analysis of her relationship to the social worker--one that was more clearly identified in her mind as marked by class- and caste-based divisions and hierarchies than by gender-based unity. It was also a critique of some of the rhetoric of the training; social workers joining hands with village women and singing songs about the burdens of hauling water and giving birth in dangerous and unattended conditions. These conditions, she implied, were unique to the village women and not shared in the daily lives of the social workers.

This dynamic, experienced several years ago at this particular meeting, resonates with ever-widening influence as the origins of program design and funding are traced today. Policies and content are established far outside the client community. They are based on strategies and problems defined in the urban centers of Rajasthan, India, and the headquarters of the funding organizations. The only thing "grassroots" about them is the transfer of this rhetoric from these global urban centers to village settings.

Chapter Summary

NGO activity in Udaipur has generated certain changes in the local social, political, and economic environment. How lasting or significant these changes will be in terms of community-wide economic and social indicators and overall quality of life of individuals is difficult to quantify or even predict. The termination of NGO services is rarely if ever included in the organizations' strategy; there is little discussion of, and no consensus as to how long the NGO should remain in an area, nor on how integral to the economic and social functioning of the village the organization should become. Different organizations have different perspectives on whether they should be a temporary or permanent part of the local landscape.

The organizational and structural problems discussed by the NGO directors and workers may reflect the relative immaturity of the local "NGO industry." My use of the term "industry" is deliberate. Although some of the NGO directors with whom I discussed this perspective bristled at its use and its connotation with business, the term is, I believe, a far more accurate one than "movement."

NGOs amongst themselves share some bureaucratic and structural components and a general but ill-defined commitment to change, but, almost by definition, they are independent and noninteractive units. Their strategies and policies are formed generally under the leadership of one individual and reflect that individual's values and goals. With a few notable exceptions, NGOs rarely act in concert with each other on a local level; alliances are formed selectively and operate for specific purposes.

All the NGOs in the study area share the common goal of social betterment for the rural poor. But in terms of their rural-based activities the work of NGOs taken as a group is more consistent with entrepreneurial and business-sector strategies: establishing a territory (or market) for their services, a "niche" that satisfies the needs of their clients, and adjusting strategy to respond to an increasingly competitive environment within which they interact with clients as well as donors. The ongoing and institutional presence of the organization brings with it all the problems faced by any business of capitalization, and equally significant, personnel recruitment, and management of organizational growth.

A phrase often repeated in my discussions with NGO workers at all levels, from the highest managers to local workers, was "people's participation." Virtually all of those involved in the development industry in this district used this phrase to describe the theoretical underpinning of their village-level activities. An operational strategy based on my understanding of this concept was difficult to identify

Chapter 4 Local Strategies, Local Histories

within the existing organizational strategies. The question of who knows what is best for the beneficiary community--the NGO or the community itself--often went undiscussed. When the community selected its own priorities for development projects (what I would consider to be a minimal criteria of "people's participation"), its choices did not always coincide with the choices and strategies of the NGO. Negotiating this conflict is a critical part of the reality of the rural development process. The semantics and rhetoric of the process of development bear strongly on the nature of the relationship between beneficiary and development communities and often belie the underlying power inequities and contradict actual programs and policies. The manifestations of these issues in the daily interaction between Bhil villagers and NGO managers and workers are illustrated in greater detail in the following chapters.

Chapter 5

The "G" in NGO:

Global to Local Politics in Development

Because of the explosion in the numbers of NGOs and the ranges of their activities, particularly in underdeveloped countries, the literature about their work has grown proportionately. Yet one aspect of these organizations is seldom noted in this enormous body of literature: their relationship to government, and the implications, both theoretical and practical, of this relationship.

Analyzing NGOs, whether in a particular country or as a worldwide development phenomena, requires examining them in the context of government, of political and economic policy on the state and even global level. This is clearly illustrated by recent events in northern India, which demonstrate the potential for an NGO coalition to challenge government strategy on a national level, as well as the global reach of such a coalition's voice.

An increasingly complex and globalized coalition of nongovernmental organizations both in India and abroad has been responsible for mobilizing a spirited opposition to the Sardar Sarovar Project, an extensive series of large dams and canals along the Narmada River in northwestern India (Fisher 1995). An NGO coalition began the antidam movement, which resulted in, among other actions, an unprecedented World Bank Independent Review report that was highly critical of aspects of the project that had been supported by World Bank funds. The report highlighted what had already been widely noted by the NGO coalition and other critics of the project: deficiencies in the project's environmental impact studies and in the programs to identify, resettle and compensate the hundreds of thousands of people, most of them Adivasis, who would be displaced from their homes by the construction of the dams, canals and reservoirs. Despite criticism of the project, and the withdrawal of some of the final phases of financing by the World Bank and other multi-lateral lending agencies, the Government of India has continually announced its intention to complete the extensive project as originally envisioned.

Income-Generating Programs: The Global Becomes Local

As Annis concludes for Latin America, NGOs are increasingly intertwined with both each other and the state. One aspect of this relationship is an unresolved dualism between NGOs and government. On the one hand there is an adversarial relationship, often borne of rhetoric and social action; NGOs are filling a vacuum created by the failures of government to provide services to the poor. And yet,

> ...at the same time that grassroots organizations are trying to wrest services and concessions from the state, the state is generally trying to break itself into finer and finer units of political and bureaucratic control. What happens in practice is a kind of interpenetration--a blending in which the so-called governmental and nongovernmental meld together. The term nongovernmental organization--though it may have meaning at conferences, in external fund raising, and in the academic literature--tends to lose its focus when applied to the tens of thousands of real-world organizations that actually do organize the poor in Latin America. [Annis 1988: 215]

The relationship between NGOs and governments does not end at the state level; the NGO activities may be related to, and in some analytic models may actually be part of, a government's participation in global economic systems of manufacture and trade. Rajni Kothari (1986), for example, argues that some NGOs in India in the mid-1980s were acting as an instrument of the government in linking the rural hinterlands into the worldwide capitalist marketing systems. He cites the global trend of capitalist nations who are shifting industrial strategies from developing industrial centers in urban areas of the underdeveloped world into the rural hinterlands. According to Kothari the textile industry in India is an example of this process. As urban-based manufacturing costs rise transnationals expand into the rural areas to develop inexpensive markets and sources of products and labor. Kothari notes that the Indian government, particularly under Rajiv Gandhi, was a partner in this process, encouraging foreign investment and expansion of the manufacturing sector in India. This process is being aided by the general perception of NGOs as independent of the government system or ruling party, and because in pre- and post-Independence India they worked closely with governmental programs setting up handicrafts, village industries, rural development agencies, credit co-operatives, and educational institutions.

By integrating rural peasants into the cash-based, commodity-based system of income generation, Kothari states, NGOs are acting as the agents of the government, on behalf of the transnational capitalist system. NGOs are accepted by the rural poor because they profess to be "nongovernmental" and working on behalf of the disadvantaged. Those organizations whose philosophies challenge this process and who take an active role in the political activities of the community are violating their charters as established by the central government. Those that limit their activities to income generation and related activities in a nonpolitical environment are rewarded by government funding and lack of interference in their activities.

Kothari's argument raises important points to consider in evaluating the larger structural implications of certain types of NGO activities in rural communities in underdeveloped countries. Many NGOs promote income-generating activities, based on the production and sale of commodities exported from the immediate area. At the very least these programs are promoting the increased participation of rural agriculturalists in an export-oriented marketing system, often encouraging the production of or growing of commodity products that will not be consumed in the community. These goods are produced based on an inequitable division of labor; the village-based labor pool, very often consisting of women, has no control over the marketing decision-making or the allocation of raw materials. Women function as household "piece goods workers" who provide only the labor inputs in a complex system of production. While the prospect of extra income is attractive, the great burden of the double and triple workday persists. In agricultural communities women already have an enormous range of subsistence and domestic responsibilities; assembly or piece-goods production is usually relegated to the late-evening hours, and often children are recruited into the process.

As noted earlier, village-level participants have no control over the production of materials or of the marketing of the products they create in such programs. Nor do these programs attack any of the structural inequalities inherent in the economic system. Illiteracy and social conventions put the SC/ST farmers at a distinct disadvantage in the marketing and sales of their products--processes controlled through better educated and more powerful middlemen and shop owners.

A local income-generating program, a sericulture project financed by UNIFEM (United Nations Development Fund for Women) in Pai, a village about 10 kilometers from Udaipur city, is described in a documentary film (Dorman 1992). Adivasi women participants interviewed by the filmmaker express great satisfaction with the increased income they derive from this program, which trains them in growing the mulberry plants that silk-producing worms live on, and also provides a source from which they can purchase the worms and to which they can sell the mature cocoons that contain the silk thread. The cocoons are then processed into dyed silk threads and woven into saris and other textile products, and sold by the sericulture center to urban outlets. These women do not wear silk saris; even if they did, the cost of the saris would make it an unreasonably extravagant purchase.

In addition, as was evident in the Pai project and discussed in the video, influxes of cash into rural households creates social problems that exacerbate gender relationships; who controls the income produced by the women, and how that income will be spent, can be a source of great conflict in these households. In Pai, for example, women complained that their husbands expropriated the cash and spent it on what the women considered to be wasteful expenditures, while they would have preferred the money to be spent on food and educational expenses for their children. The local NGO Astha was brought into the project by UNIFEM to help develop a local organizational network within which women could articulate their concerns and goals concerning the new influx of cash into their households.

I had many discussions with the directors and organizers of local NGOs about the broader implications of local income-generating programs as development strategy. These discussions, which took place between 1988 and 1995, evolved against a backdrop of rapidly changing shifts in the government of India's attitude towards foreign investment and privatization of industry--a process that had not yet begun in 1988 but was in full flower by 1995.

Although he is philosophically opposed to instituting income-generating projects, Kishore Saint, original organizer of Ubeshwar Vikas Mandal, spoke many times over the years of the conundrum of a social activist working with the poor, wanting deeply and passionately to do something to alleviate their poverty, but simultaneously reluctant to sponsor income-generating programs that link them with larger cash-based economic systems into which they are integrated at the lowest level of labor and resource extraction. He is keenly aware of the need for additional income resources as a means of meeting daily expenses and weakening the hold of local moneylenders in Bhil communities.

In our discussions on these subjects in mid-1995, Saint expressed a reluctant resignation to the local and village-level effects of India's economic liberalization and the resulting surge of consumerism at every level of local society. Even in the context of the growing penetration of commodities, cash, and globally based products into every village and phala of the district, his passion for social and political activism is unabated; he regards some of these new products, like tape recorders and video cameras, as resources for local activism and maintaining cultural identity. He is promoting their use in a program of capturing and recording local knowledge and technology systems, as well as rituals and social processes that are gradually being replaced by systems and rituals introduced from outside the rural community. His goal in these projects is to encourage the use of local knowledge and technology that will encourage more inclusive social and political mobilization. (See Ubeshwar Vikas Mandal 1992.)

Foreign Funding: Political Implications and Linkages

Foreign donors play an important part in the NGO segment in Rajasthan; one factor that contributes to the interest of foreign donor agencies in the area is the very proliferation of NGOs, many of which enjoy a positive ongoing relationship with overseas funding agencies.

Foreign funding, including the funding of local-level projects by European and American donor agencies, is not universally welcomed in India. Two separate traditions converge to taint the issue, each with a particular residue of imperialism. Both American espionage and foreign missionary activities have engendered lingering suspicion about the penetration of foreign funds and with them, of foreign influence in local affairs.

Any foreigner who takes up residence in Udaipur for more than the few weeks expected of tourists is eventually viewed as suspicious; Americans are particularly vulnerable to accusations of spying and CIA links. This suspicion can be traced in part to the well-publicized accusations in 1967 that the CIA had infiltrated and was funding social and cultural organizations in India, and was operating covertly out of the U.S. Embassy in New Delhi (see *New York Times* March 24 and October 25, 1967).

The legacy of this period of strained diplomatic relations over the U.S. involvement in the Vietnam war, and accusations of CIA infiltration into Indian organizations and political process, remains in the consciousness of those who are either familiar with the events or claim familiarity with them. After I had been living in the area for about two months, my landlady in Udaipur mentioned that a friend of hers, whose husband was a former military officer and was currently working in the private security business, had asked her how she knew for sure that I was not a spy. Another American anthropologist doing research in the district encountered similar difficulties; a late-night session of recording field notes into a small tape recorder was mistaken by villagers for short-wave radio transmission to the American government and reported to local authorities as such.

Some of the funding organizations that are now part of the development landscape in Udaipur were established as religious or missionary organizations. Their activities are now exclusively secular, but their identity as Christian missionary groups persists as part of their local identity. Following the electoral losses of the Congress(I) government in the 1989 and 1990 elections, and the formation of the coalition government under the leadership of V. P. Singh, many NGO officials in Udaipur expressed fears that the new government would more carefully scrutinize the activities of local organizations with financial ties to overseas religious-based organizations than did the Congress(I) government. The BJP, the major party of North India in the Janata Dal coalition, has a pro-Hindu appeal, and was perceived by much of the electorate as distinctly pro-Hindu and anti-Muslim and as such appealing to Hindu fundamentalist sentiments. Congress(I) was regarded during these elections as being pro-Muslim, and "soft" on issues of Hindu communal interest.

These fears have somewhat lessened with the liberalization policies, but the rhetoric of the BJP and the more extreme right-wing Shiv Sena opposition parties provides a counter-discourse, warning against the recolonization of India by foreign capital and financial investment. This ambivalence to opening up India's economy to unrestricted foreign investment resonates in the social welfare sector as well. In a 1993 interview (*New York Times* January 24, 1993) Kavel Ratna Malkani, then BJP vice chairman and identified as its chief spokesman, is quoted as saying: "In the area of social policies, the Bharatiya Janata Party is less alarmed by India's rapid population growth and 50 percent illiteracy rate than are international development agencies. Education is not really relevant to the Indian conditions...A farmer, whether he can write his name, is not important. he does not have to correspond with anyone. Education is not crucial for the Indian economy." Another party spokesman, Jay Dubashi, is quoted as saying, "The BJP is a very strongly nationalist party. It sort of harbors suspicions about foreign capital and foreign banks. Our people think these foreign banks corrupted our people" (Ibid.).

National Politics, Local Arenas

The national political events have provided the opportunity to observe the dynamics of the election process and its interaction with the NGO development process. The first round of elections in November

1989 for the Lok Sabha (national parliament) resulted in unprecedented loss of power by the Congress(I) party, which had been in power almost continuously since Independence. These elections were a turning point in the contemporary history of India, marked by increasing levels of influence of Hindu fundamentalists in local and national politics.

The importance of these elections was felt in villages as well as the urban centers of political power; in Bagdunda and environs elections and the voting process dominated all conversations for several weeks prior to the polling day. The elections were also very much a part of the NGO scene during this time. The central government's restrictions on NGO activity related to political party participation in the election process (see next section below) were balanced by NGO-based encouragement of community political participation. Policy and strategy was therefore continually renegotiated to prevent violations of the government's rules. Local-level election participation by NGO workers made the organizations vulnerable to government sanction, and appropriate organizational strategy was perceived in a variety of ways.

The elections also illuminated the process by which individual mobility for talented organizers emerges through the avenue of NGO activity, further illustrating how local political-party process, despite the necessity for many of the NGOs to remain party neutral, is an integral part of the development scene. These events provided a framework within which to examine local level political institutions, particularly those of Bhil leadership, and how these indigenous political positions and skills interface with both NGO development and state and national political party processes. The election process activates indigenous forms of political leadership and mobilization, as well as animating the values and skills inherent in them. The involvement of Bhils in these events elucidate the development potential inherent in political involvement as well as the constraints that hinder actualization of this potential. The local dynamics of the elections will be discussed in greater detail in Chapter 9; some of the broader structural implications and contractions in the relationship between NGOs and the national government are discussed below.

Local NGOs and the Government of India

The relationship between NGOs in India and the government has been complex and at times ambivalent. The Government of India's Seventh Five Year Plan 1985-90 for the first time acknowledged and encouraged the role of voluntary agencies in the nation's development process. The text of the Seventh Plan included the following statement:

Chapter 5   The "G" in NGO

> There has been inadequate recognition of [the non-governmental sector] in accelerating the process of social and economic development. These agencies have been known to play an important role by providing a basis for innovation with new models and approaches, ensuring feedback and securing the involvement of families living below the poverty line. Therefore, during the Seventh Plan, serious efforts will be made to involve voluntary agencies in various development programmes, particularly in the planning and implementation of programmes of rural development. [Government of India Planning Commission 1985 Vol. 2: 66]

The Plan identified several specific areas in which voluntary agencies "can be of great help for better implementation of anti-poverty and minimum needs programmes" (Ibid.: 67). Despite this acknowledgment of the role NGOs play in the nation's development, the relationship between them is tenuous at best, and at its worst, hostile and adversarial. By their very nature, NGOs serve quasi-governmental functions, such as delivering educational and other types of social services that the government has failed to deliver. This tension is played out at both the national policy-making level and at the local level of policy implementation and NGO activity.

Almost by definition NGOs exist by virtue of their structural opposition to government. They must register with the government to receive their tax-exempt status, and they cannot receive foreign funding except with the permission of the government. NGOs that receive foreign funding and are registered with the government are forbidden to engage in any political party activity or to support candidates for election. This regulation is generally regarded as an understandable, acceptable one, and is generally acknowledged to be obeyed. In a written statement on this subject Ajay Mehta, director of Sewa Mandir, expressed the following sentiments:

> The relationship of NGOs to politics is a delicate one, especially in so far as the politics of elections are concerned. It would be wrong for NGOs who are taking financial support from Governments or outside agencies to be active politically. Funds give them an edge in terms of support that is not fair to those who are competing without similar resources. The role however that NGOs should play is to help villagers understand the issues that are involved in the exercise of their franchise. The work of NGOs should be confined to the building up of alternatives, the self-confidence and the spirit of self-reliance of the people. This is itself profoundly political. This long term task should not be compromised by taking sides in the more immediate political struggles. Each NGO, no doubt, will have its own agenda. For those NGOs who do not take financial support a more activist role in politics would be valid. But those who do, I

feel, it would not be fair to convert this grass root support into taking party political power. The mainstream political parties have their own legitimacy and care should be taken that if they are to be challenged it can't be by taking unfair advantage of special advantages that NGOs enjoy by virtue of their access to funds in their capacity as voluntary organisations. [Mehta n.d.:5]

The Kudal Commission: The Government Strikes Back

The tension between NGOs and government is played out at the national policy level as well as on the local level. Despite the acknowledgment by the central government under Indira Gandhi of the positive contribution NGOs were making on the development scene, Mrs. Gandhi initiated a special judicial investigation of some organizations that were alleged to have been involved in financial mismanagement. An investigative commission was instituted in February 1982, under the direction of P.D. Kudal (formerly a justice on the Rajasthan High Court) and was extended through January 31, 1987. The targets of the investigation initially were two organizations charged with financial irregularities in the allocation of funds. As the Kudal Commission's investigation proceeded, it escalated its scope from making specific charges against specific organizations to including vague allegations about some unnamed organizations, and their alleged use of foreign-derived funds to destabilize or discredit the Indian government.

Critics of the commission's activities note that it was conceived in an atmosphere of political controversy; the organizations that were charged with offenses were outspoken critics of Mrs. Gandhi. The commission's final report was submitted to the government on January 31, 1987 and printed in June 1988, but it was not presented to Parliament until August 1989. Some journalists and other critics were quick to point out that this timing was politically motivated; they charged that the government of Rajiv Gandhi (his mother's political successor following the 1984 assassination of Indira Gandhi) was using the Report to divert public attention from the growing scandal involving alleged payments by the Swedish company Bofors to highly placed members of the government in exchange for armaments contracts--a scandal that contributed to the defeat of Rajiv Gandhi's government in the February 1990 elections.

An editorial in one national (English language) newspaper made the following charges:

...what ...casts a deep shadow on the dirt-digging activities of Mr. Kudal is that his whole exercise has been carried out in the spirit of a vendetta. When Gandhians had supported the Congress, as they had done when both commonly confronted agrarian radicalism, Gandhian institutions were found to be all right. However when apparently a large number of Gandhians turned against the Congress, a judicial exercise against them was initiated through the Kudal commission. Now that the commission has finally concluded its task, it is time to...end the obviously partisan witch-hunt. [*Times of India* August 9, 1989.]

Of the 116 cases submitted by the Kudal Commission to the Law Ministry and other investigating agencies, 58 were dropped immediately as non-actionable because of lack of evidence. Of the remaining cases, 16 were referred to the Central Bureau of Investigation, 12 to various government ministries and 12 to State Governments (*The Hindu* August 8, 1989).

Although few substantive actions resulted from the Kudal Commission's five-year investigation, NGO organizers and directors were alarmed by the scrutiny of their activity by the government and in the national press. Despite its failure to substantiate most of the charges, the long investigation, and its subsequent debate in the national press (including many editorials that were pro-government, pro-Kudal and anti-NGO) was a chilling reminder to NGO directors and organizers of the potential uses of the national political process and rhetoric, as well as the role of national media, within which their activities are represented and constructed.

Confronting the Government: Law and NGO Strategy

What follows are some examples of events that run counter to the majority of the strategies of organizations described in this book. These events, which were marked by violence (one in which events were shaped by its threat, the other its actual manifestation), both ensued from Bhils attempting to challenge the social norms and economic relationships of the community under the guidance of a nonresident NGO organizer. These examples provide a contrast to the prevailing NGO local-level strategy and interaction, and demonstrate, in one case with violent and tragic results, the impact of NGO policy on the lives of local villagers.

Although I did not personally experience or observe any violence against NGO workers, social workers, or social activists during my fieldwork, I was aware that a certain level of risk attaches to social activism, particularly in rural communities. Some of this risk was associated with criminal activities; extreme caution is taken when, for example, a jeep carrying workers and payroll (all cash) is taken from Udaipur to village field offices. I was continually warned not to walk alone from one village to another, nor even to go with others at night, as thievery is common in the rural areas. "Outsiders" are not targeted specifically for criminal activity; villagers always complained of theft of animals and household goods, thefts that took place either at night or when their houses were known to be empty.

Another constant threat is that opposition in any form to the local political status quo will result in violence. At the home of a friend, I met a young journalist from Udaipur whose family was in the newspaper business. Their newspaper had carried a series of stories attacking local politicians for corruption and theft, following which the office was bombed and the paper's presses destroyed. As he spoke I noticed disfiguring scars on the side of his head; I was later told that they were the result of his having been assaulted. His right ear was sliced off in the attack, which he claimed had been politically motivated.

One small team of NGO activists who ran a small organization talked often about the threats that had been made against them, particularly after they successfully orchestrated the ousting from office of a Sarpanche and the election of a Bhil to replace him. Although the threats did not alter their strategy of politicizing and organizing Adivasi men and women in the area, these workers both described some practical concessions they had made. For example, they had been offered a house on the outskirts of the village on an empty stretch of road as their field office. After the threats, they turned this offer down and instead rented a house in the center of the village, which they felt would be safer and less vulnerable to attack.

A few weeks before the November 1989 elections I scheduled a trip to their field area. They suggested that I cancel it, as they had received several threats of beatings and other violence. They did not say from whom these threats had come, but they had decided for the safety of both themselves and the people with whom they were working, that they would stay in the city for the two weeks prior to elections, and not return to the field until after the election results had been announced.

A brutal case of NGO activity-related violence occurred in Salumbar tehsil in 1990, and again in 1991. I first learned about the 1990 incident from Udaipur NGO directors who went to Salumbar to investigate the incident, and in 1991 an article about the incident was published (*Economic and Political Weekly* June 1-8, 1991). This article is sympathetic to the movement and the goals of the NGO in question. As this published report is consistent with what I had heard about the incident as it unfolded and contains far more detail than I had access to in 1990, I will quote extensively from it.

The events took place in Hadmatiya, an Adivasi village of 200 households. Like the villages of Udaipur district it has suffered from the effects of drought. Hadmatiya does not have any forest lands, but the adjoining village of Ghatet does, and Adivasis can collect fuelwood for sale in the village market from which they earn Rs. 10-12 a headload.

Chapter 5 The "G" in NGO

In Hadmatiya, as elsewhere "this source of income depends on the whims and vagaries of the forest officials" (Ibid.). As noted previously, Adivasis have been forced to supplement their land and forestry income with casual labor. "Daily wages for both men and women are about Rs. 10-12 in the region, i.e. about half the legislated minimum daily wage of Rs. 22" (Ibid.).

Over the years the Adivasi families of Hadmatiya have become indebted to a "money-lending-trading family" in Salumbar who controlled almost 600 bighas of land in Hadmatiya and adjoining villages. As a result of the implementation of the Land Ceiling Act, which sought to break up long-established land monopolies by limiting the amount of land that could be held by any one individual, 90 bighas of the family's land was transferred to the villagers "on paper" in the 1970s. "However they [Adivasi tenants] were not aware of this until recently and have been paying a one-fifth share of their harvest as rent" as well as mortgages to the moneylender of half their harvest (Ibid.).

> He [the moneylender] has also taken over the cultivable land of the tankbed which has traditionally been cultivated by nine adivasi [sic] families. A large number of the adivasis are bound by the growing burden of debt to work as *sagaris* (bonded labour) on the moneylenders' fields...
>
> Every bit of protective legislation that has been promulgated to safeguard the interests of the tribals against such exploitative practices has been flouted. Conditions in terms of infrastructure and community services in the village are abysmal. Drinking water is brought from the village well and hand-pumps. Electricity poles have been put up but the wiring has not been completed for more than two years. There is a primary school three km. away but classes are rarely held despite the appointment of five teachers. The nearest primary health centre is at Matasula, nearly 10 km away, but there is no public transport available to take a patient to the hospital. The State's developmental and welfare efforts have apparently left the lives of the tribals untouched. [Ibid.]

According to the article, at the beginning of 1990 villagers from Hadmatiya contacted the NGO Rajasthan Kisan Sangathan for assistance over the issue of cultivation rights around the tankbed to which village Adivasis traditionally had access. On March 2 they began cultivation in the tankbed area. On March 5 the moneylender filed police charges against 37 Adivasis for trespassing and theft. That same morning the police entered the village. "Some women were manhandled. The provoked villagers retaliated by throwing stones and a few policemen were beaten up. The police retreated and promptly filed cases of assault and attempt to murder against the villagers" (Ibid.). The level of violence escalated, until: "On April 2, 14 jeeps, 4 trucks and a bus load of policemen and some henchmen of the moneylender arrived at the village temple. The village was surrounded and the villagers were chased and herded forcibly in a field near Dhavda. Indiscriminate firing followed. Women were stripped and beaten up" (Ibid.).

Despite the continued threats of violence against the villagers, the Sangathan organization and its Adivasi followers continued to press their demands. They refused to pay the moneylender any rent and filed reprisal cases against police officials of Salumbar. The Sangathan also filed charges against forestry officials and forced the *patwari* (local official record keeper) to return bribe money and explain to the villagers their rights over contested lands.

The Sangathan has also antagonized portions of the Adivasi community by challenging the leadership policies of a nearby village *gameti*, a local "tribal chief...[who] traditionally has the absolute authority over the lives of the other Adivasis (Ibid.)." A dispute broke out between Adivasis of Hadmatiya and Jhadap, the gameti's village, which erupted in violence on March 1, 1991. On March 3 an armed mob reported to contain about 400 to 500 persons collected near Hadmatiya and systematically burned and destroyed the homes of Sangathan supporters while sparing the homes of others. In an effort to get police protection some Adivasis went to the police station, requesting aid early in the morning when the mob gathered; no protection was sent to the village, and this delegation of Adivasis was themselves put into custody. Eventually a total of 70 homes were destroyed by the mob. Six persons were arrested, all of them Adivasis; none of them, according to Sangathan activists, were the "main perpetrators of the attack" (Ibid.).

In conclusion the article states that while the initial conflict in 1990 was over a clearly defined issue, and that the NGO's involvement in the dispute had created antagonisms and conflicts that have galvanized interest groups outside of and within the Adivasi community:

> Last year's attack was clearly and starkly a response to the resistance of the Hadmatiya adivasis to a moneylender's usurpation of their land. If a year later the conflict and its focus are less defined it is because the dimensions of the conflict have become more complex. More importantly the range of interests antagonised by the sangathan have also become more organised...There is nothing remarkable in the story of this tribal village in Salumbar tehsil. The same processes are at work in different ways across the tribal belt in Udaipur, Dungarpur and Banswara districts of south Rajasthan. But the experience of Hadmatiya is important in that it reveals with stark brutality the repercussions of the organised attempt to the villagers to resist these processes. [Ibid.]

While the social, economic and political conditions of Adivasis in Hadmatiya are very similar to those in Udaipur district, these same conditions have not prompted such confrontative actions. In fact, the significant variable in the strategy adopted in Hadmatiya is the personality and politics of the NGO organizer.

The events in Hadmatiya galvanized the NGO community in Udaipur. Several organization leaders went to the town as soon as it appeared that violence had occurred, and returned with stories of police brutality against the Adivasis, particularly against the women, in excess of what was reported in the above-quoted article. The brutality of the police and reprisals against the Adivasis generated outrage and anger in the NGO community, but no surprise.

The events in Hadmatiya strongly contrast to the prevailing NGO strategy in Udaipur, where NGO programs are nonconfrontational and do not organize or lead participants into land seizures or other explicitly illegal actions. In the case of Hadmatiya, the organizer of the Rajasthan Kisan Sangathan was known to be a political radical who has a long personal history of confronting the political establishment and challenging, often violently, economic and political norms.

The organizer's colleagues in Udaipur understand the implications of the actions instituted, and their probable results. I questioned many of the Udaipur NGO organizers during the April 1990 incident about whether they felt the local Adivasis understood these implications and probable results. Most responded that they just didn't know. It was not an issue that had been addressed, nor did it seem to be a significant question to the people of whom I asked it.

This is not intended to suggest that the Bhils of either district are passive, uninformed followers of anyone who enters their village and holds out promises. They know better than anyone the consequences of breaching local social norms. All have personal histories as well as group histories of exploitation at the hands of landlords, moneylenders, and the police. But when the policy of an NGO involves direct confrontation the reprisals come, as they did in Hadmatiya, entirely against the Bhils--women and children included--without the distinction made as to whether or not any are members of a particular organization.

Chapter Summary

Since Independence, nongovernmental organizations in India have emerged over the past four decades as a major factor in India's national and local development strategy. These organizations are generally described as an alternative to capital-intensive and highly bureaucratic governmental development agencies, an alternative that provides both strategies and responses to local community needs more effectively than the official bureaucracies. Although the NGOs are diverse, this perception of them as a development alternative is common to all their rhetoric, as well as that of the donor organizations that fund their activities.

This rhetoric emphasizes the "nongovernmental" aspect of these organizations; yet in practice the influence of the relationship between NGO and government is pervasive and deeply affects both strategy and day-to-day operations. This relationship, and the effect of government on NGO operations in Rajasthan, thus far is relatively unexplored by the organizations themselves and by those who write about NGOs. The subtle influence by India's national government is wielded not only by the bureaucratic and fiscal regulations that the state imposes on NGOs, but also by how the government's presence is interpreted by local NGOs in their strategy and policy. The results of this complex dynamic is manifested in daily NGO operations, and on individual decision-making and alliance formation by their local participants. This role of government becomes explicit during elections, when villagers, in their multiple statuses as citizens and NGO participants, form political party alliances and cast their votes.

Village-level political party participation is a double-edged sword for NGO leadership. Theoretically, any development program aimed at raising local standards of living should encourage increased political participation and enfranchisement. Participating in mainstream politics is critical to the process of community-based action and to locally generated solutions to the problems of disenfranchisement and poverty.

The particular policies adopted by Udaipur NGOs in relationship to the government are not exclusively typical of the strategy found locally, nor are they necessarily common to NGOs throughout India. Contrasting alternative typologies and strategies in both local and national settings provides insights into the constraints inherent in these local strategies, as well as highlighting some of their implications.

Chapter 6

Household and Family:

Socio-economic and Ecological Constraints

This chapter describes the village-level environmental and social context within which NGOs intersect. Bhil communities, like Solaria, are connected with several levels of local and regional institutions. Their interaction with other villages and other caste and class groups is constant and integral to social and political organization. If phala isolation ever were a historic reality, contemporary relationships and patterns of interaction relegate that hypothesis to a questionable historicity.

Solaria has a total population of approximately 160, in 32 households. All the houses in Solaria are constructed of mud and dung walls, with bamboo roofs filled in with twigs and leaves. Some houses consist of one large rectangular room, approximately 30' x 40'. One end of this room contains the *chula*, or cooking pit. At the opposite end is a pen area for animals, most of which are brought into the house at night. As noted previously, the disappearance of animals during the night is a constant problem, almost always attributed to theft. Houses are never left empty or completely unattended; even when village-wide gatherings are held or everyone travels to another village for a wedding or other kind of celebration, at least one older child or adult remains behind to keep guard over the animals and household possessions.

Outside the house is a large verandah area, where large animals like bullocks and cows, when they are available, are penned. Another chula is occasionally located outside in the verandah area. A variation on the house layout is a smaller version, divided into two rooms each measuring about 10' x 10'; the chula is located in the inner room, and the front room, which opens onto the verandah, is used for bringing in animals at night, as well as for sleeping and storage.

All household activities are conducted within these rooms and immediately outside. Cooking, storage, food preparation, care of the animals, care of children, and visiting are all outdoor, public activities. There are no latrines; men and women use different sections of the adjacent fields. Bathing is done at a stream about one kilometer from the phala.

During village-wide meetings with social workers or politicians, men and women sit separately. Women huddle together, speaking barely above a whisper if at all, with their faces completely covered by their *chunri*, a long length of fabric generally worn over the shoulders and across the top of the head, that is pulled forward on those occasions when it is considered necessary to completely cover their faces. Within the household, however, with only family members present, a much more relaxed attitude prevails, particularly between the senior couple. Interaction and interplay between older husbands and wives is often very relaxed; although physical manifestations of affection like touching are not part of the nonverbal communication system between men and women, closeness and warmth was often evident, as well as a strong sense of partnership.

This partnership is particularly apparent in work patterns. Both men and women work in the fields, very often side by side, although plowing is generally considered to be man's work. During planting women usually handle the seeds. They carry a large basket on their heads, and drop the seeds by the handful into a funnel attached to the plowing animal. Although most people said that it is preferable for women only to handle the seeds, if no woman is present in a household planting will be done by men.

Land Ownership, Ecological Constraints

Of the 32 households in Solaria, all reported owning land. On average per household the land holdings are 1.24 bighas, supporting on average a household with 4 or 5 members.

Under ideal conditions of productivity--good monsoons, charged wells, adequate seed supply and animal availability for manure and traction when needed--three crops can be harvested. If these ideal conditions prevail one bigha yields productivity of the equivalent of approximately Rs. 2,000 (an income equal to that of a primary or secondary schoolteacher or lower-level management person in a hotel or business) if traditional local crops are planted, such as winter wheat, corn, onions, pulses, mustard, or vegetables. Newly introduced commodity crops like ginger can triple or quadruple potential income. But ideal conditions are rarely actualized and few households have enough water consistently for three full crops year after year.

Many factors contribute to land lying fallow. Even during good monsoon seasons the rains can be so spotty that some families can't even put in one crop. And even access to water will not assure that the field could be plowed. Animal mortality in this area was reported to be as high as 50 percent during the drought period of the mid- to late-1980s; some families with access to water could not plow and sow the fields because of lack of traction animals. Other factors that may prevent putting in even the rain-fed crop are lack of seeds, which, if the previous year's crop is a failure, persists as a problem the following year, or the lack of other necessities, such as animal fertilizer.

In other words, once drought sets in, the problems faced by these marginal farmers become an ever-increasing cycle of resource scarcity. The resumption of good rains may ease this cycle, but cannot provide the entire solution to the ongoing problems of marginal agriculture. Loss of animals and the loss of seed stock require the farmer to either go into debt to replace them, or to deplete whatever meager resources he has to try to get through the year. So even if the monsoons cooperate the next year, debt and lack of access may prevent putting in a crop.

The matter of land ownership is not always clear-cut; for example, families--joint extended households--may own a plot of land that is worked together. If you ask one member of the household how much land he owns, he will say, for example, "four bighas." If you ask how many of his brothers share that land, the answer may be as many as four or five. So landowning from the perspective of the individual does not necessarily mean control over agricultural resource. Land, and the produce from the land, is shared by as many as 20 individuals.

Land holdings are generally fragmented and scattered. A total land holding for a household of five bighas may actually be scattered among two or three non-contiguous plots; only one or two of these plots may be actually cultivated. On a plot of one or two bighas, a household of five people is hard put to reach even a subsistence survival level using traditional crops of maize and winter wheat.

The plots of land in a Bhil phala tend to be the least productive of all land in the area. They are located on hills, carved out of the once-dense forests. These lands were more productive when they were protected by the surrounding forests; deforestation has hit Bhil agriculturalists more severely than their valley-dwelling neighbors. The absence of forest cover and the depletion of wild grasses and shrubs has created a serious runoff problem when the rains do fall. With no ground cover or root structures to hold back the water, runoff carries water and topsoil off the hills into the low-lying valleys and river beds. Therefore their wells, also located on hills, do not recharge, as ground water does not have the opportunity to percolate below ground level. With nothing to hold back the topsoil, it runs off with the water, leaving substantially less productive soil within which to plant crops.

With all these constraints on the productivity of agriculture, it is virtually impossible for a family to support itself exclusively on the land. All households report supplementing agricultural income with other sources of income, derived generally from minor forest produce, animal husbandry, and wage work.

About half the households reported the collection and sale of minor forest produce as a source of income; household income from these sources ranged from Rs.100-300 per year in 1990-91. This includes collection of firewood for sale; collection and sale of medicinal herbs and wild flowers (particularly the *mauwa* flower, which blooms in the spring and is harvested and brewed into an alcoholic beverage); honey collection, and the sale of other wild-growing edible products.

About half the households reported the sale of animals as contributing to household income. The most frequently raised animals kept for sale are goats; they are the cheapest to buy and maintain. Goats are sold for their milking potential primarily, and on occasion for slaughter and meat consumption. In 1995 three families in Solaria have used the profits from ginger production to buy camels, which generate significant income primarily as a transport animal.

Bullocks and cows are the most valuable animals. Although a camel is the most expensive animal to purchase, at approximately Rs. 4,000 in 1990 and about double that in mid-1995, bullocks, cows, and buffalo produce far more in income and use value over their lifetimes.

The lifetime value of a female bovine animal is inestimable; she provides manure, which is a basic household commodity and fertilizer. She produces milk, which can be converted to ghee for household use and sale; also produced in the churning process is *chach* , a bitter but refreshing liquid. Yogurt is also produced from the milk, for sale and household consumption. Milk is not drunk on its own; it is used for tea when available. (Water is not used for tea- making; loose leaves are placed directly into boiling milk, along with sugar, and boiled together. This is strained through a cloth and placed in small glasses.)

The two wealthiest families in Solaria--headed by two brothers--each claimed income in 1990-91 of Rs. 5,800/year from agriculture; one household had a total income of Rs.7,500, the other Rs.10,200. Each also had 3 bighas of land, the most in the phala that one household claimed. These two families also had the largest number of animals per household: 2 and 3 bullock respectively; 1 cow each; 3 and 1 buffalo; 2 and 1 male buffalo calf; and 20 and 10 goats. Each had relatively small household sizes-- 5 and 4 household members. And most significantly of all, neither household reported any debt. Of all 32 households, these were the only ones that reported no debt.

The poorest families in the village in terms of income reported Rs.1,400 and 1,600 income for the year. They each had 1/2 bigha of land and 3 household members. The land of each yielded Rs.600 income; wage work yielded an additional Rs.800. Both families had debt of about Rs.2,500.

In the broadest of generalizations, a correlation exists between family land holdings and household income; however, other variables contribute to the income and expenditures of the household, as well as the "net" for the year. For example, one household with 1/2 bigha of land reported only Rs.200 agricultural income; they supplemented this with Rs.1,500 in wage work. There are only 3 household members, and their expenditures were Rs.2,100 with debt of Rs.2,000 rupees. Another family, with 2 bigha of land, reported Rs. 4,100 income for the year; the 7 household members spent Rs. 6,500 in expenses; in addition this household has the largest current debt of the village, Rs.6,000.

Even when a family possesses the productive resources -- sufficient land and animals for agricultural production--other forms of income are critical to "breaking even." And while more household members represent more working hands, particularly in the wage-labor income category, they also increase expenditures. So do expensive unanticipated events like illness, funerals, and death feasts, which, while they are inevitably paid for by loans from moneylenders, increase interest payments and pledges against loans.

Animals, while they are income-producing and productive resources, also cost money to maintain. Few of the households' animal-based income, when expenses were deducted, yielded any significant profit. One family with 1 each bullock, cow, and buffalo, 9 goats and 4 donkeys, reported Rs.700 income from their animals and Rs.1,000 expenses. The one household that yielded significant profit is an incredibly hard-working husband a wife with no children. Their assets totaled 10 goats and 1 donkey, with 1 1/2 bighas of land. Their agricultural income of Rs.2,400 was supplemented with Rs.200 income from forest products, Rs.500 wage work and Rs.1,200 income from their animals. Their expenses for the animals was Rs.400. Total expenditure for the household was Rs.2,700 rupees, netting them Rs.2,100 for the year, with a relatively low Rs. 900 total current debt.

Expenditures and Debt

Even under the most advantageous of circumstances--that is, access to water, seeds, fertilizers and traction animals--the yield of Rs.2,000 per bigha barely covers a household's expenses. Out of the 32 households sampled, 10 had a positive cash flow; of those 10 only two had a positive cash flow in excess of Rs.1,000 and no debt. The balance of eight households had a positive cash flow of less than Rs.1,000 coupled with debt in excess of Rs.1,000 .

Cash expenditures are an integral part of the economic cycle of the family. It does not seem possible that in today's economic and ecological environment a family can support all its needs on what it produces and its own labor. Ordinary cash expenditures are necessary for items such as salt, sugar, tea, oil, some spices, clothing, school-related expenses, medical care, and *bidi* (locally produced cigarettes).

Anecdotal evidence indicates that liquor and *afim*, a narcotic substance, draw off a considerable part of household income. If the songs that women sing when they are together is any indication, drunkenness and intoxication are a serious problem in this area, as is the expense necessary to maintain these habits, which are attributed exclusively to the men of the household. Despite the precarious financial balance these households face, hospitality to a visitor is an inviolate rule; hospitality often includes the sharing of liquor and other intoxicants among men.

As some sort of kinship connection generally exists between visitors, the sense of hospitality can be related to the ritual and social obligations of kin. Strangers--unrelated or unknown people--are neither welcomed nor protected. A stranger is generally regarded as a threat, particularly to women, and is dealt with suspiciously. But once a connection is established Bhil hospitality is boundless.

Invariably when I arrived at a house tea would appear instantly. A behind-the-scenes flurry of activity, generally sending a child scurrying to a neighbor to borrow the necessary supplies, always accompanied the arrival, as families rarely have stocks or supplies on hand of consumables other than grains. On one occasion I arrived at a village around mid-day. This was a tiny phala, a collection of only a few houses. I was immediately given black tea with sugar, and my hostess explained with great embarrassment that the goats had been milked in the morning and the milk had been consumed or processed; the goats couldn't be milked again until later that afternoon. A few hours later I was very proudly presented with a small glass of warm milk which had just been taken from the goat, an offering I am ashamed to say I could not possibly drink down, and I refused on the grounds that I don't take milk because of stomach problems.

A significant source of expenditure for Bhil households is the cycle of social and familial obligations that relate to marriage and death rituals. As cash reserves are unheard of, these expenditures are invariably met with loans from the moneylender. In addition, household expenditures may be made on credit against future harvests. Any unanticipated expense, like an illness or the necessity for travel, will be met with a loan. These cash loans are given freely, with the understanding on both sides that both a ritual and an economic obligation ties the debtor to the lender.

Although there are branches of state banks in some villages, Bhils avoid them. Many reported that they were subject to extortion and corruption when they approached the banks. Under the reservation benefits, SC and ST members are entitled to up to 50 percent government subsidy on some loan transactions. Nevertheless, many people reported that the bank managers demanded a rebate or cash payment for exercising this subsidy.

Bank transactions further require the "signing" of papers and documents; this often was accomplished by the placing of a thumbprint on the loan document by those who cannot read or write. Even if someone can scribble their name, they do not understand the documents nor the details of the conditions of the transaction. I observed one such loan transaction. An old man came into the local bank office requesting a loan. The bank manager rattled off a long, involved speech to him in Hindi about the conditions, terms, obligations, etc. that were attached to the loan. I watched the old man carefully, and could not discern any kind of understanding or communication with the bank manager, nor did he at any time respond to or question any of the conditions. At the conclusion of the bank manager's speech the man placed his thumbprint on the documents and left. I was told later by a regional manager for the state bank in Dungarpur/Banswara that the default rate on loans in the rural communities is about 50 percent; the bank, he said, rarely pursues these defaults because of the complexity of the legal process and the scant value of the possessions of the defaultee.

As noted, only two households in Solaria reported no debt in 1990-91; the average household debt was Rs.2,595. Most debt is incurred because of the expenses related to life-cycle rituals and celebrations. These expenses are continuously being discussed by the NGOs and other development and social reform agencies, and are an ongoing theme in the village-level discourse on poverty and social reform. I have continually observed a gap between the discourse and practice; although people continually talk about the deleterious effect of these events at meetings and in NGO-led discussions they still feel obliged to participate in them. In Solaria, one man reported the following as the cost of rituals: participation in Gavri Rs. 500 (a cycle of dance-drama performances discussed in Chapter 10); Navratri festival Rs. 100-150; *dapa* (bride price) Rs. 2,000-10,000, and Holi festivities, Rs. 900.

The same person said, "If our daughter has given birth to a child then we have to buy clothes for the baby, the mother, and more. If it is their first son then we take fifteen to twenty people with us to her in-laws' house, and eat and drink with them." Elsewhere he discussed the high expenses of death feast rituals, particularly the *nukta* feast, held about a month after death. If the feast is held in honor of a senior male member of the community, jati members from literally miles around will attend and will be hosted by the family of the deceased. Several people with whom I discussed this issue told me that they opposed the practice in principle as an expensive and wasteful ritual, but as their fathers died they still felt compelled to honor them in the traditional, and expensive, form of hosting a large gathering of their jati mates from several villages.

Marriage Rules and Exchanges

Marriages are generally village exogamous and follow a virilocal postmarital residence pattern, in that the bride goes to the village, and usually the household, of her husband's parents. They are also gotra exogamous. Exceptions to the rule occur in several different types of marriages. Some phalas contain two gotras or separate patrilineages; marriages between these two groups is acceptable but not preferred. Elopement with a mate from one's own village and gotra also occurs on occasion; these marriages are grudgingly accepted by the families after a show of disapproval. A small percentage of marriages follow the reverse postmarital residence pattern, and the husband moves to the household of his wife. This is generally motivated by either a lack of brothers in the wife's household or more frequently by the new husband's lack of resources on his own. He is referred to as *ghar jamai* (literally house son-in-law), a term that carries with it some derision, as it indicates that the man could not meet the ideal set of responsibilities--both financial and social--to his village, his family, and his wife's family.

Households consist of senior male and female, unmarried children, and usually newly married couples, son and daughter-in-law. Women marry out of the village, although they maintain close ties with their parents' village and visit back and forth regularly. The composition of the family is not fixed over time but evolves as the individuals themselves pass through various life stages; the ideal pattern is for the son to build his own house close to his father's--usually within a hundred feet or so. In some cases the father will merely extend his own house to increase the amount of room available, and keep one chula to feed the extended family. But once the son begins to have children of his own, the ideal is that he build his own home and his wife has her own chula.

Poverty and restraint of resources often distort this ideal form. Lack of money with which to build a new house is often cited as a restraint in a couple establishing their own household. In addition, it was explained to me that in families with only one son it would be silly to

Chapter 6 Household and Family

go to the expense of building a new house for the son and his wife, when the parents' house would eventually be inherited completely by the son.

Most marriages take place between partners who live within the village's "marriage circle," referred to locally as *chowkla.* McCurdy states that the marriage circle around Ratakote is a 25-mile radius, or one day's walk from the village. This circle may encompass 50 to 75 villages, but in actuality marriages tend to cluster between a smaller number of villages. Local Bhils generally replied in response to my questions about it that the size of a chowkla is "ten-fifteen-twenty villages." This smaller number of interacting villages is more likely for several reasons. One, as McCurdy indicates, is practicality--villages that are connected by some sort of passable walking trail or road share frequent and varied forms and sources of communication. Although a village may be within the geographic marriage circle, if it is cut off by a waterway or a particularly arduous pathway, it is unlikely that regular communications between any village members would take place.

McCurdy also describes what he refers to as the "social sector" within the marriage circle. Members of a social sector interact often; villagers pass through one another's villages walking to and from markets, town, and bus routes. They interact at fairs and *melas* (large gatherings) regularly and are likely to participate in Gavri and other local ritual activities. The social sector is likely to include two villages linked by marriages in previous generations.

Social-sector villages may also be linked by shared religious or political activities. Followers of a particular guru or reformer may form close linkages that will include the marriage of offspring. And the frequency of NGO-sponsored inter-village meetings, bringing together often hundreds, and on rare occasions, thousands of villagers from one region, also becomes a factor in re-defining the social-sector parameters.

Most marriage discussions are initiated by the parents of the boy seeking a marriage partner. Marriages that are arranged by both sets of parents are accompanied by a complex set of exchanges of money, food, and other goods. Marriage negotiations begin with a middleman bringing together the fathers of the boy and girl; they meet, share a meal and drink, and agree to the wedding. A betrothal ceremony takes place about six months before the wedding. This ceremony is the beginning of the wedding ritual cycle, and the point at which affinal terms begin to be used between the families. The betrothal ceremony also marks the beginning of the gift-exchange and visiting exchange process between the two families.

In analyzing the dowry and bride price payment process in India, many observers, from colonial administrators onward, cite the onerous expense to one side of the marriage, most frequently the dowry expense, as Hindu dowry payment is the prevailing form of marriage payments. The tremendous cost of dowry to a family with only girls is often cited as the cause of female infanticide and other forms of mistreatment of female children, generally in northern India (Miller 1981). While dowry is certainly a tremendous burden for families, the focus on it often obscures the value of the ongoing flow of money, food, and gifts in both directions throughout a family's life cycle.

Among Udaipur Bhils, the prevailing system of premarriage payment is dapa, or bride price; the groom's family negotiates a bride price payment approximately one month prior to the actual wedding. This payment is only one of many exchanges of gifts and goods that take place between the two families.

Hosting of one's affines--and affines often seem to travel in large retinues--involves feeding and housing large groups of people, during which time all their needs are met by the hosts. The total cash value of this hosting and gift exchange goes toward equalizing the marriage payment expense. A longer-term analysis of this process in the dowry context may provide some economic equalization and rationalization to what is often referred to as an "irrational" economic ritual expense. In addition to the value of exchanges within the households themselves, feasts and meals for the entire village are part of the expense, thus the benefits of a single wedding are spread throughout a village, and will be whenever a wedding takes place within that village. Many villagers spoke of a system by which all the households contribute a certain sum to meet the expenses of the wedding, knowing that in time whatever is contributed to the "pool" will be repaid in kind.

A few months prior to the wedding the mother of the groom, accompanied by female relatives and friends, visits the bride's house and makes gifts of clothing. About a month before the wedding the groom's father and retinue travels to the bride's village to decide on the bride price payment and actual date of the wedding.

Bhil informants in Solaria told me that dapa payments can range from Rs. 2,000 to 10,000, depending on the resources and loan capacity of the family. During the 10-day period prior to marriage, the bride and groom, in their respective villages, are feasted and feted by their families. Girls are given a new set of clothes and travel around their village with a procession of other unmarried girls (their unmarried sisters and cousins), singing alternately bawdy songs about marriage and mournful dirges marking the end of their childhood and leaving their natal homes. They are given pure *ghee* (clarified butter) to drink, a treat marking their special, but transient, status as brides-to-be. Young men are garlanded and turbaned, and often carry knives or swords around their waists.

Chapter 6 Household and Family

Bhil women marry at around age 18 and go to live with their husbands immediately. Other caste groups betroth their children as early as in infancy; some may actually go through the marriage ceremony before puberty. This may occur when wedding celebrations can be "bunched"--two or three siblings marrying at one time to help defray wedding costs. The "brides" will then return to their natal homes immediately and reside with their families until they are 15 or 16.

When early marriage among rural Bhils takes place, it seems to be motivated by social pressure on the part of the bride's family to fulfill the cycle of responsibility to marry off their daughters or to remove a relatively unproductive member of the household.

At one large meeting sponsored by Sewa Mandir, one young woman spoke of the miseries of an early marriages--at age 12 or 13--and the emotional pain and physical suffering it brought to her.

> When a son is born the parents are very happy. Their hearts are filled with joy and they shout in the village that my wife gave birth to a son. When a daughter is born people think they have come into crisis. When the daughter begins to grow her father thinks about her marriage. He talks with the son's father and settles her marriage without asking his wife or daughter. Her father takes no pains over whether she is happy in the marriage or not. But a mother-in-law never thinks about her daughter-in-law's childhood. She thinks that she is too little to do all the work in the house and fields. She never treats her daughter-in-law like her own daughters. When her husband becomes a little older he no longer believes in the arranged marriage. He wants to marry by his own choice, and leaves her. She comes to her parents. They can't help her. After the death of her father, father's brother sends her back to the husband's house. In this way her whole life is spent in misery. She gives birth in childhood. She loses her health and her beauty. Mothers should be more bold. They should not marry their daughters in early age. It totally destroys the life of a woman.

Another woman at the same meeting described the early marriage scenario in this way:

> If a girl is born to a family it becomes a problem. When she is ten or twelve years old her grandfather says to his son, marry off your daughter. The son may refuse, but the pressure on him becomes too great. The grandfather says that the marriage is an occasion of happiness and if I die I will not see it. So the daughter is married at an early age. In her in-laws' home she has to do all sorts of work. In early age she becomes a mother. Her mother in law does not take care of her. So she looks like an old lady even in young age. Her

father won't take her back. She has no home. Where should she stay?

Elopement, Adultery, and Social Conflict

Elopement is generally cited in the existing literature on Bhil marriage practices as a relatively common marriage form; McCurdy states that 30 percent of the marriages in Ratakote occurred as a result of elopement; his informants were quick to point out, he says, that while their marriages were "regular," many other relatives were married by elopement or other irregular means. Elopements generally occur when a couple decide spontaneously to marry. They generally go to the boy's parents home, where, after efforts to dissuade them are unsuccessful, all parties agree to a quick marriage.

Sexual liaisons outside of marriage are tolerated as long as they do not escalate to the point of family involvement and breaches of social contracts. Adultery, for example, seems to be significant not so much for the sexual breach as for the resulting conflict it can cause between families and villages. It is likely to be regarded as a breach of contract, or a breach of promise, which results in interfamily feuds, which can then result in violence and police intervention, which is generally avoided by rural Bhils at all costs. The police, the courts and the legal system are rarely viewed as avenues of recourse, only as sources of exploitation and danger, particularly to Bhils who are unable to understand the written documents that invariably accompany police or court actions.

One event of adultery reported to me illustrates this. A couple in a Bhil village, both married to others, ran off together with the intention of setting up a household. They were captured by the family of the woman's husband and forced to return to their village. The woman was tied up, hung from a tree, and periodically beaten for several days (the punishment also meted out to women accused of witchcraft). The man decided that he wanted to leave the village, which he was permitted to do. He was escorted out of the village by a group of men when he suddenly bolted and in desperation jumped down a well. A policeman was called to the scene to aid in the rescue. The concern of those who related the story to me was that the case would now turn into a police action, which would be investigated further.

Multiple Marriages and Widow Remarriage

Second marriages for Bhil men with a living wife do take place, generally motivated by lack of offspring, or lack of male offspring. I interviewed one household in Khewara within which this occurred, and the two wives lived together with the husband. In this case the first wife did not produce any children during seven years of marriage. The husband then took in a new wife. The first wife was not pleased but she agreed to it. The second wife gave birth to two sons and enjoyed a high status in the household. To her surprise, however, and to the great delight of the first wife, *she* then gave birth to a child. The second wife fell into a deep depression, while the first wife was overjoyed. When I met this family for the first time, the second wife sat in a corner quietly with her head covered, while the first wife, playing with her baby on her lap, spoke openly and confidently about the household situation.

This was a fairly uncommon situation, however. The family had a relatively large plot of land and a well-constructed house; the husband had a salaried job in addition to the family's agricultural production and was relatively well-off. More common is the situation of another woman, who was living with her teenage daughter in a tiny but well-maintained house in a Bhil phala near Bagdunda. After several years of marriage, during which only their one daughter was born, her husband left her and went to live with another woman in the same phala.

Among Bhils, widows are generally free to remarry. The widow's parents again collect a bride price (called *natra* for a remarriage). Bhil women reported however that it is unlikely that an elderly widow would remarry; remarriage, they said, "is for women below thirty years." If a woman is widowed late in life, and has sons, in all likelihood she will remain in her husband's house and her sons will inherit the land. If she has only daughters, or has no children, her situation is more precarious.

A female informant explained the situation of Bhil widows in this way:

> The custom here is that if she becomes a widow and has a daughter then the family members don't give her the land. But if she has a son, then whatever share her husband would have got is given to her. The woman also has to be strong. Even if she has two daughters they won't give her the land. If she has daughters and her father-in-law allows her to stay with the family, once her daughters get married the woman starts facing many problems. Life becomes very difficult for her and she has to go to another man.

Bhil women reported to me that married women are occasionally forced by their parents to leave their husband and go to another man's house in remarriage. This is motivated by the natra payment to the woman's parents. In such a case the children remain with the husband and the woman loses any claims to either her children or possible inheritance on the death of her first husband.

Another difficulty older women may face is the accusation of witchcraft (*dekani*). Although both males and females can be accused of witchcraft, the accusation often falls on women in events of unexplained illness or other unfortunate occurrences, accompanied by the torture and beating of the victim.

Carstairs (1983) describes accusations of witchcraft in Bhil communities, pointing out the seeming contradiction between prevailing attitudes towards women and interaction between the sexes, and the accusation of witchcraft later in life. Although the economic and material motivation of this process has not yet been examined it would be a fruitful avenue of future research to correlate accusations of witchcraft with conflict over land and inheritance. It may also be related to postmarital residence patterns; in this virilocal system, an unrelated woman enters her husband's village as a relative stranger, and although she usually has kin in the village she is in some ways an outsider--her affiliation to the village is through her husband's family. As in caste Hindu society, her integration into her husband's lineage may be incomplete; but unlike caste Hindu society, no elaboration of ritual and behavior controls a Bhil widow in her husband's household and community. Her status as an outsider--and a witch--may be brought to bear particularly if it is in the interests of her husband's patrilineage to drive her out of the community, or at least the realm of respectability, in cases of dispute over property and inheritance.

Death Rituals and Expenses

While all contemporary ethnographies note that the Bhils cremate their dead, earlier works about the Bhils in other areas are not as clearcut as to burial/cremation practices. Malcolm, for example, states, "The Bhills [sic] always bury their dead" (Malcolm 1827:86). Enthoven describes in great detail the burial practices of the Bhils of Kandesh (1975 (1920): 169). J. K. Doshi, in his study of the Bhils of Pai (a village about 20 kilometers from Udaipur city) states that the general rule is to cremate; "some categories of people are not cremated but buried...children below the age of seven; insane persons; epileptics; persons who have died of small-pox and professional ascetics with yellow robes." (1969: 102)

If Malcolm's observation on burial practices in his 1827 publication is accurate, there has been a transition, presumably in emulation of caste Hindu practices, from burial to cremation over the past century. I was told that all Bhil dead are cremated. The one time burial was mentioned was by a particularly frank older woman--and she was immediately thereafter scolded by her daughter-in-law as being too outspoken--who said that these days the expense of wood for a cremation fire was causing some poor families to bury their dead, a source of great shame and embarrassment to them.

The death of an adult begins a 12-day period of active mourning and related rituals, most of which involve the gathering of villagers and kin.

Cremation takes place quickly after death, usually within 24 hours, at a cremation site outside of but within a short walk's distance of, the village proper.

Preferably the death feast is held 12 days after the death has occurred. If the deceased is a prominent male, and the death feast will involve the gathering and feeding of several hundred or several thousand people, it may be postponed for up to six months until resources and money can be gathered to fulfill the ritual obligations to kin and jati members.

Levels of Socio-Political Organization

As noted previously, the most significant unit of organization in Bhil communities is the phala, the smallest settlement unit. The term phala is used for both the "village" designation as well as subwards of a village.

This lack of precision of boundaries and demarcation is probably the result of the dispersed household distribution typical of Bhil villages, as well as the growth of individual households over the generations since the village was settled. What is clear is that the Bhils of each of the phalas make the distinction between their geographic community and that of the multicaste village closest to their location.

Bhil households are generally built on top of hills in a dispersed residential pattern. Some observers attribute this pattern to security; from the vantage point of the hilltop house adjacent paths and access routes can be carefully watched. As noted, animal theft is a constant worry, and the disappearance of animals during the night is a common occurrence. In Solaria the houses were built on the hills, overlooking agricultural fields, which were all located in the adjacent valleys between hills, or on plateaus behind the house settlements. There is daily interaction between the Bhils of Solaria and the multicaste village of Morwa. Men travel back and forth almost on a daily basis; children walk the approximately 2 kilometers to the school and back every day. Women travel there less frequently, and tend to go in the company of men, or at least in the company of other women. A range of services and products is available in Morwa, including some shops, a grain grinder, potter, blacksmith, and a shopkeeper who is also the middleman in agricultural commodity sales and moneylender. In addition, Morwa (a census unit) is the closest center of government services: there was a primary health center (most recently run in conjunction with the SWACH health project) which subsequently closed, and the primary school. There is no regular government bus service to and from Morwa; a private bus connecting Morwa to Bagdunda and Udaipur runs only in fair weather as it moves along a river bed that can be flooded during the monsoon season.

In addition to regular contact with individuals and groups in Morwa, most Bhil men from Solaria travel to Bagdunda by bus or on foot on a somewhat regular basis. As these outings may be a combination of shopping expeditions, family visits, and ritual events, women often accompany their husbands. The trips may involve the purchase of manufactured goods, such as tin plates (considered more valuable and of higher status than locally produced clay); foodstuffs, which are more expensive than in Udaipur but less expensive than in Morwa; silver or other jewelry; fabric; or clothing. The travelers also use these expeditions to sell produce on occasion; transport small animals for sale or purchase; or conduct business with the *tehsildars* or local government officials.

The same bus that travels to Bagdunda goes on to Udaipur. Travel to Udaipur is less frequent than to Bagdunda, but also occurs on a regular basis despite its cost, which is the equivalent of more than a day's wages. Trips to Udaipur may also be made for purchase of textiles or commodities, as well as transporting an ill person to the city hospital-- a medical strategy of last resort because of its expense. These trips to Udaipur from this area are now increasingly connected with the activities of NGOs, whose headquarters were all in the city.

The visit of city and town people *to* Morwa takes place on a much less frequent basis, but this flow of people to the countryside is important, because it symbolizes the increasing presence of Udaipur-based political institutions in the Bhil community, as well as the significance of Bhils to these organizations. These "visitors" generally represent one or two overlapping institutions: politics and development.

Local Political Organization: From Phala to State

The phala, a named residential unit, may have an informal leader, but individuals within phalas interact with each other with an equality reinforced by constant interaction and kin-based equality. Phalas cluster around a village, a more centralized unit of identification and organization. Each village has a headman, or *gameti*, who represents that village cluster of phalas in social, ritual and political affairs within the Bhil community. The village headman has the authority to make decisions on behalf of the village and to enforce those decisions, particularly in the area of payment of fines and jati-related decisions like boycotting or out-casting.

McCurdy describes for Ratakote two types of headmen: the *gameti*, which is an inherited position going to the eldest son of the headman, and the *khas gameti*, which is not necessarily an inherited position, but goes to a person who displays true leadership qualities. The khas gameti becomes most important and assumes most of the leadership role when the inherited title passes to a weak or undeserving individual.

Chapter 6 Household and Family

The gameti is counseled by a group of male village members, usually about five in number, who advise the headman but do not have any authority on their own. In issues of particular importance, all male heads of households of the village will meet with and advise the gameti, who alone has decision-making authority in the village. One informant mentioned two additional levels of organization to me, *betak* and *somaj* which he explained as meetings of village headmen on larger, more inclusive levels but was not able to clarify these terms further. Most people, when asked about organization and Bhil government, only spoke of village level gameti, but I was present at several meetings, many of which were sponsored by NGOs, which brought together representatives of local Bhil villages from a very large area; the organizers of one such meeting claimed that representatives from over a hundred villages attended. This regional level of political organization is being mobilized increasingly to address social and political issues of significance to Bhils of the area.

In addition to these local, community-based political institutions, the Bhil phalas and villages are part of a state and national structures. Coyers describes the political structures in Rajasthan state as follows:

> Rajasthan's elected Chief Minister, the head of the regime party...in the state's Assembly *(Vidhan Sabha)* makes policy decisions. Most policies are formulated by a Cabinet of elected members of the Assembly who are appointed by the Chief Minister.... Policy is implemented by a hierarchically-arranged administrative network.... At the district *(zila)* level, I.A.S.[Indian Administrative Service] officers serve as Collectors who perform a multitude of functions from being the districts' chief judicial officers to being the District Development Officer. At the sub-district *(tehsil)* level members of the Rajasthan State Administrative Service (R.A.S.) perform supportive and some discretionary duties. The tehsil level functions include maintenance of revenue and land records and action in minor civil actions. Below the tehsil a government employed village level worker (VLW) serves as an extension agent and a *patwari* keeps village land records....
>
> Parallel to the elected administrative hierarchies...are *panchayati raj* structures. ...Groups from one to five villages are organized and authorized to formulate policy programs, submit budgets, and administer funds disbursed from the state government.... The local village-level council is called a *panchayat*, is directly elected and is chaired by a *sarpanch*....the *panchayat samiti* ...includes representatives from each *panchayat* at the tehsil level [and is chaired by a *pradhan*].... Each *panchayat samiti* is combined at the district level into the *zila parishad* (district council) which includes the *pradhans*, the chairmen of the panchayat samiti....

> The panchayat samiti is responsible for important expenditures and receives relatively large amounts of money from the state government through the Development Department. These funds are distributed in the forms of loans and grants, and are supervised by a Block Development Officer and the *Pradhan*. [Coyer 1975: 30-34]

The district of Udaipur is divided into tehsils, the smallest administrative unit of the state. The tehsildar is the tehsil authority; the patwari is the local representative of the tehsildar and he keeps all land records and collects taxes; the patwari is the one official the Bhils interact with regularly, as he visits all villages several times a year and keeps records concerning land ownership, crop output, and taxation.

In addition, all villages in rural sections of India are included in the Panchayati Raj system, the goal of which was to provide an administrative apparatus for decentralizing and implementing state rural development programs. Panchayats were conferred powers and functions that decentralize the government through a democratic system of locally elected representatives to administer development programs and dispense allocated funds.

The police system is organized at the district level. From the perspective of the local residents, police intervention is avoided assiduously, even for the most serious of crimes. Bhils regard the police presence as threatening and dangerous under any and all circumstances; the perpetuation of local systems for settling disputes (including those stemming from murder and other serious crimes) is regarded as preferable by far to involving the police.

The Forestry Department and its local officers and officials play a significant role in the life of village Bhils. All government policy concerning the use of nationalized forests and their resources is administered and executed through the local Forestry Department bureaucracy. This includes enforcing restrictions on access to forest lands under the direct jurisdiction of the Forestry Department as well as the enforcement of restrictions on access to minor forest produce. Many people throughout the rural areas of the district related stories about corruption in the administration of these policies; for example, those who can afford bribes to the forest guards are permitted access to forest lands, and engage in activities that include unauthorized squatting and tree-felling.

The Panchayati Raj system has provisions that require seats to be reserved for members of scheduled castes and tribes, as well as women. Most people with whom I discussed this provision in 1989-90 believed that this system, despite its structural access, was weighted against them. Because the Sarpanche has the authority to dispense funds directly, they said, the money intended for community projects inevitably ends up in the pocket of the Sarpanche and his cronies. Upper-caste members tend to exert undue influence over the panchayat, they say. Even when a panchayat has an SC or ST Sarpanche, some informants claim, he is usually hand-picked for his cooperation level and is quickly corrupted by what little power he is allowed.

This skepticism, expressed widely in 1990, subsided somewhat in 1995. During this five-year period several events have transpired to activate local participation in, and confidence in, the panchayat raj specifically and the electoral process generally. These issues will be discussed in greater detail in Chapter 9.

Water

When I asked villagers, men and women, what their biggest problem was, they would immediately answer, *pani*, "water." The lack of water for planting and harvesting is by far the greatest perceived obstacle. Most people believe that the rains have become much more scarce and unreliable in recent times. "Monsoon anxiety" is often expressed particularly in the pre-rain summer months, although stoically and with resignation.

Water supply in the study area is primarily through wells. Although there is a hand pump in Bagdunda and one in Morwa used only for household water, they are unreliable because they are continually breaking down. In the village of Bagdunda, wells are divided up among the families and by jati. In Solaria each family has access to a well that is either entirely owned by them or is shared in a corporate fashion. As many as eight families may have interests in one well; most families have interests in more than one well. The people in Solaria say that everyone has access to all wells for drinking water; exclusive rights and ownership of the wells and the water contained within it apply specifically to agricultural and irrigation use.

The collection of water for household use is generally the work of women and young girls but this division of labor is not always observed; it seems to have no ritual or social sanction attached, and men often carry water. The full sized water jugs that the women carry on their heads hold 25 liters and weigh about 50 pounds when full. A common sight throughout the area is of young children carrying smaller water jugs, sometimes more than one, on their heads, learning the skill of balancing these weights without spilling or dropping their burdens.

Water is used very sparingly in the household. It is used for cooking pulses, and in making the dough for *chapatti* or *muki ki roti*. Vegetables, when available, are cooked in oil. A small *lota* that holds about one pint is taken into the field or presented immediately upon returning from the field during morning ablutions; guests are also presented with a small container of water (a lota can be made of clay or sometimes metal, but usually is a rusted tin can) on arrival for drinking and washing. Bathing is done in the stream. Dish "washing" is either done sparingly with water or is accomplished by rubbing the tin *thalis* (plates) with dried chula ash and then removing the ash carefully by hand. Where possible, waste water is retained and used to give to animals.

Ecology, Household, and Gender

Deforestation in Bhil agricultural communities sets off a chain of ecological events that impacts dramatically on residents' quality of life. It is becoming increasingly apparent, however, that deforestation is not an "equal opportunity" disaster--its effects are felt far more profoundly by those segments of society who are already marginalized by low socio-economic status. And within these marginalized groups, gender and age are further significant factors for evaluating the impact of ecological degradation. (See for example, Shiva 1988, Fernandes and Menon 1987, and Fernandes, Menon and Viegas 1988).

The ecological consequences of the rampant destruction of the forests of the Aravalli hills in Rajasthan follow an all too familiar scenario: monsoon irregularities, intermittent drought, loss of human life and livestock, crop failures, and the out-migration of able-bodied men into urban or factory settings. In periods of lowered agricultural output, nonagricultural income-generating activities--particularly those of women--become increasingly significant But the competition produced by the intensified labor efforts of poor women in an area of relatively fixed outlets for their efforts results in still greater instability of income, and an expanded necessity for relying on traditional forms of caste-based interaction. The net effect of this process is to perpetuate the ties of the entire Bhil family to its upper-caste patron.

From the perspective of potential development, and the weakening of traditional caste-based ties, another significant aspect of this household-based dependency is that it discourages alliances between and among Bhil women that would potentially aid them in establishing better prices and conditions in their marketing efforts. What begins as a woman's poverty-driven effort to generate more household income during agricultural crisis results in a much more encompassing dynamic of social and economic dependency, perpetuating exploitive caste-based socio-economic relationships.

Drought and deforestation are obviously felt by all residents of the area, but the effects are particularly profound on Bhil agriculturalists. They are the first to feel the effects of monsoon irregularity; water shortages hit their wells first, and last the longest. The Adivasi plots tend to be the least productive of all land in the area. As noted, they are located on hills, carved out of the once-dense forests. More fertile low-lying farms, owned by Rajputs and Jains in the valleys, benefit from the runoff from the hills. These valley wells have more of an opportunity to recharge, protecting the more affluent farmers from the effects of monsoon irregularities.

Recent efforts to enclose and protect land from grazing and forestry have yielded some positive results; the local grasses, when there is adequate monsoon and protection, quickly regenerate. NGO-sponsored projects to plant tree saplings have been only marginally successful; during the drought period of the 1980s one organization's efforts yielded only a 20 percent survival rate for the saplings. Programs in later years have seen a 40 to 50 percent survival rate. The long-term outcome of these re-plantation programs, which include introduction of new plant species to the area, is still questionable, for it will take at least 20 years of care and protection to produce mature full-grown trees.

Deforestation particularly effects the day-to-day lives of Bhil women. The paucity of agricultural production has necessitated supplementing household income with other activities--specifically the collection of minor forest produce, firewood, and the care of animals. These are all women's work, as are weeding, harvesting or buying food, cooking it and replenishing supplies.

Women rely on minor forest produce as a source of cooking fuel, supplementing it with *gobar*, dried animal dung, when available. They collect dried twigs and other forest produce, often assisted by small children, and as the problem of deforestation has intensified, so has the burden on these already overtaxed women. What took their mothers one-half to one hour to collect now takes them six or seven hours a day.

Some family case studies illustrate how the burden on women's time and energy has increased as a direct result of deforestation and wood scarcity. For example, one household of two people--a woman in her forties and her teenage-daughter--consumes 40 kilograms wood per week and 30 kilograms gobar per week. The daughter collects 10 kilograms of wood at a time, and it takes her 6 hours to collect the 10 kilograms

Another household, consisting of six household members, uses 1 quintal a week of wood (100 kilograms) and 50 kilograms of gobar per week. A daughter collects 7 kilograms each trip, which takes her 8 hours.

A third household, with three family members, collects 1 quintal of wood per week. Two children (two girls aged 6 and 8) collect 7.5 kilograms in 8 hours, some of which is sold in Bagdunda at Rs.7 a headload. This involves 3 days' work for 2 children to collect the wood and one full additional day to walk to Bagdunda and back, about 12 kilometers away (they aren't permitted to carry wood on the bus).

Another household of 7 members uses 100 kilograms of firewood per week. One woman collects 10 kilograms in 8 hours. They buy the deficit--about 50 kilograms per week. This woman reported that the 8 hours she devotes to collecting the firewood are from 4 am to 12 noon.

The poorest households are the largest consumers of wood. They cannot afford to purchase an alternate source of fuel like kerosene, which is used to operate kerosene stoves. Limited numbers of animals also restricts their access to dung.

The majority of women I interviewed sell wood regularly to the same Rajput family that they have worked for over the years, and for whom their families had worked before them. Women reported to me in 1989 and 1990 that when they sell firewood to Rajput women locally in Bagdunda and surrounding villages they received payment of Rs.2-3 per headload.

For some Bhil women, the small payment they receive for wood also includes performing other services as well. On an average of three days per week, they go to Rajput homes early in the morning with a small headload of wood. They also carry a clay pot on their heads to collect chach as part of their payment. They work the entire day for the Rajput household, cleaning animal stalls and performing other menial tasks. At the end of the day they get the pot filled with chach, and 2 to 3 rupees for the wood. This process is repeated a few days each week. Other women reported that they would simply go to the Rajput house and sell their wood, receiving only the same small number of rupees in return.

I asked why they didn't charge more for the wood; they replied that there are always other women who would sell it for less. If they demanded a higher price they would just be told to go away. When I asked them about the possibility of organizing all the women in the village to get together and sell the wood at a higher price, their responses revealed details of other gender-based behavioral norms.

Women tend to interact only with their phala mates and women from their natal villages. It would be unseemly for a woman to travel to another phala to conduct business, or to try to organize women in several villages. Suspicion would fall on her intentions immediately. Fear of violence against women by men of both their own and of other caste groups places limits on their physical mobility. Social constraints, such as accusations of witchcraft, are commonly used against women who step outside of the norms of socially accepted behavior.

Other factors are also cited for the tendency of Bhil women to stay close to their homes. The heavy silver wrist and ankle ornaments Bhil women wear are part of their marital payments, as well as being the family assets. Any cash accumulated by Bhil families immediately gets converted into silver jewelry, much of which is worn at all times by women as ankle ornaments are usually sealed closed permanently. These ornaments, particularly older ones, have become increasingly valuable over the years, and are found for sale in the shops that cater to foreign tourists in Udaipur. Many of the women I interviewed reported having heard of gruesome attacks on Bhil women in which their jewelry was ripped from their bodies--even of the amputation of feet to forcibly remove the anklets.

These are all potent constraints against organizing and confronting economic and social exploitation. And if the women of one phala managed to organize and set prices among themselves, they said, there would be no way to compel women in other phalas to do the same. So, the women explained, it is better to keep things the way they are...and maintain long-term relations with the nearby Rajput women with whom they can safely interact.

Why Are We Poor?

For many villagers I met, the flexibility of migration and access to unlimited lands is part of the general image of the "good old days." Some now account much of their contemporary poverty to their inability to acquire more land from which they can support their expanding families. In one meeting organized by workers of UVM, contemporary poverty was attributed in part to lack of access to land and in part to illiteracy and lack of access to educational resources. One man summed up his situation this way:

> My grandfather was the only son of his parents. He had enough land in Morwa and he had enough to eat, as he was only one family. But then my father and his brothers came. So the same land is supporting four families which was earlier enough for one. Is not so for four families and thus we have become poorer. And now those three families have turned into ten families. The land has not increased. It is the same. The family has increased ten times and the land has been distributed equally among the ten of us. So the land which supported one family is now supporting ten. This way we have become poor. Secondly our parents didn't think what will happen to our children. They never gave a thought to it. Because of increase in population, poverty has increased. If our father had educated us, then one would have joined the panchayat, the other the forest department or the police or become teacher etc. but they never thought of it. If they had educated us this poverty wouldn't have come.

During another meeting in a Bhil village located in an interior area not yet penetrated very deeply by NGO activity, one of the speakers made the following statement:

> Without salt food has no taste. In the same way we are nothing without education. This helps in developing people's understanding. For this formal education is not necessary. When twenty or twenty-five men sit together they can find out a way to understand why poverty has spread and how we can overcome it. But we don't educate our daughters and sisters. We have this feeling that they were born to work and all these things [like education] are for boys. We should consider both boys and girls as equal.

These themes were reiterated over and over again in my conversations with people who generally view lack of education as a primary impediment to their own progress, and place literacy and among their first priorities when they discuss their own personal and community-based development agendas.

In an effort to address these self-identified priorities, Bhatia set up a nonformal educational program in several villages around Solaria. The teachers, recruited locally from among the few Bhil men with rudimentary literacy skills, were paid a relatively small salary of Rs. 200 rupees/month. In a discussion among some of the teachers and other village members on the subject of "why should we educate our children?" the following responses were elicited: "So that we can develop an understanding in children. So that the children will not be afraid to speak and then will be able to talk boldly with others;" and "To get a job. And after education we can earn more money."

As of mid-1990 six nonformal education programs were in operation. The meeting rooms had all been constructed with supplies donated by Bhatia and labor donated by the villagers. In villages with no schoolroom, teachers and students meet on the verandah of the temple or some other central meeting place. The schools met for one and one half to two hours each evening, six days a week, a schedule determined by the necessity for the children to work in the fields and tend to animals during daylight hours. As noted previously, there is great fear of allowing girls, particularly unescorted, to walk to the schools, so the attendance in these nonformal schools is, as in the government schools, mostly male. In one location the school met during the day to accommodate this problem.

I observed several nonformal educational programs during fieldwork, whose students included adult women and children of just about every age group. The pedagogical process was generally the same in all settings. The students were memorizing multiplication tables by rote, but didn't seem to be learning anything about the concept of multiplication. Younger children were barely able to keep their eyes open as they struggled to listen and squinted to see the chalk markings on their dirty slates as the daylight waned. All these schools were eventually closed down because of lack of local participation and regular attendance by the children.

Despite the lack of local participation in this particular nonformal educational program, verbal and literacy skills are highly respected in Bhil communities. Leadership is closely associated with the ability to speak well, aggressively and forcefully (McCurdy 1964: 412). As detailed in Chapter 9, these skills are often the road to upward mobility, both through NGO employment and political party participation.

I did not observe any women whose verbal skills were honed to the same degree as men's. At some NGO meetings in Bagdunda one older woman from a near-by village spoke comfortably in a mixed sex audience, and for long periods of time, with grace and ease; but she had not asked for, nor has she been offered, a leadership or organizing position. The one woman in Bagdunda who sought a leadership/organizing position did not have the public speaking skills required.

Bhil women are so unaccustomed under any circumstances to speak out in public that they are constrained from quickly stepping into such a role. Most Bhil men can converse comfortably in Hindi, while women generally speak only local dialects; those who wish to converse with women must do so in Mewari.

Chapter Summary

The patterns of social and ritual interaction within and between caste groups are constantly shifting. To label any one set of dynamics as "traditional" with its implied opposite of "modern" is to establish a false dichotomy; a more accurate description of these patterns would be a field in constant flux. The structural aspects of the relationships--hierarchy, dependency, and obligation--are relatively fixed, but actual behavioral practices, and their motivations, are constantly being renegotiated and redefined, as are the social, developmental, environmental, and political forces that come to bear on life histories in this local landscape.

NGO programs, policies, and activities are one of those forces and will be detailed in subsequent chapters, particularly in the context of these ecological, social, and political issues that dominate contemporary Bhil life. One continuous theme of these programs, and of reform deriving from within the Bhil community, is the expense of fulfilling a nearly endless cycle of ritual obligations to one's family members, particularly to one's affines.

These expenses are particularly burdensome around the time of marriage; families routinely go into debt to meet the expenses of premarriage payments, rituals, and ceremonies. But these expenses, and the public, visible nature of these village-wide rituals, are also a village-wide forum in which Bhils craft their social identity.

Public display of the expenditures of social rituals is a matter of pride not only within the Bhil community but also in the image of Bhils projected to other groups. This was evident from the comment of one Solaria resident, a man in his fifties, when describing plans for the up-coming wedding of his nephew. He described how his brother's family was going to the significant cash expense of renting an audio system and speakers so that recorded cassette music could be played at the wedding, a practice Solaria residents have observed at the weddings of other caste groups but up until this time had not themselves done. One of the reasons for going to this expense, he said, was so that "the Rajputs would see that we can do this, too."

Chapter 7

Comparing Programs and Strategies

This chapter focuses on contrasting organizational strategies, which, by their differences and similarities, illuminate some of the characteristics of the local NGO landscape. "Big" development is contrasted with "small" development here, by looking in detail at local programs and strategies. A multilateral project with a five-year life span and a multimillion dollar budget is described, along with the local programs of smaller NGOs, both from the perspective of Bagdunda and Solaria residents' relationships to these programs.

Solaria is fairly typical of Bhil communities in Udaipur district; by any standards it would be characterized as "underdeveloped," considering its relatively low household income as well as access to basic resources and services. But the underdevelopment of Solaria's resource base and infrastructure does not by any means equate with isolation from the multiple forces of development in the area, particularly NGO activity. Solaria residents are either active participants in, or are indirectly influenced by, a wide variety of programs and projects that have positively affected their quality of life. These programs range from a one-man free lance development worker to active participation in the capital intensive community health project. Solaria's residents share a high level of awareness of the programs and projects of all the organizations in the area, including Sewa Mandir, Astha, and now Alert, which is currently operating in a cluster of villages near Solaria, started in the early 1990s by a former employee of Ubeshwar Vikas Mandal.

The phala of Solaria is within three hours' walk to Bagdunda and the field offices of Ubeshwar Vikas Mandal (UVM) and Sewa Mandir; over the years UVM has made efforts at involving residents of Morwa and Solaria in its activities. Solaria Bhils have marital ties and social interaction with Bagdunda residents and surrounding phalas. Men therefore travel frequently to the UVM centers of activity (women less frequently), and have knowledge of all the NGO activities in the area through regular participation in meetings and gatherings.

The primary direct development influence in this phala is Mr. B. N. Bhatia, the free-lance social worker described previously who has "adopted" this and several other nearby villages. He believes--and the projects he undertakes in Solaria reflect this strategy--that household income generation is the primary strategy for local development. To this end he has arranged for the funding of local cooperatives through the microgrant program of Trickle Up. He has also co-funded projects through loans to the villagers of Solaria for capital expenditure projects, particularly well deepening. The goal of these projects is to enable villagers to increase agricultural productivity, and plant commodity crops like ginger. He has also supervised and helped finance the training of a few young men as tailors, and arranged for the purchase of sewing machines and fabric so they could "set up shop." Other projects he has facilitated in this village include arranging financing through Trickle Up for a sugar cane crusher, a mechanical device that produces sugar cane juice, which is cooked down into *gur* (also known as *jaggery*), a highly marketable sweetener used throughout the area. As noted in the previous chapter, the nonformal education centers instituted in this area have not been successful, and have all been disbanded.

The UVM strategy (described in greater detail below) is to facilitate the organization of larger units of villages into self-sustaining and self-generating action groups. UVM's primary goal is to motivate the residents to undertake and support environmental protection of the area. A relatively small organization with 30 to 40 full-time employees, it stresses mobilization of the community to meet shared goals--particularly the goal of environmental protection. As part of this vision, UVM is opposed to making cash grants or loans for capital improvements to individuals or households. In the 1990s, their policy and strategy has evolved to include facilitation of agricultural development and irrigation programs, and helping their membership to gain access to state funds to increase the productivity of privately owned lands.

In his initial stages of operation in the late 1980s, Bhatia was affiliated with UVM. When conflict arose over organizational strategy and approach he terminated their official connections, a move of which all villagers are aware. The break has also created a somewhat tenuous relationship between the villagers and the UVM workers in the area, which spilled over into open conflict during the 1989-90 elections. I did not personally observe the following incident, but it was reported to me by several different people on various occasions that a Bhil UVM worker, known to be a Congress party organizer, came to Solaria to campaign for the local Congress party candidate. The phala spokesman in Solaria, a BJP supporter and local agent, is reported to have become very abusive of the UVM worker, and a fistfight ensued.

This kind of open conflict between two Bhil men in view of other members of the community was very unusual, and it was shocking to those who observed it. The rift was somewhat healed a few weeks later when the two men met and spoke cordially to each other at a two-day meeting that was being sponsored by UVM. This particular rift seemed to blow over, but the multiple forms of factionalization, and its implications for other forms of alliances, remains a part of the landscape.

This event also illustrated the territorial "franchise" structure of village NGO activity in the 1980s, a characteristic that is increasingly less prevalent. Based on the fact that the development workers and organizations made, and continue to make, a significant commitment in terms of time, effort, and resources to a particular area or village, they assumed that an implicit understanding of "exclusivity" would be observed by all sides in return: the program participants seemed to make an implicit commitment to their NGO sponsor that by availing themselves of the benefits of a particular organization they would in turn extend exclusive allegiance and support to that NGO or individual. While NGO affiliation was not the exclusive cause of conflict, it did create an alliance that may be evoked from time to time under other circumstances, like electioneering or other factional events. NGO affiliation therefore becomes one aspect of alliance formation in a complex arena of alliances based on multiple identity issues.

Locally Based Development: Ubeshwar Vikas Mandal

In 1995 UVM completed ten years of activities as an organization engaged primarily in facilitating ecological recovery amongst the Bhil communities of Girwa and Gogunda tehsils. According to the organization's documents, its first members were a dozen young Bhil men of Dhar village who were motivated by the growing ecological crisis of their area to form a local voluntary association. The organization is named for Ubeshwar Mahadev Mandir, or temple, in Dhar. (Ubeshwar Mahadev is the name of the deity; *vikas* translates approximately into "development" and *mandal* means "circle" or "ring," but has also has the connotation locally of group or organization.) This temple is located at the source of a once-perennial stream, it stands as a dramatic reminder of and symbol for the devastating degradation of natural resources in the Aravallis. Since its inception UVM has been concerned primarily with educating people about the environmental situation, and particularly the consequences of unabated deforestation. To this end UVM has instituted eco-reforestation on 2,500 hectares of land in 50 communities.

UVM has established funding relationships with Intercooperation-Switzerland and Danchurchaid, the latter facilitated through CASA (Church Auxiliary for Social Action), an Indian private funding body. Additional funding support has been generated from Sri Dorabji Tata Trust, the National Wasteland Development Board (NWDB), and Campaign for People's Action and Rural Technology (CAPART) (the latter two are Indian government funding organizations). UVM's work has been evaluated by research teams from NWDB and CAPART , and the Ford Foundation, and was recommended for India's prestigious Indira Priyadarshi Vrikshmitra (Friends of Trees) Award for 1991.

Beginning in 1993 UVM undertook an ongoing research program in and around Bagdunda to document people's knowledge of land and water management, as well as the local socio-cultural institutions through which this management is facilitated. This research program is an effort to document the technologies and strategies of local resource management that are often being replaced with technologies developed and introduced from "outside" the community, using more complex technologies and chemical inputs. The first of these projects documented traditional water and irrigation systems.

UVM's local organization strategy is to form community groups with elected leadership who have the responsibility to coordinate with the UVM staff and other agencies, convene village meetings, plan and execute development activities and ensure accountable use of support and resources for people's initiatives. Approximately 30 such community groups now exist; 10 around the village of Dhar and 20 around Bagdunda. These village community groups meet at least once every month. This Gram Sabha (village assembly) is the local forum of decision making; UVM's staff members are usually present in these meetings as facilitators.

Local staff members have also assumed more complex roles, linking their communities to UVM and other local institutions to take advantage of opportunities for obtaining resources and wage labor. The organization regularly holds structured learning and training events, as well as follow-up meetings and camps, and monthly meetings of all lead workers in Dhar and Bagdunda. Village-level loan funds, managed by the membership, are encouraged by the organization and have been instituted in several communities: each family contributes Rs. 5 to 10 each month, which is deposited in the local bank.

Since its inception, UVM's activities have focused on maintaining, creating, and upgrading long-term natural assets with a high emphasis on making irrigation better available to rain-fed farms. Specific programs include protection and regeneration of common pasture lands; construction of protective walls and checkdams; and sapling plantations.

In the early 1990s UVM began to research and expedite programs to maximize water availability for irrigation. A lift irrigation project was commissioned and funded by the state's District Rural Development Agency in Khera, the Bhil phala adjacent to Bagdunda. This project, recently completed, delivers water to previously nonirrigated private fields from sources in adjacent hills, through a system of electrified pumps and pipes.

These projects are significant for a number of reasons. They represent one role of the NGO as being a linkage to governmental services, guiding local villagers through the process of research and application preparation for state funding. They also acknowledge the necessity for developing individual household resources and income bases, as well as community based initiatives.

When questions of financial mismanagement and individual accountability arise, they are confronted both locally and in organization-wide meetings. Some individuals in local communities have been forced out of the organization, resulting in further community fragmentation and factionalization. Construction of several small dams was suspended in 1991-92 when the village-level leadership did not fulfill the organization's financial accountability standards. Other dam projects failed because of technical or design limitations, or unanticipated escalation of construction costs. And even the most sophisticated, well-organized projects, particularly in the area of planting and introducing new plant species into the ecosystem, can be short-circuited by the unpredictable monsoons.

Other initiatives are constrained by personnel limitations, particularly evident in the area of gender-based programs. Women have been involved in all UVM-supported development initiatives since its inception, but despite its efforts, the organization has not been able to recruit and maintain skilled, professional full-time female social workers who would commit to living in the villages--a necessary factor in generating and sustaining a consistent program that would have the capacity to organize local women and sustain their participation. UVM's experience is that local male workers are unable to sustain the involvement of women in the community meetings. (See Chapter 8 for a detailed discussion of the gender aspect of local development programs.)

An experimental project to help women supplement their income by learning to stitch and embroider was begun in April 1992; nine women were trained to stitch cushion covers, purses, and other articles that would be sold at local retail outlets marketing "Tribal" artifacts. The women learned the basic techniques quickly, but the articles they produced lacked the quality and consistency required to be commercially viable in this highly competitive market.

Another priority in the UVM strategy is local education; the schools in its operating area are understaffed and teaching quality is poor. Even where schools exist, children often do not attend because of household and agricultural needs; in some villages girls do not attend at all. The organization has therefore developed two kinds of educational initiatives. Where schools exist but are not functioning properly, the organization supports local efforts by villagers to demand corrective measures to secure teachers and to ensure their regular attendance. Encouragement of attendance by children on occasion involves public disclosure in group meetings when a male worker, for example, is not sending his own daughters to school. Nonformal education centers established in the early 1990s by several communities were all eventually disbanded because of lack of attendance, an experience that parallels that of Bhatia's nonformal education centers around Morwa-Solaria.

UVM has encouraged traditional cultural activity since its inception, including sponsorship of a local team of singers, dancers and musicians in Bagdunda region. The team uses the local styles and idioms in music and dance to create short skits and plays, and is extremely popular in the region. UVM annually hosts a performance of Gavri, a dance-drama performance cycle unique to the Bhils of Udaipur district.

UVM is particularly interested in revitalizing the traditional institution of group work and shared responsibility for village members, known locally as *adsi padsi*, or give- and-take (Saint 1989). Kin-based cooperative projects are commonplace, such as brothers joining together to plow their respective fields or help build a house. The adsi padsi tradition of cooperation extends beyond kin-based obligations. McCurdy, for example, describes in detail tile-making activities undertaken during the months of May and June by both men and women, and the building of a schoolroom, with the labor donated by the villagers and the cost of materials met by the government. (1965: 141-142)

This tradition is often alluded to by Bhil villagers when they speak of the "good old days." Many described how the entire community would gather and help one member build a house or plow his field. Although community-based labor projects are still undertaken, women particularly seem to think that the spirit of adsi padsi is a thing of the past. Again and again, particularly in NGO-led group discussions, they would say that people have become selfish, and look out only for themselves.

I observed several adsi padsi building projects, road clearing and other types of water-control construction, all undertaken and completed within a few weeks. The villagers showed these construction projects with an enormous amount of pride in their accomplishment--deservedly, as one stretch of wall I saw, about 1 kilometer long and 3 feet wide, was formed of carefully placed stones that made a level, table-straight edge, and had been constructed in just the few weeks prior to the onset of monsoon.

The structure of adsi padsi in progress showed a marked gender bias. On walking from one village to the next, several times I passed wall-building projects in villages that were taking place spontaneously, that is, not under the direction or supervision of an outside NGO worker or staff member. As I had been present at many UVM meetings at which adsi padsi was discussed, and which these local residents attended, I was greeted enthusiastically by male villagers as I passed by, with shouts of greeting and "adsi padsi"--a reference to the work they were doing. I noticed invariably that the work was being supervised by men, and the actual carrying of stones from other areas to the wall was being done by women. Once the stones reached the wall-building area, they were either placed on the wall by men, or the women were instructed by men as to where to place them. This exclusively female transport of stones by hand was a pattern I saw repeated in many other types of construction projects in the area.

The activities, successes and failures, of UVM are well documented and discussed within the organization, candidly and at length. The group's history and strategy is somewhat typical of the small organizations in the region. UVM is unique, for an organization of its size, in one significant respect; UVM's founder, Kishore Saint, has a global reputation for commitment to environmentally related social service and development. Within the NGO community, UVM shares with Sewa Mandir and Astha a supporting and networking role to many other smaller organizations, whose organizers are not fluent in English and do not have the same level of skills or connections to funding and academic institutions around the world. This networking role links UVM with other NGOs in Udaipur and throughout India.

Large-Scale Strategy: SWACH

A water, health, and sanitation project administered by UNICEF in conjunction with the government of Rajasthan provides a vivid contrast to the programs (and budgets) of UVM and other locally organized NGOs. The project's organizational infrastructure, focused goals, and nearly unlimited funds made it a unique aspect of the local NGO landscape. It was also unique in that the program was designed to be completed within a specific time period, and then phased out by 1995, consistent with "exit strategy" guidelines that govern most large-scale development programs.

The reach of the program was impressive; even in most interior Bhil phalas people were familiar with it, particularly with those aspects of the program that relate to the treatment of guineaworm, an endemic disease. The program is still widely recalled as SWACH (Sanitation, Water, and Community Health), whose acronym means "clean" or "pure" in Hindi. An extensive community health program in several districts of southern Rajasthan, it was funded in part by the Swedish

International Development Agency (SIDA) and co-funded by the state government. Its budget for 1986-1990 was US$7 million; the project "was designed as a conscious attempt to address a number of related problems within the fields of Safe Water Supply, Sanitation and Public Health" (UNICEF nd: 6). The prevalence of guineaworm disease, known locally as *naru*, was first and foremost among the identified problems.

Guineaworm is a disease associated with rural stepwell use. A painful and debilitating disease, it erodes the health of its victims in a number of ways. The presence of the worm itself is painful and destructive to muscle and connective tissue. If not surgically removed, the worm eventually works it way to the surface of the skin, and this eruption creates an open wound that, without medical treatment, becomes infected and ulcerated. Many village-level workers recruited for the program wept during training sessions as they described the slow, agonizing, and often fatal progression of the disease in their family members.

Guineaworm is found in arid regions of Africa, the Middle East, South America, and India, although the south-central region of Rajasthan is described by a local expert as the most affected region on earth (Joshi 1991: 33). The disease is caused by the worm *Dracumculus medinensis L.*, which lives in open tanks, ponds, and in stepwells. Its larvae are ingested by cyclops crustaceans that also live in the well water; they are then ingested by humans who drink the infected water. When the cyclops is digested in the stomach, larvae are released, penetrate the intestinal wall, and mature in connective tissue. The young worm migrates to the victim's extremities, where the life cycle of the disease culminates in the formation of a long adult worm, sometimes as long as two or three feet, which grows in intramuscular and connective tissue below the surface of the arms or legs. During summer months the worm edges closer to the surface of the skin and erupts, causing an open wound accompanied by intense pain, irritation, and itching. Bathing the infected parts in water provides minimal relief, and in many areas the stepwell is the only available water source. In this eruption phase of the disease, worm larvae are expelled into the well water from the open wound of disease sufferers, and the disease cycle begins again when the well water is ingested by others.

No drug can kill the worm inside the infected patient. The chemical Temephos can be applied to infected well water to kill the water-borne larvae; effective use of Temephos requires a very high concentration applied repeatedly over several months. According to informants who worked in the SWACH program, this procedure was rarely carried out to precise specifications because of inefficiencies in the program's technical and training infrastructure.

Once the worm begins to grow, the only way to cure an infected person and prevent the spread of the disease is to extract the worm just before it erupts. A local doctor, working on the SWACH team, perfected a process by which the worm is extracted physically--a dangerous and difficult process analogous to removing, through a small incision in the skin, an unbroken strand of cooked spaghetti embedded in muscle tissue. If the worm ruptures during this delicate process it releases a fatal flood of toxins and larvae into the body.

As disease transmission and control is so closely related to stepwell water use, the SWACH program was designed as both an engineering and educational program. The engineering phase involved removing of steps from the interior of stepwells and resurfacing the inside of wells, as well as installing a pulley and pail system for retrieving water. This reconstruction was designed to eliminate the possibility of guineaworm sufferers bathing their feet in the well and releasing larvae during the eruption stage. The engineering and construction budget also included the funds for the installation of hand-pumps throughout the project area, to supplement the use of open wells as a water source. In another phase of the project, local women were trained to maintain and repair these hand pumps.

An extensive and integrated educational program accompanied SWACH's engineering and training efforts. This aspect of the program, which involved the recruitment and training of hundreds of local women, was designed to communicate information about the life cycle of the disease as well as more general water and sanitation techniques throughout villages and phalas in the area.

The program introduced the use of double-layered straining cloths, one side green, the other white, which, if regularly used when transferring water from the well or hand pump into household-use vessels, would supposedly strain off the cyclops carrying the larvae, thus preventing ingestion. This procedure is of dubious value however. "There is no convincing data to show that [cloth straining] is really an effective method. There are doubts about the size of the mesh, and that people will remember the message to use only one side of the cloth" (UNICEF n.d.: 84). Nevertheless, the use of the straining cloth was a pivotal aspect of the village-level training program. It was unclear to local coordinators and trainers why it remained so important in the program's training aspect when its medical value was dubious; one reason for its continued emphasis was rationalized as being a reminder to people, particularly to women, to take constant care with their treatment of water, and be aware that the water contained harmful things. The reality of the situation remains, however: these cloths are ineffective in addressing these problems, a fact that was never communicated to village women.

The primary strategy for the educational/training aspect of the program was the recruitment of village contact teams, mostly women, who were trained as educators and village-level information sources, to conduct household-by-household surveys of those ill with guineaworm, and train household members in the use of straining cloths and other water sanitation techniques. In addition to the ongoing village-level educational activities, periodic meetings were held with coordinators and higher-level organizational staff, to reinforce the local-level animators' training and communication efforts.

In the program's initial stages, local NGOs were integrated into its structure; although in practice the actualization of this participation was limited. NGOs eventually withdrew because of conflicts between local NGO strategies and SWACH goals, and their participation was eventually phased out of the project design. In 1992 the UNICEF medical and organizational consultants were shifted from a project office in Udaipur to Jaipur according to plan, and the was taken over entirely by the government of Rajasthan in 1995 and phased into the state government's health program. Its local activities have disappeared from the scene, although villagers widely attribute the program with having successfully eliminated guineaworm disease.

Contrast and Dispute Over Strategy

I attended many SWACH meetings and training sessions throughout the district; one particular meeting that stands out in my memory was held near Bagdunda in 1990. I attended along with two women who were then full-time employees and women's organizers for Ubeshwar Vikas Mandal. As it was taking place in a community in which I knew virtually all the participants, it brought into sharp focus many of the conflicts and contradictions inherent in the structure of the project. This meeting also provided a revealing contrast in style, format, and agenda to UVM's gender-based programs and strategy (detailed in the next chapter).

The SWACH meeting was one of several that were held in Khera, the Bhil phala about 1 kilometer from Bagdunda. As is customary for group meetings in such a setting, the group gathered under a large tree outside the temple. When Vina and Reka (pseudonyms; both used only their first names as identification and were most often referred to as Behenji, a polite form of "sister."), UVM's women organizers, and I arrived, about twenty women from Khera, Bagdunda and other nearby villages had already gathered. I recognized the woman leading the SWACH meeting--a ubiquitous and very talented organizer, speaker, and trainer from the headquarters staff of the project in Udaipur. She was assisted by two women, also SWACH employees from Bagdunda. They were all dressed in saris and wore watches and other types of gold jewelry that distinguished them from the Bhil women. I learned later that one of the women was the daughter of the Sarpanche and the other the daughter of a well-known moneylender.

The SWACH organizer led the assembled women in an enthusiastic discussion of, and songfest about, health issues. At one point during the presentation some of the village women became restless and one started to get up to leave. The meeting organizer stopped her, and asked her pointedly if she were leaving because of a dispute she apparently had with the Sarpanche's daughter. This was very embarrassing to the woman from Khera, but she did as she was told, sat down and stayed for the entire meeting, as did all the other women from Khera.

Only after about an hour and a half did it become apparent that this meeting had another agenda, besides local education, which explained why the women had been forced to remain. A large delegation suddenly arrived in one of SWACH's air-conditioned vans. Five people emerged--three Indian women dressed in saris, an Indian man dressed in a Western suit, and one European man who was identified as an important visitor from overseas. He spoke briefly through an interpreter and said, "I am only an ignorant man; like your husbands, I am ignorant. You have to show me how to do things." The women laughed as he mimed the awkward and incorrect use of the straining cloths that had been distributed to the meeting participants. He then asked if any of the women had any questions for him.

To my surprise, the same Bhil woman from Khera who had attempted to leave the meeting raised her hand and asked him about conditions in his country. I found it very difficult to believe that any woman in Khera would, in such a setting, raise her hand and ask about conditions in a foreign country; Bhil women rarely if ever speak in front of males within their community, let alone an outside male, and Vina, Reka and I were sure that this question was "planted" by the meeting organizers, as part of the "show" for the visiting dignitaries.

Whatever its origin, the question provided the European man (who I subsequently found out was a top official of SIDA) with the opportunity to recount a story about his grandmother, a rural woman who taught herself how to read by marking letters with charcoal on a tree stump. He concluded his presentation with an acknowledgment of the work of the NGOs active in the village. After about half an hour the visiting delegation got back into their van and left.

The meeting continued for another two hours, with more lectures and more songs about local health conditions that had been composed by the SWACH team based on variations of local women's folk songs. The meeting concluded with the distribution of a few biscuits and bananas to the assembled women.

At the conclusion of the meeting, a heated discussion developed between the two UVM workers and the organizer of the meeting from SWACH. Vina and Reka were very angry and asserted that the women from Khera had been used and manipulated during the course of the meeting. They criticized the distribution of SWACH supplies to the women as counter-productive, observing that if the women had gone to the trouble of collecting and preparing these supplies themselves, from their own meager resources, it would engender a much stronger commitment to their use and adoption than if they were given out free of charge. They also strongly objected to the lack of acknowledgment during the meeting of what the Khera women had accomplished. They expressed resentment over the meeting organizers' failure to encourage the participation of the village women, who during the entire presentation were expected to take in information but supply no information or input on their own.

This dispute between representatives of two different types of organizations encapsulated a conflict inherent in the rural development process: two approaches, two strategies, two separate philosophies, very much at odds with each other, despite the deep commitment to what they are trying to accomplish on the part of all concerned.

The UVM social workers believe that if development agencies are to make change that is significant to the community, then program organizers must make a long-term commitment to that community-- spending time living within it and finding out how community members think, feel, and respond. This information will then serve as the basis for programs and strategies that emanate from, and are based on, local resources, strengths and priorities.

These two social workers have met with women in adjoining villages and hamlets in small groups and in private discussions; very slowly the women have become accustomed to them, have learned to trust them, and have begun to speak candidly and openly, a process that had just begun and was far from completed. The only tangible outcome of this time- and labor-intensive process thus far was a few women's self help committees whose members had begun to deposit money as a group in the local bank.

This approach contrasts with the SWACH program, which has the financial and personnel resources required to blanket an area with information by speaking to as many different women as possible. Local trainers and organizers attempted to revisit contacted villages every two months. They trained local women as volunteer animators to visit local households and communicate to their neighbors the details of the health maintenance message. The program organizers did not establish a relationship with the women in the village; this was the role envisioned for the volunteer village workers. SWACH's overall strategy was designed by medical doctors and development/aid administrators with little or no local input. The medical protocols and administrative structures were intended to be used and applied in multiple countries around the world, and designed from the perspective that they could be rapidly duplicated for use in other geographical settings.

The SWACH strategies approached eradicating disease as a biological and medical problem rather than a socio-cultural one. The training and communications systems were designed to alter behavioral practices, not take in information from the communities. The project designers did not take into account, for example, the caste-based dynamics of well ownership and access. A study was eventually commissioned and executed by SWACH to assess local perceptions and social structures relating to water use and well ownership, but this information was compiled and completed five years after the program was instituted in Rajasthan (Deegan 1990).

The project designers and implementers have a highly specific goal: eliminate guineaworm disease, alleviate suffering, and avoid unnecessary deaths. This can be accomplished, they believe, by dispensing information on the nature of the disease quickly and effectively to as many people as is possible in as short a time period as possible.

In 1995, when I returned to the area, I asked about guineaworm and SWACH. The program is part of local memory, recollected selectively and symbolically. The overall consensus among villagers in Bagdunda and Solaria is that the disease has been eradicated. Follow-up epidemiological studies will be needed to confirm this; from the inception of the program, SWACH officials acknowledged to me problems relating to the accurate reporting of disease incidence and cure rates, particularly in the more physically remote and inaccessible areas of the district. The same problems remain for verifying claims of eradication, particularly for the long term.

In 1995 I saw no straining cloths in use. But even more significantly, I revisited some well sites that had been reconstructed by SWACH, and which had had their steps removed. I was confused to see steps in two of these wells that I knew had been reconstructed. They still bore the SWACH name and the date of the reconstruction embedded into the well wall and their owners reported to me with pride that the SWACH officials had come to their wells and to their homes several years ago, to examine the newly stepless wells. "Why," I asked, "are there now steps leading down into the well?" The well owners explained that it was simply more convenient to use the steps for access, and that they had put the steps back in.

The SWACH program illustrates many of the strengths as well as the weaknesses of "big" development projects. As a focused attack on one medically defined local problem--guineaworm disease--it seems to have been successful. But from its inception the program neglected the social and cultural contexts of the disease, and it is thus an example of a lost educational opportunity that had the potential of having significant long-term quality-of-life effects, an observation made in follow-up evaluation of the project SIDA 1994).

While the structure of the program was designed to integrate women into every level of the educational process, and a concerted effort was made to hire local women animators at the village level to be trained as hand pump repair mechanics as well as educational advisors, the wages that they were paid were considerably lower than those of men doing the equivalent work. The majority of the women who actually participated in village level SWACH activities were recruited as volunteer workers, thus perpetuating many of the local gender biases and inequities (Ibid: v).

Despite its continuous rhetoric of "people's participation" and local "grassroots" involvement, the program was extremely hierarchical and centrally organized. The project was designed and structured at UNICEF headquarters in New York and New Delhi and based on a protocol first developed by UNICEF for Western Africa; it was only minimally modified to accord with the complexities of the social structure of water use in Rajasthan.

Chapter Summary

Comparing the strategies and content of local programs as they are delivered to villagers gives evidence of some of the disjunctures between rhetoric and reality on a local level that are inherent in the global development undertaking. These discussed cases are not unique, nor are they cited because they especially represent a problem not present in other organizations. Quite the contrary: they are surveyed here because of the near-universality of the issues and conflicts they represent.

No matter what the size of the organization, or the budget of the program, the rhetoric of "grassroots" development and people's participation is inevitably executed within a structural hierarchy. Goals and strategies are established at "headquarters" and then delivered to rural villagers. Priorities are defined outside the village; villagers then have the option of accepting or rejecting that strategy, an option that is often limited by their personal financial constraints. From the perspective of local villagers, an imperfect NGO option is better than no NGO option at all.

These two cases also illustrate the constant and ongoing tension between short-term focused problem solving and the slower and far more complicated issues of enduring long-term social and economic change. Both "big" and "small" organizations explicitly share the same goals: improving the quality of life and resource base for individuals and communities. But developing and implementing strategies that are appropriate, effective, enduring, and integrated is far more elusive.

Chapter 8

Women's Programs, Women's Voices

I go to the hills and get fire wood. I get the fire wood.
   Who will listen, poor women?
I sell the wood and bring home one kilo of grain.
   Who will listen?
I get up early in the morning and grind grains.
My fingers all have wounds.
   Who should I tell, helpless women?
I go to the hills and bring grass.
   Who should I tell, oh poor women.
Children die of hunger but husbands just sit and drinks.
   Who will listen, oh my poor women?
The husband beats us after drinking.
   Who will I tell?
They sell the utensils of the house and bring more liquor to drink.
   Who will listen?
      --Verse of a song sung by Bhil women of Bagdunda in 1990

There is an enormous body of literature on the systemic and structural marginalization of women within the development process, and on the necessity for gender-specific strategy to address structural and analytic impediments. Books, professional journal articles, and popular journalism continuously address the economic and social inequities that poor women globally, and Indian women particularly, confront on a daily basis; women in India who are both low caste and lower class are truly the "poorest of the poor" (see Sen and Grown 1987, Gender and Poverty in India 1991). In Rajasthan, rural women bear all the economic burdens of poverty exacerbated by social conservatism (Raghuvanshi 1983); Bhil women in rural communities, as has been previously noted, are victims of multiple forms of economic and social exploitation (see, for example, Singh, Vyas and Mann 1985).

According to the stories village women relate themselves, domestic abuse, social oppression and low household status, throughout an endless day of domestic and financial responsibilities, are just some of the factors that threaten their well-being on a day-to-day basis. Gender-specific programs are a feature of virtually all the NGOs of Udaipur; women's programs are integral to the operational strategy of these organizations. Ideally, the programs provide rural women with a forum for discussing problems to which they immediately can relate; a single-gender forum is the only one in which Bhil women will discuss such problems openly, and then only after a long period of encouragement and confidence building.

Bhil women rarely go out in public, even when in a group composed of only women; men therefore literally speak for the community. In mixed-group meetings, women's voices are heard only in song, such as the one quoted above, and then only after the men disperse or the participants regroup in gender-specific meeting areas. These songs therefore serve as powerful representations of their gender-specific perspectives.

While the necessity for a female forum and strategy is acknowledged and integrated into the development perspective of the NGOs, in practice the sexual segregation of these programs and the structural divisions within organizations reinforce gender hierarchy. In addition, gender-based programs reflect some differentials in the organizational and mobility potential of male and female workers, a topic discussed below.

As noted, extensive programs in place are aimed at women in the areas of health, community sanitation, literacy, and other forms of education in Udaipur. A steady stream of development messages are directed at them, as are a large variety of projects and programs. In the process of observing NGO meetings, gatherings, and discussions at every level of the organizations, I found points of conflict emerging between these various organizations, as well as within them, over strategy and appropriate long-term approaches to identifying and addressing women's problems.

The literature on women, gender, and development supports the conclusion that Bhil women of this area are caught in two binds that constrain the prospects of changing their lives: poverty and low social status, which affect both men and women, and the social oppression specific to their gender that intensifies the social manifestations of these conditions. There is, however, an alternative perspective, emphatically articulated by the Adivasi woman described earlier at a meeting I attended in the western part of the state in the summer of 1988. Her problems, she said explicitly, have nothing to do with being a woman, but are the result of exploitation by landlords and moneylenders--a burden that falls equally on men and women.

This woman's comments fell outside the feminist rhetoric of the organizers of this particular program as well as outside certain norms of the scholarship of gender and development. But I am unable to dismiss her remarks as easily as did the organizers of this particular meeting; her comment is a reminder of the necessity of continuously examining the assumptions and biases of gender-specific development policy and strategy, as well as their relevance to how issues and priorities are perceived at the local level.

Theoretical Paradoxes, Strategic Implications

The low social status Bhil women describe in their own households and communities presents somewhat of a paradox; Bhil women are depicted in much of the ethnographic literature as relatively independent and sharing equal household status with their male partners, particularly in contrast with caste Hindu women (see for example Carstairs 1954 and 1983). Their visibility in markets and at public functions and fairs have contributed to this "outsiders'" view that Bhil women enjoy a higher status and freedom in their communities than do women of other groups.

At first glance this assumption would seem to be supported by the bride-price system of premarriage payment. Dapa, in contrast to dowry payments *from* the bride's family, is an infusion of capital *into* the bride's household, a transaction that would seem to make daughters valued members of that household (as opposed to the dowry system, in which all daughters, and their marriages, represent a financial liability). Ethnographic data on Adivasi women in Rajasthan, however, belies the linkage of female status with bride-price payment. As Unnithan-Kumar (1991) observes, the status of Adivasi women as devalued dependents in both their natal and postmarriage households is constructed from birth, and is structurally similar to the dependence of caste Hindu women. Despite the financial value of the bride-price transaction and Adivasi women's participation in economic and social activities, they do not have personal, discretionary access to valued resources in the community. "In effect then the inverse economic transactions of bride-price and dowry may in fact disguise the similar structural inequalities of both the women in caste and 'tribal' communities" (Ibid.: WS37).

The status of Adivasi women is further hampered, according to some observers, by Sanskritization and other roads to social mobility, which, while elevating group status, simultaneously intensifies gender hierarchy. The very process by which groups seek to lessen the disparity of caste hierarchy intensifies the disparity of gender hierarchy:

> The most severe gender inequalities of all are found among poor, low-caste groups which are striving for upward mobility in the traditional, ritually defined hierarchy, through Sanskritization.

> Women there have the worst of all worlds: they do not have gender parity because of the strictures imposed by Sanskritic status emulation, they do not have economic sufficiency and security because of their caste (ritual) status. Put another way, they suffer discrimination unique to their gender status as defined by Sanskritic ideology, together with poverty and denigration which they share with their menfolk as a result of their class and caste statuses respectively. [Berreman 1993: 370-371]

Other theoretical models, while not directly formulated in reference to Adivasi women in India, explain gender marginalization in terms of agricultural production systems (Boserup 1970, Miller 1981). While Bhil women participate actively in the agricultural production system they do not "control the plow," nor do they have direct ownership rights to land, which is inherited by men through their father's lineage.

Gender inequality in Bhil communities is therefore the result of a complex of economic, ideological, and processual factors. No one factor--not caste, not economic status, not gender--fully explains or predicts the complex manifestations of a Bhil woman's contemporary and historical exploitation. This complexity is further nuanced by the wide range of explanations women give for their own poverty and marginalization.

Women's Perspectives on Poverty

Often during group meetings, when women were not able to express themselves in conversation they were encouraged by social workers and organizers to sing a local song, the content of which then became the focus of discussion; the song quoted earlier was often sung by the women in and around Bagdunda at meetings and NGO-sponsored gatherings.

During an organizational meeting at a village near Bagdunda in 1989 Vina and Reka, then organizing local women for UVM, led a discussion on the topic, "Why are we poor?" The meeting was led by Vina, Reka, and Lal-ji (a pseudonym), a male worker for the organization. Some of the assembled women gave their views on this subject and on their perspective of "the old days":

> Lal-ji: Where has your poverty come from? Have you thought about it? In the olden days the Rajputs, the Zamindars [landlords] used to take away whatever you reaped. But these days there is no one taking away your lands. You have your own land. Are you happy now, or were you happier in the old days?

> One of the oldest women in the group replies:

Chapter 8 Women's Programs, Women's Voices

We were happier then. We did everything, all the work. Milking the cows, working in the fields. And we were happy. Earlier everyone used to work all the time. Now people don't work, they idle their time away. Even old men worked in the past. Now they don't work.

Lal-ji: How many fruit-bearing tress do you have in your home? How many mauhua trees? You are the ones who will pick the fruit. Why does your husband take the fruit you have picked and make wine out of it?

Another woman replies: Our husbands don't listen to us.

Lal-ji: You have to make him listen. If your husband comes home tomorrow and wants to set your house on fire, will you let him? No. But now you have given the main reason for your poverty. Your husband is not listening to you. And because of that you are not happy...Tell him if you want to drink, go ahead, but drink in limit. You need clothes, you need for your children, you need food. You ask him for that, but he doesn't give a thought to these things. He is only thinking about drinking. Now I ask you to think together, because no one else is going to come and help you. You have to help yourselves. Can your parents help you now? Have they helped you? You were happy at your parents' place. You got two meals every day and clothing. But then your parents got you married and sent you to your in-laws' house. If you are not happy now, will they come and help you?

The same woman replies: No, they will not come and help us.

Lal-ji: Now that you have come to your in-laws' house, whether they kill you, they strangle you, they throw mud on you, or give you new clothes, whatever they do to you, no matter what happens your parents are finished with you. When you got married your parents must have given you some new clothes. For one year your needs were met. But after one year, when you start needing new things...then you realize the truth. No one else is going to come from outside and fill your drums with grain. You will have to work for yourself. And even if you are unhappy, you are the one who has to suffer. No one else will suffer for you.

Vina: What is the difference between now and then?

A village woman replies: In the past there were not that many fields. There was jungle, and in the forests were animals.

Q: What did you grow at that time in the fields?

A: We used to grow maize in the fields, and we took water for irrigation from the wells. Whatever we reaped one year was held in store for the next year. Now whatever we reap we use this year. And if what was stored went bad, we used it for fertilizer.

Q: How many crops did you take?

A: We mainly took three crops--maize, wheat and barley. Side by side. We took crops of pulses and grass for cattle. There was plenty of water.

Q: You have grown old since then. Have you seen any differences? Did the people drink at that time?

A: No, they used to work all day, and eat their dinner, and dance gavri and go to sleep. They didn't drink. They entertained themselves with dancing.

Q: When did conditions start changing?

A: Slowly, the men started drinking and conditions started changing. The men started seeing other men doing it, their brothers drinking, so they started drinking and they started beating their wives. Even if we try to make our husbands understand, they don't understand. They don't realize. Women among themselves, even if we talk to them they go to their friends and say my wife is talking about these things. It creates tension in the house. We work for the whole day and we bring in money and then our husbands take it away.

Q: What is the difference between then and now?

A: Whatever we had, a little or a lot, we shared it with everyone. Our daughters were married off but we would keep them well. If anyone came, any guest came, we would give them food. But now if a daughter comes back to her parents house nobody will keep her. Our children are dying of hunger. They will say, so where should we get food for you? If a stranger comes we don't offer him food now.

Q: You are making it clear now. The people are not abiding by their traditions now. The thinking has changed. People have become more self-centered, more materialistic now. They don't think of helping others or giving to strangers.

A: Even if someone came to beg for food people never used to turn him away. Now they turn him away badly. Human behavior has changed. Sin is increasing. People are not abiding by their religion. That has brought us poverty and shortage of water. People are more sinful now and that is the cause of all our troubles. In our times people were not materialistic. There was cooperation. They never thought, "Why does that man have better crops? If we had good crops we would share. If another man had good crops, they would share. We never thought this is his, this is mine. People are selfish now...If you think good thoughts you will get good results. Good crops, good clothes. Think good of others and good will come to you.

Question directed at a group of younger woman: "You heard what the old woman said. What do you think?

One younger woman stands and says: Earlier there was love and affection between people. But now they don't maintain their relations. There is no affection. No love between people.

Contested Spaces: The Dhurrie

Many issues regarding status and behavior are physically and behaviorally manifested around the spatial distribution of people during a meeting on the *dhurrie* (also referred to locally as *jejum)*, the mat laid out at the beginning of a group meeting. When social workers or organizers arrived in a village, the dhurrie was laid by local women in front of the temple and the visitors sat on it; villagers slowly gathered and seated themselves on the ground, around the dhurrie. On those occasions when men and women gather for village-wide events, men sit on the dhurrie, and the women do not. This was a point of discussion at several of the women's meetings I attended, and gradually, through long and often difficult exchanges, the organizers engaged the village women in the process of challenging this practice. Part of the process of engaging women in the activities of organizing and discussing women's issues generally began with getting women to sit on the dhurrie with the social workers.

This message was successfully communicated in one village near Bagdunda. After working for about a year and a half in that village, Vina and Reka were told by women there that during a village ritual, the dhurries were spread as usual, but that the women tried to join the men on them. The men resisted, and insisted that the women sit on the ground as usual. Several of the women got up and told the men that if they could not sit on the dhurries they would not perform any of their tasks associated with this ritual, nor would they cook the food necessary to complete the event. The men agreed grudgingly, although only to having a second dhurrie laid for the women.

The Rhythm of a Meeting

The following is a description of a meeting held in a Bhil phala about 4 kilometers from Bagdunda; it was similar to many other meetings of its kind organized by Vina and Reka, who were never addressed by name, but as *Behen-ji* , an affectionate term that means "sister" with a respectful honorific suffix attached. This village is about an hour's walk from Bagdunda.

I arrived at the village with Vina and Reka, and we spread our jejum under the enormous tree that forms a shaded canopy over the entire temple and gathering area. We arrived at about 11:00 am; the first of the village women started to appear at about noon. When three or four of them had gathered, Vina began reading a story to, an Aesop's fable translated into Mewari, and discussing it with them. Slowly, over the next two hours or so, more women gathered; a few were from Bagdunda and the rest from two nearby Bhil phalas. By 1:30 pm about forty women, two men, and at various times, six or seven children had assembled. This meeting was the seventh monthly meeting of Bhil women held in this village.

The first event of the meeting was asking the women to stand up and one-by-one introduce themselves to the visitors from Bagdunda. Most refused to even attempt it.

The women who finally did stand up and speak to the group were older- -in their late thirties or early forties. One younger woman, about 20, who was goaded by the others to stand, covered her face with her long scarf and barely got out in a whisper, "*Mera nam...*" (My name is...) before she exploded into paroxysms of nervous laughter, which everyone joined in. It was all done in good fun, but provided a "starting point" for a discussion about self and the power of saying your own name. Only a very few women --those who had been working with the social workers for several months already--could speak out and contribute to the conversation with any ease.

Later Vina, Reka, and I talked about this reluctance to stand up and speak one's name; they believed it to be the result of several different factors. Bhil women are not accustomed to interacting with outsiders-- people not of their immediate village and therefore not related to them by either natal family or affinal ties. While Vina and Reka were by this time a familiar sight in the women's social landscape, some women cited my presence as particularly daunting to them. More significant is the fact that these women are not encouraged to identify themselves as individuals by name in any circumstances. Identifying themselves by a given name, and not as the daughter of or wife of someone, is an unfamiliar experience to them; not something they do in the normal course of events.

Storytelling was another very effective way of conceptualizing issues with women during meetings. Vina, who was fluent in Mewari, was particularly adept at using Aesop's Fables as a starting point for discussion. She repeatedly told the story of the thirsty crow who could not find water anywhere. At last he sees a jug, but the little water it contains is concentrated at the bottom and his beak cannot reach it. So he throws pebbles into the jug. The water level rises, he drinks the water, and flies away happy. After reading the story Vina suggests that the crow, like people, can solve any problem by thinking about it and trying to come up with a solution.

The Bhil women responded enthusiastically. One woman said: "He could solve the problem and he's just an animal. We don't have confidence these days. That bird thought so much--at least we can think that much, to make ourselves happy."

Vina continued the discussion by broadening its implications. "You have to think about it this way. If the government underpays you for wages and such, you have to ask why is this so. Also think about the problems of your village and why your husbands drink so much and beat you. If your husband doesn't beat you but your neighbor is beaten will you help her? Women responded together: "Yes."

Vina related another story, also enthusiastically received, to gender, deforestation and local political hierarchy.[1] After telling it, Vina suggested a parallel with a Sarpanche who stands for election. "If there is one woman who will convince fifteen others he will talk only to her, and make promises to her, like the way the swan thought the crane would bring all the fish to him."

She added, "The empty lake is like your forests. You have cut all the trees in your forest. Now it is empty. In the same way some Adivasis are waiting to be turned into swans. They have cut all their wood and turned it into charcoal or timber for others. And how many of your women have turned into swans?"

One local woman replied: "Our lands are all empty now. We have to take care of our woods. The men did all this. They are the cranes waiting to be turned into swans. Only village people can protect our trees."

Vina then asked some of the women to repeat the story. Some repeated bits and pieces, others repeated the entire story with great detail and enthusiasm. It was obvious that, when given the opportunity and some practice, these women have very good memories and verbal organization skills.

At about 4:00 pm the meeting broke up as casually as it began. With no formal announcement the assembled women gradually got up and either headed back home or began the preparations for our tea. The women broke into groups and began singing and dancing. For the next hour we sat, danced, sang and talked, until Vina, Reka and I, with several women from Bagdunda, walked back at a brisk pace to reach home before dark.

Volunteerism vs. Paid Labor: Women's Perspective

On the morning of the meeting described above, before our departure from Bagdunda, two Bhil women well known to Vina and Reka because of their participation in UVM activities came to the room Vina and

Reka shared, and where I also stayed on occasion. They had a rather intense and somewhat heated discussion which I could not hear. When the Bhil women left I asked what the discussion had been about, Vina replied that it had to do with money. One of the women regularly participated in UVM meetings and had organized the local *Mahila Samiti*'s (woman's group's) small bank account, to which members contributed Rs. 5 every month. This woman told Vina that she wouldn't come to meetings any more, including the one scheduled for later that morning, unless she got paid for her work, like the men employed by UVM. When discussing this with me later Vina said that, while she was distressed by the confrontation, it was overall a positive thing because these feelings were being expressed by the local women in a direct and candid way, and that moreover, the subject of remuneration warranted further discussion within the organization.

Since the inception of women's activities in Bagdunda, mahila samitis had been formed and were envisioned by UVM as the root of women's self-help groups; participation was envisioned to be based on the women's desire to participate, not on the promise of any financial reward.

But the village women knew that some male workers were paid employees of the organization, and that all the other organizations operating in the area paid their male workers. During meetings on women's organization, Vina discussed with them the difference between "members" as of a samiti, and "workers" for wages. She stressed that a mahila samiti should build its membership as a women's self-help organization, with the goal of unity and participation. This is a subtle difference that makes sense within the philosophy of local NGO strategy, but one that did not seem to be relevant to all of the local women.

Despite their threat to boycott the meeting, they did appear a few hours after the meeting began and continued to participate in subsequent meetings and gatherings. The larger issue of integrating women into the structure of the organization remains unresolved to this day; repeated efforts by UVM to hire a full-time female employee to work with the local women have been unsuccessful and the women's self-help programs, including the mahila samitis, have gradually dispersed.

Women and Education: Enacting Cultural Norms

There is strong and often stated consensus among Bhil male adults about the importance of literacy, particularly for children. A small number of women in Bhil phalas--those who were most involved with the UVM programs--expressed a desire to learn to read, and a few have learned to recognize the characters that form their own names. But the task of educating the rural women is daunting, primarily because of the

Chapter 8 Women's Programs, Women's Voices

economic, social, and political realities of their marginalization. These constraints follow them throughout their lives.

Children of both sexes are highly productive members of their households. Both boys and girls are given responsibility for grazing household animals in the fields and on common grazing lands almost as soon as they are able to find their way back home again from them. Girls also contribute a substantial amount of labor to household chores: throughout the day they work in the fields, weed gardens, gather firewood, clean and prepare food, providing a whole range of domestic duties.

Many villagers are now encouraging their boys to attend school, and are freeing them from their productive responsibilities to allow them to do so. They point out with great pride the accomplishments of their sons, and urge them to use their battered slates to show visitors what they have learned in Devenagri script and multiplication tables. Yet there is still little acknowledgment of the necessity for girls to be educated. People often discuss in public educating their girls, and at meetings they take pledges and make affirmations that all children should be educated. But privately they do not encourage it, and will cite several reasons for not doing so.

As mentioned previously, danger is associated with girls traveling from their phalas to village schools -- in some cases three, four, or more kilometers away. The danger of kidnapping and molestation of their girls by Bhil men is widely believed to be an ever-present threat, one that may result in a forced or unplanned marriage. Informants also talked about the fear sexual assault and the theft of silver jewelry from Bhil women, both of which often take violent form and result in severe injury and in some cases death to the female victims.

Many people expressed the feeling in private that it is simply not proper behavior to educate girls outside the home. For many people the belief persists that educating a girl decreases her marriageability; by local standards, an educated girl is considered a liability, not an asset.

The conflict between social norms and public rhetoric was evident in a series of meetings held by UVM in Bagdunda and attended by over two hundred people from several surrounding villages. As usual, despite the actual theme of the meeting, which was the environment, other social issues became part of the agenda. And also as usual this meeting, which took place over three days and nights, took on the festive characteristics of a *mela*, or fair, as it drew kin together from several different villages and included two cultural programs of songs and plays along with the educational agenda.

During one session, literacy and children's education was discussed. A local village UVM worker (male) was leading the group discussion, urging villagers to encourage their children--both male and female--to go to school. After the meeting several of the women said in private conversation that this particular worker was being very hypocritical, as it was well known that he was sending his sons to school, but not his daughters.

Another incident during the evening's cultural program literally enacted the community's ambivalence to educating girls. The program, which was well attended and lasted for several hours, consisted of the performance of *bagins* or hymns, puppet shows, and dramatic presentations of plays and skits performed by four local men--two performing male parts and two performing the female roles, consistent with local performance norms. All are well-known in the area as very skilled performers who are adept at singing, dancing, and dramatic presentations. The male performers who portray females do so with great sensitivity and skill. Although there was much light-hearted banter during the preparatory dressing and make-up period, the men all took a great deal of pride in their final appearance and the manner in which they portrayed women.

These performances are part of community tradition. The gathering for the singing of bagins and other songs is a regular occurrence, particularly when there is a visitor to the village. Every major NGO meeting or gathering included an evening "cultural program" that included singing songs and playing musical instruments well into the night. Men are the only performers, leading the songs, dancing along where the song-skit lent itself to dancing, and playing musical instruments. Women enjoyed these sessions as much as men, and in their own section, with covered faces, sang along. Often these sessions, which began with bagins and songs of a serious or religious theme, ended up after several hours with bawdy songs about illicit sexual liaisons between men and women, elopements, and "henpecked" husbands.

Three skits were prepared for that evening's cultural program. One skit involved the interaction between a husband and wife. She, an educated woman, was portrayed as overbearing and abusive, making escalating demands for money, jewels, and clothing. When her meek husband objected she hit him, and demanded that he go to the city to buy her more fabric and jewelry. The audience enjoyed the performance enormously, and laughed loudly whenever the woman hit her husband or made her increasingly outrageous demands of him. The next day the subject matter of the skits was criticized by several of the Udaipur-based staff members who had been present; they expressed their dissatisfaction over the content of the cultural program. A long discussion was held, reiterating the necessity for educating both boys and girls, and for portraying educated women in a more positive light.

Even where there is a strong desire for education, outside constraints often interfere with the process. For example, in Morwa, the state primary school that children from Solaria attend opened in June 1989.

Between June and December, five separate teachers had been assigned to it; all had come and gone. Even when there is a regular teacher assigned to the school, informants claim, they rarely appear. No efficient supervisory network exists in these more remote rural areas, and the teachers tend to reside several miles away in towns with better facilities, so they appear sporadically. After about three months of the students' walking to the school and finding no teacher, one of the older boys from Solaria who has an 8th-level education began teaching the younger children for a few hours each day.

Even in villages where NGOs have no active presence villagers cited lack of education and lack of literacy skills as one of their three major problems (the other two being water and poverty). But realization of this goal is difficult, given the indifferent infrastructure and the socio-economic constraints, particularly for rural girls of school age.

Reproductive Control and Health Issues

Despite the information "blitz" delivered by the SWACH program to this area, basic sanitary hygiene, such as washing hands after bowel movements or touching children's feces, is generally not observed locally. The contamination and disease-bearing potential of human feces is not yet fully understood by local residents. On several occasions I observed women rinsing off their children's bottoms with a tiny amount of water and with the same hand then wiping the child's face. No villages in the area have latrines or even designated areas to contain human waste. Women in villages where SWACH animators were present told me in 1990 that they all use a straining cloth when collecting water for household use, and that their children will not drink water unless they see it strained. As mentioned previously, the use of the straining cloth is of minimal value; and more often than not after being used at the well or hand pump, it was then rolled up and placed on the woman's head to help balance the heavy water jugs they carried back to their homes. Diarrhea and related intestinal illnesses are very common; other people reported suffering from tuberculosis and malaria, along with the long-term effects of untreated broken bones and other wounds.

With the exception of indigenous healers, there is no stable source of medical care. Although primary health care stations exist "on paper," they rarely operate on a continuing basis. When they do operate, according to informants, drugs and contraceptives that should be distributed free of charge are sold by local workers.

A hospital in Udaipur supplies free medical care, but "free" care carries a high price tag. In order to get to the hospital, the sick person must travel there by bus. He or she will be accompanied on this journey by several family members. If hospitalization is required, the patient must be attended to at all times throughout the hospital stay by a family member. On several occasions when walking through the hills from village to village, I saw a procession of people carrying on a string cot either an ill person or a woman experiencing difficulty in labor. This requires at least four people, and depending where they are from they might have been walking for several hours before reaching the bus route. If a woman requires medical care she is accompanied by both male and female relatives.

If the patient survives the journey by bus, and sometimes critically ill people expire during this two-hour phase of the journey to Udaipur, the family then faces the necessity of at least one family staying with the patient throughout the entire period of hospitalization. This person, who sleeps under the patient's bed, is needed to assist, feed and bathe the patient, as nurses only dispense medication. "Free" hospitalization does not include food for the patient's attendants, nor does it include the cost of medicines, drugs, and any and all medical supplies, which must be purchased in cash by a family member from a drug store outside the hospital. Nor does it include the payment of bribes to staff physicians, whose salaries are paid by the state-run and operated hospital, some of whom demand personal payment directly from the patient's family before completing surgical or other medical procedures.

Unfortunately, because of the illness of the father of my research assistant from Bagdunda, in 1995, I was an active participant in, and observer of, a month-long hospitalization in the state hospital in Udaipur. Throughout the process, which I guided for this rural family, I continually confronted the intransigence and indifference of the medical bureaucracy. Despite my influence and connections, which I exploited throughout this experience, I found myself continuously intimidated and overwhelmed by the local hospital system, and could easily imagine how intimidating the experience would be for a rural, illiterate villager. We were occasionally assisted by hard-working, committed and honest medical professionals working under greatly challenging conditions. The care my friend's father received throughout his hospitalization was, however, greatly improved and expedited by the presence, noted by staff and other patients alike, of a foreigner who visited the hospital every day and took an unexpected and active role in the care of a rural, illiterate SC farmer.

Because of all of these factors the decision to hospitalize an ill person is a critical family event. The serious financial nature of the decision, as well as the risks and dangers associated with the journey and the confrontation with an indifferent and undersupplied medical establishment, make it in some cases a major community decision-making event. I was in the home of another family when a discussion about whether or not to hospitalize a man suffering from tuberculosis took place. More than twenty people of all ages gathered to debate the pros and cons of hospitalization. Once it was decided to proceed and bring the man to the hospital, it was simultaneously decided to go to the village moneylender and borrow Rs. 500 to cover the expenses.

The major illnesses Bhil families confront regularly, according to informants in 1990, were guineaworm and related infections; tuberculosis; childhood diseases exacerbated by malnutrition and lingering infections; diarrhea and other health problems related to the water supply; childbirth complications; and anemia. As discussed previously it is widely believed now that guineaworm has been eradicated by the SWACH program, although the other diseases remain endemic.

Reproductive health, sexually transmitted diseases, and contraception are difficult issues to address with local women. They are very reluctant to discuss sexually related problems or disease out of modesty and fear that they will be perceived as being barren or unable to bear sons. The question of availability of contraception came up spontaneously only once, when I accompanied Vina on a visit to a Bhil woman whose infant daughter, her only child, had died suddenly during the night of unknown causes. She was the only Bhil woman with whom I had contact in the field area who was educated; she had been educated to 10th level, although she failed her examinations and did not have her certificate indicating her educational level. She had been trained as an *anganwalli* worker (a child care and maternal health para-professional) and had briefly served as a SWACH worker.

This woman was originally from Bagdunda, where she had managed to learn to read and write with her parents' cooperation. When she turned nineteen her family decided that she should marry. A marriage was arranged with an illiterate Bhil agriculturalist in a village about five kilometers from her natal village. Although she said her husband was a good and kind man, he didn't encourage her to work or continue her education.

During our visit she said she was very eager for us to obtain birth control pills for her, as she did not want to have another baby right away. When we asked her if she could get them from the local health workers she said they will only sell them to her for very high price. She said she wanted to do some work for the next five or six years before she had another baby.

Based on my limited access to information on birth control in the area, it appeared that the primary method of contraception practiced in this area is female surgical sterilization. Both men and women are paid to have the operation; some reported receiving as much as Rs. 350 (the equivalent of a month's wages for day labor) for surgical sterilization. Local state-employed health care workers are given quotas for sterilizations and report that they can be terminated if they consistently fail to reach these quotas.

The vast majority of people with whom I spoke who had the operation were women. There is a belief, expressed by both men and women, that a vasectomy is bad for a man's general strength. As a man's physical strength and endurance are deemed to be more important than a woman's, it is the wife who usually agrees to the operation. Most women said that they required their husbands' permission to have it, although some said they had the operation without permission, believing that the money they received for having it would offset their husbands' disapproval. One woman reported that she had been approached by a doctor who convinced her to have the operation, which she reluctantly agreed to even though she had only two children. She feels generally weaker after having had the operation, she reported; her husband had previously refused to have the operation because he said that there is even more weakness for a man than a woman after sterilization. As other women reported, she received Rs. 350 after the operation and spent the money on household articles.

I asked an unmarried woman of eighteen who lived with her parents in Bagdunda if she knew about family planning. She replied that she knew nothing about it, and because of her unmarried status it wasn't considered good or proper that she have this kind of information.

In some areas, particularly along highways and major trucking arteries, Bhil and other Adivasi women are becoming drawn into the practice of prostitution. Social workers and social activists believe that this is done with the knowledge, and presumably the consent, of their families or husbands' families. Sexually transmitted diseases among these women, who generally lack access to medical facilities, go untreated. In this socio-economic setting the transmission of AIDS is, according to some observers, a medical disaster of tremendous proportions that is just beginning to be addressed by local NGOs.

Chapter Summary

The persistence of gender bias in planning, organizing, implementing and evaluating development policy is itself evidence of the structural impediments and biases inherent in the process. Nevertheless, despite overwhelming evidence for the necessity of addressing the role of gender bias as both a theoretical and a practical issue, the words of the Adivasi woman in Jodhpur, who emphatically attributed her problems to poverty and exploitation, not gender, are telling indeed.

A development strategy that targets only one group in a village also has the potential of fragmenting the community; development programs that target SC/ST groups and exclude the poor of other caste groups and communities foreclose an alliance based on common poverty and lack of state resources. An exclusively gender-based development strategy may therefore prevent the formation of strong cross-gender village-based alliances.

A strategy and ideology that derives exclusively from gender-based exploitation offers village women organizing issues that are readily identifiable and familiar; but contemporary poverty has its roots in factors other than gender. Identifying those problems requires confronting the full range of social, economic, and political constraints that are unique to women as well as those that supersede gender. A development strategy that attacks these constraints must therefore encompass the full realities of rural oppression and position gender within its larger socio-political context.

---

[1] This story is called "The Crane and the Swan" and takes place in a land with a beautiful lake surrounded by hills. There are many cranes living in the hills, and many fish in the lake. The cranes eat the plentiful fish, and everyone is happy. One day a swan (*hansa*) flew over and saw the lake, and thought how beautiful it was. The swan started thinking to himself, "How can I take all these fish to my lake? He became greedy. He saw the cranes swooping down and carrying away the fish. Only the cranes, he said, can take the fish to my lake. The swan thought of a way. He took one crane aside and said, "I will make you as beautiful as a swan if you will bring me fish." The swan said he would take the crane to see the Swan King and the crane was very happy. The swan brought the crane to the king and told him about all the fishes in the lake.

The crane said, "I am alone and cannot take all these fishes. I will ask another crane to help." The king agreed. The crane said, "We have had enough fish; we will go to another place." So the cranes started taking fish to the swan's lake. Soon their own lake was empty, and the swan's lake was teeming with fish. One young crane said, "Our lake is now empty but the king is not making us swans." He told the other cranes and they all went to see the King, but he made excuses and didn't go to meet them. When they finally got to the king they said, "We have brought fish, you must now make us all swans." The king replied, "I promised to make only one crane a swan." The crane who had delivered all the fish to the swan king stayed there and reaped the rewards of all their labor; the others went back home and banged their heads in despair. In another version of the story a deluge comes and destroys all the cranes. The swan is a locally recognized symbol for an influential but dishonest person.

Chapter 9

Elections, Alliances, and NGOs

"Congress has gone. We brought down the government in Delhi!"
--Bagdunda residents describing election results November 1989

The national events that transpired during 1989-90 were a turning point in the contemporary political history of India, marked by increasing levels of influence of right-wing Hindu fundamentalists in local and national politics and unprecedented shifts in political party power. The elections of November 1989 were very significant to local perception of the political process. Villagers experienced, many for the first time, casting a vote whose impact resonated all the way to New Delhi; they felt and joyously expressed that they had brought down the government with their efforts.

This set the stage for their more active political participation, mobilization, and pursuit of local office in subsequent elections, fueled in part by increasing confidence in the impact of local voters on the electoral process. One result has been the necessity to offer more complex and refined NGO services, strategy, and policies to accommodate this increasing political sophistication in the communities in which the NGOs operate. One such program was instituted by Sewa Mandir in 1994; the organization offered consultation and training services to newly-elected Sarpanches throughout the district, whether or not they or their villages had any previous connection with the organization.

The election period also illuminated the process by which local villagers emerge as talented organizers through the avenue of NGO activity, and acquire upward mobility, further illustrating how, despite the efforts of the NGOs to remain neutral, local political party process is closely linked with organizational development programs and individual mobility strategies.

These events provided a framework within which to examine local-level political institutions, particularly those of Bhil leadership, and how these indigenous political positions and skills interface with both NGO development and political party activities. Indigenous forms of political leadership and mobilization, as well as the values and skills inherent in them, are being activated in this process. The involvement of Bhils in election-related events underlies the development potential inherent in political involvement as well as the constraints that hinder this potential.

Elections and Electioneering

This election period marked a particularly aggressive stance by Solaria residents. People from Solaria and surrounding villages told me that a few weeks before the elections the residents of Solaria learned that the MLA (state legislative assembly) candidate of the BJP would be passing through the area. He did not intend to stop, they said, but 300 community members gathered on the road and formed a roadblock in front of his jeep. They refused to let him pass until he agreed to sign a statement promising that if elected, he would see to it that the road to Morwa was improved and that broken hand-pumps in Morwa and Solaria would be fixed. The candidate was reluctant to sign the pledge, but eventually he did, and was allowed to proceed on his way.

"Election fever" seized most of the villages around Bagdunda and dominated all conversations for several weeks prior to the first round of elections; the issue was also very much a part of the NGO scene during this time. The organizations were explicitly working to balance their active encouragement of community political participation against the restrictions the central government places on NGO political activity.

The elections for the Lok Sabha, or national parliamentary elections, were held in Rajasthan on November 22, 1989 and state assembly elections in February 1990. The Congress(I) party, which, except for a brief period in 1977, had dominated state elections since 1952, was ousted from power by a coalition led by the BJP (Bharatiya Janata Party). In an aggressive effort at coalition-building, the BJP achieved great success in rural communities by recruiting support among the SC/ST groups. They were traditionally supporters of the more liberal and secular Congress party, which is closely associated in the minds of local voters with Nehru, Gandhi and Indian Independence. (See Hall 1990 and Rajasthan Election Atlas 1990 for an analysis of the 1989 election results.)

As noted previously, political process is a delicate issue for the NGOs, as they are forbidden by law to engage in party politics. Nevertheless, the linkages between NGOs, government and political process are intrinsic to the village level development process, and this linkage becomes particularly vivid around election time.

During the pre-election period, most of the organizations in the study area organized meetings and discussions around election issues and urged all participants to take active part in the election process. I observed, around election time, several scheduled discussion sessions during which the differences between the parties were explained, along with the basic mechanics of voting and ballot-casting. This was particularly important because many of the participants, particularly women, were voting for the first time in their lives and were very fearful of confronting the bureaucracy and the strange mechanics of the process.

Play-acting was a particularly effective technique for women. At one such session I observed, sponsored by two NGOs jointly, a few older women acted out a scene in which they confronted a mock political "candidate" and asked him direct questions about promises that he had made in the past, and what would be done about specific issues in the future. This was played out with a great deal of banter and humor from the audience and it was an opportunity for these women to practice their powers of assertion and communication skills in public, and for the women in the audience to observe their peers engaging in public speaking activities. The question session with the "candidate" concluded with the women attacking him and causing him to run away. The speed with which this educational session degenerated into a light-hearted physical attack on the "candidate" indicated a ready willingness on the part of women, in a relatively safe environment, to "turn the tables" on the (male) candidate.

At another session during the same meeting, NGO organizers talked about the structure of government, the functions of the government officials that would be elected in the upcoming elections, and about the differences between the major parties running candidates in the area. The participants were shown the symbols for each of the parties--a lotus for the BJP, a raised hand for the Congress party, a plow for the local Communist party, etc. At another meeting a facsimile of a paper ballot was passed around and the mechanics of the voting process enacted. The use of symbols to represent the parties, and the necessity of voters to recognize these symbols, is critical to the voting process in the area because of the high rate of illiteracy there.

The outcome of the election was, prior to ballot casting, uncertain. Predicting the form that caste or other social group alliances would take was a far more complex process than was first assumed by local party organizers. It was assumed that Congress would maintain its traditional support among the local SC/ST voters, as it is the political party associated with the Independence movement and with the benefits and reservation programs. This assumption proved to be false; alliances on the basis of caste group affiliation alone did not take into account the many variables in the process. Political alliances were formed on a localized level and were driven by many other issues besides political party history. For example, there was aggressive support for both major political parties within all caste groups.

In the 1989-90 elections the BJP's Hindu nationalism rhetoric gained considerable support among Scheduled Tribe members; Bhil informants reported with a great deal of pride that what they perceived to be the political party of the Rajputs and Maharanas was courting them on the basis of "pan-Hindu unity."

Lal-ji, a Bagdunda Congress party organizer (and UVM staff member) had told me a few days before the Lok Sabha elections that in Bagdunda about 60 percent of the total population was for the BJP. That party, he had explained, was the party of the wealthy, the moneylenders and large land-holders. Congress, he said, is the party of the Adivasis and the poor. Given the election strategies and results, this analysis proved incorrect, and did not predict the success of electioneering efforts by the BJP among the Bhils.

NGOs, Politics and Upward Mobility

Both NGO development programs and political party participation rely heavily on verbal communication skills, and in Udaipur district the primary NGO source of disseminating information is group discussion and meetings, held in a nearly endless stream throughout the year. A man who can engage his listeners by speaking well, with ease, with passion and with logic, will be able to parlay these skills into a local leadership position. As Bhil leadership is generally not structured by hierarchy or lineal descent, a compelling speaker almost automatically emerges as the community leader. The NGOs tap into this indigenous system to find its local leaders and organizers; but in many cases the individual with leadership and verbal skills does not have basic literacy skills.

In Bagdunda, the experiences of Lal-ji illustrate some of the complexities of the election process viewed from the perspective of NGO activity. Lal-ji, a Bhil agriculturalist with little formal education, was a salaried member of UVM and part of the managing board. He was a very important member of the organization as a whole, and an influential member of the area in which he resided.

Lal-ji was an extremely talented speaker and organizer; I observed him delivering speeches over the years on several occasions, and was often spellbound by his ability to speak extemporaneously for long periods of time on a wide range of subjects. He was soft-spoken yet very forceful in his delivery, and communicated equally well with men and women. In addition, he was a shrewd negotiator of local power and politics. All these skills were major factors in his importance to UVM as a community worker and organizer.

For example, in 1988 the organization sponsored a *pad yatra* (parade and gathering) on the environment; the attendance at this event ranged, according to various sources, from 2,000 to 5,000 people. Whatever the actual numbers, by all reports Lal-ji was credited with gathering this crowd, and his organizational skills attracted the attention of the local political leadership. Soon thereafter he was approached to work for the Congress party as an organizer in the following year's elections. He became a very active Congress worker, and there was talk that in the future he would be asked to stand as the MLA in this district.

As the 1989 elections drew nearer it was impossible to separate out Lal-ji's two statuses: NGO worker and political party representative. Some of UVM's workers in other villagers were also drawn into the electioneering process as representatives for the Congress and BJP parties. These individuals were also known to be associated with the political parties they represented as well as UVM. The organization did not wish to restrict the political participation of these individuals, but was mindful that there was nevertheless a potential conflict between their political work, on the one hand, and the government's restrictions against NGO political party activity on the other. To allay the conflict, the organization leadership decided to suspend all its activities for the month prior to the elections, and put all workers on a one-month hiatus.

Another NGO working in a different part of the district at the time had a more explicit policy; they forbade their local workers from engaging in any type of political party activity. The leadership of this organization believed that it was impossible to separate their day-to-day activity from the political process of the villages in which they worked, and that their workers would therefore have undue influence on the voters if, in addition to their regular activities of education and organization, they were to represent a particular political party.

During an informal discussion one of the directors of this organization related his experiences working on literacy programs in the early 1970s.

> We trained many bright young men to be teachers in the non-formal sector; they became trainers and teachers of teachers. And then they became elected officials. They moved from the voluntary segment into mainstream politics. Not necessarily helping the community. We didn't realize what we were doing; if we had we could have influenced a whole generation of politicians and political activity.

We were committed to non-political activities. We didn't realize what was going to happen.

As a result of this experience when he began his own organization he established the firm policy that his workers could not simultaneously be NGO employees and organizers as well as political party representatives.

Another organization founder stated the following:

I do not have a problem about people running for office. They have to decide what business they are in, and stick to it. NGOs can't be political. It will destroy their credibility in the field. While it would be good to have someone in government sympathetic to the NGO situation, one would never know where their first loyalties were--to their party, which is related to their own careers, or to the NGO community.

This speaker also expressed the belief that overt political activity on the part of NGO workers is very confusing to the local community, as it may not always be clear which hat they are wearing; that is, what segment these workers and their activities are representing at the moment--NGOs or government.

Election-Period Turmoil

As is generally the case in India, the elections in 1989 took place over a three-day period; election day in Rajasthan was November 22. Throughout India, a great deal of violence, well publicized in local-language newspapers, arose around the elections, including the attempted assassination of a BJP candidate in Rajiv Gandhi's home district of Amethi. The newspapers were filled with reports of communal/political party violence; by November 22, 1989, 40 people had been reportedly killed in election-related violence. Re-polling was ordered in hundreds of districts because of electoral irregularities such as ballot stuffing, voter intimidation, or the theft of ballot boxes.

There was therefore some tension in Bagdunda during the election period. Each of the village's major political party representatives, surrounded by a half a dozen followers, kept a careful watch over the polling place (the school building) but the process proceeded peacefully throughout the day. I asked the polling inspector if I could go inside and observe the actual voting process; he let me in but then asked me to leave immediately, obviously nervous about my presence and his responsibilities for maintaining order during this tense period.

Each of the five villages in the voting district had a different room for polling. The first step of the voting procedure is to have one's name checked off against a master list of eligible voters. To get a ballot the voter then fills out a small slip with name, husband's or wife's name, village, and voting center; illiterate people had this information filled in for them by an election worker. After providing this information the voter is given the actual ballot which consists of sheet of thin paper listing the symbols of each of the parties with the name of the candidate (written in Hindi) directly underneath. The voter goes to the far side of the room to a table and places the rubber stamp mark over the appropriate party symbol. The voter then folds it and puts it in the ballot box.

After they voted, several Bhil women expressed great fears about the process. Giving their names to officials, and interacting with political organizers and local power brokers, appeared to create great anxiety for them. They were fearful of doing the wrong thing, of making mistakes, of not carrying out the process correctly or the instructions they had been given accurately. Later, a BJP polling-place monitor told me that he saw at least twenty-five women put the stamp on the wrong side of the ballot, thereby invalidating their vote. According to official statistics state-wide 2 percent of the votes polled were rejected as invalid (n.a. 1990: xi).

Women were also easily manipulated by those who were better informed than they. I was told by a man who supported one of the opposition parties that he convinced a group of women who had never voted before that to cast a ballot for the Congress(I) party, whose symbol is a hand, the voter should put the rubber stamp mark on her own palm, not on the ballot.

Election posters were prominently displayed on the outside walls of shops, homes, tea stalls, and abandoned buildings throughout Bagdunda, and were important tools for associating faces, names, and party symbols. The Congress symbol was a particularly effective one; when I saw one woman after the elections and asked her who she had voted for, she raised her hand, palm out, and said, *Hat ke liye* ("I voted for the hand.")

I was told by both Congress and BJP representatives immediately after the elections that the voter turnout in Bagdunda was about 50 percent of the registered voters; state-wide the official turnout was computed by election officials to be 56.5 percent (n.a. 1990: xi). Both local party officials said that for the election of the Sarpanche and other local officials the turnout is usually close to 100 percent.

Three days after the elections, Bhatia called a meeting to discuss the experiences of Bhil BJP supporters from Solaria and Morwa during the election. Among other issues, these party workers, expressed their opinions about effective electioneering techniques. They all agreed that a mass gathering, while important for public shows of party strength, was not the most effective political tool. Some men said that many people came to rallies sponsored by the political parties only because of the food distributed afterwards. One of the men said, "If you want to sing a song then you need a big gathering. But when you want to gain knowledge then you need only two people and discussion between them."

During this meeting the theme of intercaste relationships arose and the ensuing discussion seemed to indicate that politics, at least during the time of elections, can be a social leveler. Questions were put to the group by Bhatia:

Q: When you go to talk to the Rajputs [about politics] do you feel afraid of them?

A: No, earlier we did. Now we don't. The Rajputs are like this--if we go to talk politics they will give us a mat to sit on, but they won't allow their Bhil laborers to sit on a mat. That means they are not against Bhils, but they don't respect their bonded laborers.

Q: What about Meghwals. Whom did they vote for? And why?

A: They voted for Congress. They say we don't follow the system of changing our masters. Congress is our master. But some Meghwals of Morwa were with us. Some of them were diplomats--if we went they said, yes I will vote for you and if the other party went they would say yes, I will support you.

Meghwals, more than Bhils, expressed fears about the repercussions of the outcome of the election. As Scheduled Caste members they were concerned that the resurgence of Hindu religious rhetoric, now a part of political process, would be interpreted in conservative villages like Bagdunda as sanctioning some of the overt discrimination, and perhaps even some of the violence, associated with inter-caste hierarchy of the past. The election results also indicated the lack of consistent and enduring political alliances in the area between Scheduled Caste and Scheduled Tribe groups, and the factionalization between members of these two groups (see Mencher 1974).

Alliances and the NGO

The position of the NGO in the community can be illuminated by examining the multiple sets of alliances that cross-cut social and political groups in a rural village. As noted previously, the NGO neither creates nor destroys existing relationships; its activities in most cases coincide with existing conflicts, fissures, alliances and hierarchies. The NGO is one of many vertical and horizontal sets of alliances that order village-level social and political relationships (see Attwood 1974).

A protracted event in one of the villages in which UVM, its members, and its executives participated, illustrates the complexity of village-based alliances and how the NGO fits into, but does not in itself create, factions or fissures in the social landscape. This event also illustrates the interaction between the NGO and a local political institution, in this case representatives of the Forestry Department. The NGO acted as an ally to and spokesperson for the local community and provided it with leverage and authority in the confrontation that took place.

These events arose from a dispute amongst the residents of a Bhil phala a few kilometers from Bagdunda. A plot of several hundred bighas of land controlled by the Forestry Department was under dispute. The land was currently being used as public grazing, with access allowed to women for the collection of dead wood and fodder. The Forestry Department wanted to enclose 250 bighas to do some plantation and reforestation work, and proposed to hire villagers and pay them at the minimum wage rate first to build enclosure walls and then to plant saplings on the enclosed plot. The local Forestry Ranger said that the work must begin immediately, as the department's fiscal budget was due to end within about a month of these discussions and the project had to begin during the current fiscal year.

Some of the residents of the village did not want this work done. They claimed that all the land was being used for the grazing of cows and goats, and that their unlimited access to this grazing pasture should continue. Opponents of the project also claimed that the villagers were already busy with their own agricultural work and adsi padsi projects building check dams and bunding walls. (I subsequently learned that twenty Bhil families had encroached on the land in question and had built a bunding wall around it, preventing others from grazing their animals or having any other access to the land. This subject was not discussed in public at the meeting.)

A meeting was convened in the village to take a vote on the Forestry Department issue, which about 175 people attended, including the UVM director from Udaipur. Prior to the actual commencement of the meeting the Forestry Department guard from the area arrived, according to informants, and was drunk and abusive. He said the work would be done no matter what. When the Forestry Ranger (the guard's superior) drove up on his motorcycle, the guard ran off.

The tone of the meeting as it proceeded was the most directly confrontational I had ever observed. There was acrimonious debate about each issue raised. Some villagers, under the leadership of a UVM worker who lived in the phala, said that they did not want the land enclosed, nor would they work on the project. They claimed that they had too much of their own work to be done, as well as UVM work. Unstated, but understood to all, was that this faction didn't want any of the land enclosed and placed off limits to grazing or minor forest produce collection.

Much of the dissension was emanating from two brothers who were the leaders of the two opposing factions in this dispute. One, who was coincidentally also the representative of the NGO, was against the project, and his brother sided with supporters of the Forest Department's program. I later found out that these two brothers, who had a long history of feuding, also supported different political parties; the NGO worker was a Congress party worker and his brother was a supporter of the BJP.

After a great deal of discussion a five-point compromise was presented, and despite the heated debate leading up to it, quickly agreed to by all the parties. The enclosure and plantation project would go ahead; villagers would work on the project and be supervised by a "mate" (the supervisor of a labor project who controls the "muster roll" or work and payment records) from their own village. Limited access to other forestry lands would continue for grazing and fuel collection.

Considering the acrimony of the debate, which had on for about two hours, the final resolution and agreement was reached very quickly. I think it was a foregone conclusion, known by everyone but not stated, that the Forestry Department would have its way. But the event was significant in that it was the first time that the Forestry Ranger, who was supervising the project, actually sat down with Bhil villagers and negotiated terms with them. It is difficult to know whether he would have agreed to a negotiating session without the presence of the NGO director and several outside observers from the organization.

The Forestry Ranger was reported by informants to have said that if the villagers did not cooperate and provide the necessary labor he would bring in workers from outside the community, under the supervision of a Rajput from another village who had already been designated as the project "mate."

Virtually all informants spoke of the corruption and deceit with which the muster role is maintained. Payment day--when funds are dispersed to individual workers--is rife with fights, arguments, and dissension. Accusations of false entries abound on both sides--workers claim the mate makes entries for individuals who do not work so the mate can pocket their wages. Mates charge that workers were no-shows or didn't put in a full day's work. Record-keeping on the list is generally "signed" by the workers' thumb print; as most cannot read the entries being made concerning their work, it is not surprising that there is constant dissension over the payment.

But even more significant than the daily wages is the muster role's symbolic importance for the Bhils. It is seen as the instrument of continuous exploitation. The mate on a wage labor project is invariably of a dominant caste. His ability to read and write provides him with an additional advantages. He also has the power to hire and dismiss--a power that is quickly exercised when he is challenged, particularly over appropriate wage payments. Bhils constantly report that when they contracted for work, including work from state-sanctioned funds, they receive about half the actual minimum wage.

Villagers see the muster role and the mate as a representation of their powerlessness and their poverty. The following song was composed and sung by the women of one of the Adivasi villages during a regional meeting of several NGOs and their constituents in Udaipur. It illustrates how the villagers express, through irony, the connection between their powerlessness and the web of poverty:

> Oh my sisters, come let us make the muster-roll and write down false names.
> Write down false names and decrease the laborer's wage.
> Reduce the laborer's wage and kill the poor with hunger.
> Kill the poor with hunger, but give a funeral feast.
> Give the funeral feast and make a loan from the Mahajan.
> Take a loan from the Mahajan and make Hansa [the swan, a symbol of corrupt local leadership] more powerful.
> Oh my sisters, bring the rule of the muster roll and increase the power of the mate.
> Increase the power of the mate and dishonesty will reign.
> Oh my sisters, vote for Hansa and bring the rule of dishonesty.
> Oh my sisters, for whom will you vote so that power remains in your village.
> Oh my sisters, vote for the poor and bring them to power.

Prior to this confrontation with the Forestry Department representatives, the villagers there formed an intercaste organization. The village consists of 160 Adivasi families, 10 Gujar families (a middle-range jati of cattle- and other animal-breeders); and three Rajput families. A Gujar was elected head and spokesperson of the group. Bhatia, a long-term observer of the community, mentioned that this structure was common; when Bhils interact with higher-caste groups they look to others to serve in leadership positions, and never take it on themselves. I asked whether he thought the formation of this intercaste group might not be evidence of some common-interest organization. He replied, "Not at all. The Gujars and Rajputs are joining with the Adivasis because they want access to the NGO money and benefits that are directed at the Adivasis."

Chapter Summary

The ability to speak out in public convincingly and mobilize the support of other local residents is cultivated by NGOs among the local people who work for/with it. Talented organizers are an asset to the organization, which presents these people with potential routes of personal mobility. In addition, their organizational and mobilization skills do not go unnoticed by the local political parties, who also cultivate talented individuals for political positions. This latter avenue of personal mobility comes into direct conflict with the government-sanctioned role of the NGO as a nonpolitical entity.

As has been described, each of the NGOs operating in the field area had a different strategy for dealing with this potential conflict, a policy that was not negotiated with the community but was imposed from the management level.

Several avenues of personal mobility may become available to a local NGO worker, although this potential in and around Bagdunda does not extend to women. A man may be hired by the organization on a full-time basis, and be given a position of power and authority. In addition, this individual may attract the attention of outsiders interested in cultivating his skills for other purposes. Pursuing these avenues of personal mobility may be labeled "selfishness" or "lack of commitment" to the NGO or the community. Reconciling the mobility and success of one individual with the goals of the group or village community was a constant theme of group meetings and, more heatedly, private discussions. And if an individual did reach some level of economic or political success, much discussion ensued--both in public and privately--about whether the benefits of his success would be shared by the rest of the community.

The NGO is only one of many local institutions around which personal and group factions mobilize; NGO-based alliances also operate in concert with those shaped in other institutions and settings. Alliances formed around the NGO, like other alliances in the community, may shift and reorganize. As in the case of voting blocs, the circumstances that trigger alliances and the composition of the local group that mobilizes, are not always based on class, caste, or NGO affiliation. And what might look like village-wide, or intercaste alliance formation does not always turn out to reflect common or shared interests; it may be a mechanism by which individual families can gain access to NGO resources.

Chapter 10

Perspectives on Decision Making and Hierarchy

All the NGOs in Udaipur describe their strategies as reflecting the needs of the beneficiary communities as articulated by those communities. This is referred to variously as a "bottoms-up" or "grassroots" approach, and in more recent discourse, to "people's participation" or client-driven development management. Nevertheless, this philosophy of participatory management rarely seemed to make operational in the field. Instead, decisions, particularly critical decisions about how money was to be spent within the villages, were generally made by organization management; the extent to which villagers participated at all in decision making and financial allocation varied from one organization to another. Sometimes village participation was virtually nonexistent, and other times it was limited to simply obtaining consensus for organizational policy.

The explicit nature of hierarchy and centralized decision making was therefore apparent in many of the organizational processes, such as fiscal allocation, project identification, strategy, and hiring and firing decisions. Pursuing financial resources, and the representation of the organization to external and/or foreign funding sources, are invariably the sole domain of the organizations' headquarters staff in Udaipur.

This structural hierarchy is informed with a diffuse and subtle set of behavioral norms with symbolic and cultural expressions. The significance of these symbols is far more complicated than merely clarifying the operational framework, and exploring it illustrates many of the more subtle cultural norms of hierarchy that all the participants share. On occasion some of the participants articulated a full, rich analysis of these symbolic messages; on most occasions, however, they were explained only as evidence of "the way things work."

Sharing cultural norms does not result in smooth consensus. These cultural patterns, while providing a basis for motivating actions or events, are also subject to differing interpretations, and these multiple interpretations were often flash-points around which conflict arose between village-level participants and NGOs as organizations.

This chapter details a series of unrelated themes and events culled from observations of several different organizations, to illustrate how varying perceptions of the prevailing social and cultural norms provide points of conflict, as well as the culturally defined norms for resolving those conflicts. They also demonstrate how acts motivated by the very best and altruistic intentions can result in unanticipated conflict and frustration, because of different interpretations of those acts by different participants.

Why Participate with NGOs? Multiple Perspectives on Mobility

While it is the goal of organizations to include as many families and households as possible in their programs, the choice of whether to participate or not is, of course, an individual or household decision that, as previously discussed, brings to bear a wide range of social, cultural, and political considerations.

Very often villagers see their associations with the NGOs as a route of upward mobility. Employment by the organization will result in steady, regular income to supplement the uncertainties of agricultural production and day labor. But more important are the multiple linkages the NGO potentially represents, linkages with people and institutions of more power and influence than can be otherwise cultivated in the normal course of events. And indeed, I observed a marked difference over the years in some NGO-associated villagers in terms of self-esteem, self-confidence, and the increased ease with which they associate with people of upper castes or classes.

This kind of motivation for affiliating with an NGO does not correspond with the motivation that NGO directors and managers envision as appropriate or desirable, however. They focus on building community-level associations and village-wide programs with shared social, political, and--not necessarily direct--economic benefits spread equally among all participants. Although these two sets of goals are not necessarily mutually exclusive, most of the NGOs assume that participation in their programs will be based on a commitment to community-level service, as opposed to upward mobility or personal economic benefits.

These potential benefits are visible; over the years the villagers witness those that have derived to individual participants in the NGO process. They see how forming one's own NGO, for example, brings with it some of the rewards of "middle-class" life that are modest by most urban standards but highly desirable from a rural villager's perspective. The motorcycles that bring NGO workers based in Udaipur or other towns to the villages, or the telephone in an NGO field office, are symbols of middle-class prosperity that are out of the reach of most village-based participants.

The theme of individual gain through NGO participation is used by all the participants at different points in the discourse. In times of open conflict between villagers and NGO management, no matter what the specific issue, invariably the villager will make charges of financial mismanagement against the NGO organizers. Disgruntled former employees or NGO associates in the villages inevitably point to the middle-class "prosperity" of these individuals and their families as evidence of the fact that they have personally benefited from the NGO by misappropriating funds intended for the rural poor.

Throughout my research and association with NGOs in Udaipur I have not come across any substantiated case of sustained and tolerated financial mismanagement within the organizations with which I have had any contact. Quite the contrary. The organizations are extremely sensitive to the ramifications of such charges and act quickly and publicly to confront any individuals so accused. That the theme of financial mismanagement arises so often is due in part to the expectation of corruption, the dynamics of which all villagers are very familiar with, within local institutions generally.

The perception of NGO formation as a direct route to a middle-class lifestyle is not limited to villagers; the growing visibility of the NGO community in Udaipur is not always perceived favorably among city dwellers. Conversations in 1995 with middle-class residents of Udaipur city reflected a general tone of cynicism about the motives of these "do-gooders" and the perception that starting an NGO is an instant route to individual financial success.

Many middle-class Rajputs, for example, expressed dissatisfactions at the benefits of the caste-based reservation system from which they are excluded; they perceive NGOs as part of the same system that provides unfair advantage to the SC/STs. Many middle-class city dwellers accurately see themselves as economically privileged but with limits to their spending capacity. Many expressed to me their perception of the benefits system as dramatically impacting on their own children's futures--for example, that they will be forced out of state-run educational institutions by "unqualified" or "undeserving" SC/ST candidates. The influx of development funds through local NGOs, much of which derives from foreign sources, further stirs middle-class resentments against, and cynicism about, these organizations and their organizers.

On a village level, local dissatisfaction and cynicism with NGO activities often reflects another reality of local development: that there are both winners and losers in the process, and that the losers are those who may have joined up with the NGOs full of hope and optimism but were later dismissed or quit out of dissatisfaction with the procedures, priorities, or benefits. The disgruntled losers are often individuals who attempted to utilize their NGO position in ways that the organization deemed to be unfair or dishonest, but which, from their perspective, was consistent with familiar and acceptable norms, such as rerouting a percentage of supplies meant for public distribution to private hands.

As one who was not accustomed to the public expression of this kind of corruption as a way of life, I was often amazed at the way in which people spoke of it as their right, or as just compensation. This view was expressed by an engineer who had worked briefly on a local state-sponsored construction project. He told me he felt that he deserved to steal supplies from the project because he had not been hired by the state as an engineer, a job he had expected and believed he deserved by virtue of his having attained, at state expense, his engineering degree.

As previously discussed, an unresolved theoretical conflict as to how to view their own participants lies within the structures and strategies of NGOs. Some, like Sewa Mandir, foster the professionalization of the NGO sector, and actively recruit people who are seeking to develop careers, with accompanying rewards. UVM's Kishore Saint, on the other hand, believes that the goal of community service (as articulated by the Gandhian concept of *sewa* (spiritually-informed service) should drive NGO work at all levels, and that financial reward or personal mobility should be among the last considerations for entering the field.

Both organizations, while offering different perspectives on the professionalism of the NGO salaried worker, share the belief that individual upward mobility is not an appropriate motivation for villager participation, whether as volunteer or salaried worker. Both organizations see themselves as mechanisms for community development, not individual development. While this vital theme is as yet unresolved in NGO work, these and most other organizations in the area are now actively supportive of members who seek to pursue local public office, particularly through election to the position of Sarpanche or as village panchayat raj representatives. Sewa Mandir has expanded its support of individuals, particularly women, pursuing elected office by offering workshops and training sessions to all rural elected officials who choose to participate, whether or not they are members of the organization or from villages that participate in NGO projects.

Multiple Perceptions of Problems and Strategies

NGOs identify deforestation as the most critical problem of the area; community-based reforestation and plantation projects are the major strategies in and around Bagdunda. Bhil villagers have a strong spiritual connection to the land, as well as an historical and economic one, particularly to the forests and its resources. UVM draws on this connection explicitly in the name of their organization, which refers to a temple and local deity. But villagers articulate these problems, and therefore their appropriate solutions, differently; they consider the scarcity of agricultural water as their primary problem, and do not spontaneously link it to deforestation. A series of events surrounding a well-deepening project illustrates these strategic and ideological conflicts, as well as the structural relationships inherent in the local-level dynamics between villagers and NGOs.

The general concept of conservation as intervention that the NGOs practice is not always consistent with the Bhil belief in the regenerative powers of the earth's resources. Many villagers asserted that, despite the visible damage to the environment, "the earth will take care of us." They expressed faith that despite monsoon failures, which are an accepted part of the agricultural cycle, the rains will continue to fall. They believe that the grasses and trees will regenerate and new water sources will be found using indigenous technologies. They do not make a link between deforestation as a human-caused process and resulting water shortages, which the NGOs explicitly link as parts of the systemic cycle of tree destruction, floods, and monsoon failures. (See Gold and Gujar 1989)

The practices of enclosing, and therefore limiting access to, common grazing land, and planting tree saplings are not indigenous ones. The NGOs have introduced these active interventions, as well as banning the harvesting of live trees. These strategies involve changes in traditional access to productive resources, and they require adopting new household practices that particularly affect the time and labor expenditures of women, as previously discussed. These new strategies also require changes in animal-grazing patterns and access to grazing lands, critical resources for the maintenance of agricultural animals and for the income potential they represent.

Another strategy encouraged by the UVM is the building of enclosure walls across gullies and around fields to slow down soil and water runoff that, if controlled in this way, will aid in the recharging of wells. Based on its interpretation of technical and engineering analysis, UVM believes that well-deepening in itself will not increase well water retention without these area-wide interventions to affect the regional watershed levels, a strategy referred to as micro-watershed management.

Chapter 10 Perspectives on Decision Making and Hierarchy 191

Supported by the advice of state-employed engineers and water specialists, the organization is convinced that the wells are not recharging because deforestation has prevented the collection of monsoon waters in underground aquifers. They argue that if bunding walls and saplings are planted, the collection of water will be improved throughout the watershed area, by natural percolation processes into the underground aquifers that feed the wells.

Local agriculturalists have their own preferred strategies for dealing with the problem of water scarcity. It is a direct intervention strategy of locating new wells and deepening existing ones, either manually or through the use of explosives.

Bhils in several of the communities in the area have actively pursued well-deepening as a priority when they have access to the money and labor necessary for these projects. This is a capital-intensive undertaking, and one that cannot be done without financial assistance: dynamite charges in 1990 cost about Rs. 400 per round of twenty blasted holes; anywhere between three and ten rounds are needed to deepen an existing well. The rental of a tractor greatly reduces the labor needed for clearing the debris, and a pneumatic pump, also rented, draws off mud and silt. These expenses are far beyond the resources of local Bhil households. In order to undertake such a project, outside funding must be found. Banks do not finance well-deepening; even if they did, most Bhils are reluctant to enter into these institutional loan transactions.

Although anyone can also potentially locate an underground water source, the presence of underground water is often detected by a local *bhopa*, or medium, aided by his special skills of communicating with the spirit world. It is believed that this knowledge, expressed through the medium, is the result of spirit intervention; the information is received by the bhopa during spirit possession or is transmitted through dreams. The villagers' faith in the validity of this information is firm and unwavering.

I visited a village about six kilometers from Bagrunda in 1990 where an underground source of water had been recently identified. This village was within the operating territory of UVM; workers from the organization had visited it and adjoining villages, and were in the process of integrating them into their activities. At the time of this event several meetings had already been undertaken and discussions held with the villagers, although no substantive UVM activities had begun there.

This village consisted of approximately 100 families, about 70 percent of the families were Bhil, about 20 percent Meghwal, and the balance Rajputs. There seemed to be a great deal of unity and cooperation throughout the village; UVM meetings were attended by almost all the village men, and the villagers in general seemed to be willing to participate equally in adsi padsi projects.

A Bhil villager had had a dream that water would be found in some solid rock hills approximately one kilometer from the village. He and other villagers were convinced that this dream was a positive omen, and they consulted a local bhopa. The bhopa listened carefully to the details of the dream, visited the area it indicated, and showed the villagers precisely where to dig, near an existing well. They manually dug down about 20 feet and found water. An altar was immediately built at the site and images of various deities were installed.

Once the well was dug, the villagers wanted to deepen it to tap farther into the underground aquifer. Vina, a UVM organizer, had visited the village approximately one month prior to my visit. There was no road or path to the well, and she suggested that the villagers clear a path and start building bunding walls around the area, so that ground water would percolate into the underground aquifers more effectively. She was assured that when she returned the work would have been done with adsi padsi labor. When I accompanied her there a month later, both jobs had been completed. A road about one kilometer long had been cleared, and several bunding walls crossing the gullies had been constructed. All this labor was done entirely by hand by villagers.

With those tasks completed, the villagers told Vina they needed money to deepen the well. They explained that they had done as much as they could by hand, and needed some financial assistance in renting and purchasing the necessary equipment and supplies. She promised she would present their case to UVM's management in Udaipur. She did, but the request was ultimately turned down on the basis that (at that time) the organization did not finance individual capital intensive projects, and furthermore, based on the input of engineers and water specialists, did not believe that individual well-deepening was an effective strategy.

The community members then told the UVM workers that they would go to Sewa Mandir for assistance, as that organization had recently completed a dam-building project in the area. All the UVM workers urged the villagers not to do this. Many discussions were held between villagers and local workers (which I heard about subsequently). When I discussed this event with several local UVM workers, their responses were similar: all were offended and angered by the villagers attempting to approach a second organization after having established a working arrangement with theirs.

I subsequently questioned many of the UVM people to ascertain what precisely was wrong with what the people of the village had done. None gave me a detailed explanation; all said in one form or another that it was simply wrong. The NGO workers, its social

Chapter 10 Perspectives on Decision Making and Hierarchy   193

workers, and its management all believed that the villagers of this community had violated an unwritten, unstated trust between them and the local NGO--a trust I interpret, based on this and many other events, as implying exclusivity and loyalty: By approaching a second organization the villagers were violating the implied exclusivity of their "contract" with the first organization.

These events became well known throughout the UVM operating area, and the outcome --the rejection of their request and the subsequent criticism of them by the local NGO workers--was frustrating to the villagers in which the event took place; they felt that they had completed their end of the bargain by building the road and check dams, and that they had been unfairly denied further capital assistance.

This event was also of interest to me because of the history that had preceded it. The villagers had defined and articulated their own development strategy. They had two immediate goals, water management and organizational support for a non-formal education center, which they stated unequivocally during their meetings with UVM workers. They wanted a teacher in their village for their children; they wanted slates, a lamp and kerosene, and a mat for the students and teacher to sit on. And, they said, they wanted their new well deepened.

UVM had been sympathetic to all these goals, but had asserted that none of these specific requests were consistent with the operating strategy of the organization. UVM workers held long discussions with the villagers about the local political administration, and how their demands should be put to the Sarpanche, as he was in a position to help them meet their own stated goals. The villagers had replied that the Sarpanche, based on past experience, would not be of any assistance to them. There was no resolution to this incident during 1990. Nevertheless there was continued dialogue between representatives of the organization and the villagers about the potential for arriving at a mutually agreeable development strategy.

Five years later this event would have had a different outcome. The local NGO landscape is now far more "consumer-driven" and the organizational participants have shifted their strategies, in part as a response to an increasing awareness level among local villagers of NGO dynamics and services. One long-time observer of the local development scene commented to me in 1995 that the villagers now select from "a menu" of NGOs and NGO services. She said that the villagers in and around Bagrunda know who to seek out for different types of NGO products: "If they want plantations they come to UVM; if they want anicut dams they go to Sewa Mandir; if they want to plant ginger they go to Bhatia."

Gavri: Bhil Dance Drama and the NGO

Gavri (alternate forms are *Gauri or Gouri)* is a religious dance-drama enactment that takes place over 40 days in August and September, in and around Bhil villages in Udaipur district. Gavri is performed by Bhil villagers and is a complicated and extensive cycle of intervillage performance and traveling during this period, unique to the Bhils of this district. It is clear from the few studies of gavri (see Chauhan 1963 and 1967; Weisgrau Forthcoming) that these performances express both Bhil identity and inter-group concepts of hierarchy and reciprocity. The symbolic vocabulary of the ritual is well known locally; although they are not clearly articulated by participants, the interactive patterns of gavri are ingrained on the social landscape. The performance of gavri is tied into a social and economic network among the Bhil villages; the hosting of gavri performance by an NGO is consistent with the traditional aspects of these performances that symbolically express the linkages between kin and affines, as well as obligations to traditional patrons.

The historic origins of this complex ritual cycle are obscure and difficult to place with certainty; it is generally believed that the Bhil gavri is linked with the Mewari festivals celebrated in Udaipur honoring the goddess Parvati, also known locally as Gouri, in the month of Vysakh in the Hindu calendar (April-May). According to Chauhan and Chelawat, these springtime festivals were taken up by rural Bhils, but were adapted to the labor demands of the planting cycle, and now correspond to the period after maize plants first appear in the fields, and harvest time (1966: 5).

Because of the large commitment of labor and village resources required, the actual performances are rotated among villages over a cycle of several years; when a village does make the commitment, however, it requires the participation of virtually all Bhil households as well as financial contributions from all households of all castes.

Consistent with local performance patterns, all roles in gavri are played by males; women are forbidden from participating except as members of the audience, although they play an important part in the ritual structures and preparations surrounding the performances. The roles of *Rai*, or female deities, are especially coveted; the right to play these and other parts is inherited through patrilineal descent. On some special occasions gavri characters may be portrayed by men who during the course of the previous year promised deities that if they recovered from illness they would offer themselves to play the female roles. Supporting and nonritual roles are open to any males from the village.

The decision for a village to perform the gavri cycle is communicated through the bhopas; the deity Parvati is invoked in a prayer session, and she herself speaks through the bhopa in trance, indicating whether or not the village should undertake the performance cycle. This decision has important financial ramifications for the entire village because of the significant expense involved, including the purchase of costumes and jewelry and the gathering of actors and musicians. A village will therefore undertake the performance only once every several years.

The social and economic features of the 40-day festival reinforce intra-village and inter-caste relationships; the actual performance sites fit into one of two general categories: Bhil villages where the performers are related through affines, and villages to which the performers are called to perform and in which the Bhils have economic relationships and obligations. The first category includes villages into which the daughters of the performing village have married and are now living; the households of the Bhil women host the gavri performers and provide them with both food and money. In the case of mixed-caste villages, the performance is held in recognition of the women of both the Bhil and other caste groups; here the performance is hosted by non-Bhil households into which women from the performers' village have married.

The gavri performance is also made for creditors and those with whom the Bhil villagers have "business" relationships; inevitably that business relationship is with their creditor and moneylender:

> When the Bhil of this area observes Gauri festival, they visit their Hajies village for a day and dance before his house. Every village of this Bhilwar area is connected with certain Hajies. They have permanent relations with them. It is claimed that their fore-fathers were connected with fore-fathers of those Baniyas...Some of the Bhil work as Halis (servants at the field of Baniyas). The Bhil...also take loans from their Hajies. [Chauhan and Chelawat 1966: 15]

McCurdy states that the Bhils of Ratakote "dance for the Rajputs and Mahajans of Nagar" for a full day (1964: 276). When I expressed to Udaipur Rajput and other upper-caste residents a desire to see gavri performances, I was told that this could be arranged by them "calling" to the city the Bhil performers of the villages to which their families had historic ties.

As is apparent from this brief description, gavri is a complex social and economic ritual system. The procession of villagers to other villages re-enacts not only a ritual story of deities, but also the movement of women from one village to another during the course of their lifetimes as well as the cycle of exchange and obligation established through marriage. Most significantly for the present context, the festival also re-enacts the social obligation and hierarchy inherent in the relationship between Bhils and other caste groups, particularly in their economic and social relationships with creditors and patrons of other classes and castes.

The hosting of a gavri performance in any setting symbolically expresses social hierarchy that is noted on some level by all participants. In a village, gavri is a celebration among jati cohorts-- Bhils visiting other Bhils. But even in this interaction of jati mates a subtle hierarchy and ongoing pattern of reciprocity and obligation exists. The wife givers in the traditional Hindu caste marriage system have a higher position and status than the wife takers. The villagers who perform for their daughters' affines are the wife givers; the wife takers are reciprocating the "gift" of the performance by giving food and money. And the performance establishes the necessity for a reciprocal performance, an obligation that will be fulfilled when the hosting village in subsequent years performs gavri themselves.

Structural hierarchy is even more apparent when the performance is for other caste groups; it reaches its pinnacle of inequality in the annual performance of gavri for creditors and patrons. The "obligation" of the performance by the Bhils for their patrons is never fulfilled; the performance must be repeated each year, much as a form of tribute is repeated over and over and does not fulfill the obligation, nor does equality ever become established between the two parties. It is the performance of the "tribute" that in fact perpetuates the inequality between the two groups, as does the gavri.

These structural implications of the performance of gavri in the rural local social setting are therefore also present when the relationship is between development organization and development beneficiary. The organizations perceive their hosting of these performances as the fostering and encouragement of local cultural traditions. From the perspective of Bhil performers and rural traditions, a performance hosted by an NGO in Udaipur has different implications, which, while not articulated, are implied by the different perspectives and histories of the participants.

The NGO as Dispenser of Goods

During the drought period of 1985-88 the NGOs distributed grain and animal fodder as part of the state's famine relief program. As noted earlier, this "legacy" of the NGO as donor of goods has been problematic in the evolution of the relationships between the organizations and their beneficiary communities. The organizations resist perpetuating this strategy of donations, as they believe it to be counterproductive to establishing local initiative and independence. But the acute needs of the community, particularly the needs of children in poor households, prompt occasional acts of donation.

Chapter 10 Perspectives on Decision Making and Hierarchy   197

Observing one such distribution, which was motivated by purely humanitarian intentions, illuminated some of the multiple interpretations of such activities, and the conflict that resulted. This event was unique, and it was the only time I observed any organization involved in the distribution of clothing, an activity that is not part of any organization's ongoing strategy. I note it here only as an illustration of the multiple perspectives within which events and NGO activities are interpreted.

On one of my regular trips to Bagrunda I accompanied the UVM workers who were traveling to the village, about 50 kilometers away, in a rented jeep. When I arrived at the office to meet the jeep I saw a huge pile of about 200 children's sweaters that had been donated to the organization by a relative of a senior member of the organization.

I asked more about the sweaters and was told by the UVM workers they were to be given away in the villages we were visiting, where several meetings and cultural programs were scheduled. I immediately anticipated conflict; I knew that Vina, who would be participating in the programs, was an outspoken critic of "giveaways" in the villages, and was philosophically opposed to hand-outs in any form. They serve, she had said in our numerous discussions, only to foster dependence and do nothing to create any sense of empowerment or independence within the community.

I pondered the situation on the hour-long ride out to the village. Here were hundreds of sweaters for children who undoubtedly needed them, as winters in Udaipur can be cool, particularly at night; village children usually wear shorts and short-sleeved cotton shirts and little else throughout the year.

It was the intention of the UVM worker organizing this event that the sweaters would be distributed only to children in regular attendance at the local school, a strategy he believed would encourage school attendance. This strategy presented more potential points of conflict; the children who attend school are a selected group. They are generally boys, and are from families that can afford to send them to school, in the sense that they have somehow managed to compensate for the lost labor of their children as workers in the fields or animal tenders. Very few girls regularly attended the village school, despite the continuous discussion of the importance of education for all children.

On our arrival a meal was prepared and the cultural program began. Eventually over one hundred people gathered. Women and men were seated separately in the audience as they participated in the songs, plays, puppet shows organized by the NGO. These all contained themes of political awareness, social dynamics, claiming political power, and gender relationships, as did the meetings throughout the following day.

The second afternoon the sweater distribution began. First, children from the government school were brought to the meeting area, which was at the temple, where all of the organization's meetings in the village take place. There were about thirty-five children in all brought from school--all boys. They were told to join their hands, and say *namaste* (respectful greetings) and were led in prayers and singing bajins (hymns) by the NGO worker organizing this event. Then each boy's name was called by the school teacher, and a sweater was handed to him by the village's oldest resident.

Children who were not in school gathered on the sidelines and watched quietly, as did their parents. The NGO worker who had orchestrated the event announced to the group that they would return at another time with more sweaters and give them to the children who were not in school.

The next day we went to Morwa; a much smaller group attended the meetings and cultural programs. Again, the school children were brought to the meeting area and the sweaters were distributed. But this time some of the children who didn't get them cried. One mother demanded a sweater for her daughter and was refused. In private conversations with some of the UVM workers later, they said they believed that the whole event had created more hostility than good will and doubted that it would be repeated.

Petitioning the Patron: NGOs and Me

In conversations with Bhil villagers about "the old days"--pre-Independence Udaipur--they talked about what they perceived to be one positive aspect of the local socio-political hierarchy: it was a system by which they could directly communicate with and personally petition the thakur, their local patron, and be heard. Even more importantly, the thakur would make an on-the-spot decision in response to the petition. If a petitioner waited long enough and patiently enough, sitting on the ground outside the patron's residence, he received the answer to his request.

Villagers, in conversations with me, contrasted this direct access and response with today's layered bureaucracies and indifferent bureaucrats who are either unable or unwilling to act with any speed or decisiveness on individual requests. From the local perspective, the post-Independence government replaced a far more efficient and responsive system of direct petition. At least, they said, you knew where you stood in the old days; today you are far less able to deal with the new bureaucracy, where no direct response can be elicited, and action and decision-making are replaced with forms and paperwork (which they cannot read or understand).

Chapter 10 Perspectives on Decision Making and Hierarchy

It was difficult to escape these parallels with the past when observing the occasional interactions of NGO management-level staff and "petitioners" who come to the Udaipur offices. Often I would see villagers sitting patiently on the floor outside the offices of the decision-makers. Once inside, most villagers would sit on the floor and speak to the person seated on the chair behind the desk. The petitioner would make his request in a soft voice, and whatever reply was given would express no direct response and leave quietly.

Whatever the result, going to the NGO office was far preferable to attempting to find the right government office in the city and then locating a sympathetic bureaucrat within it. Even if one succeeded in finding the right person to speak with, the response may be unintelligible. It might be given in Mewari, but it would be in bureaucratic Mewari "governmentese," alluding to an array of acronyms, programs, and departments--a "language" not comprehensible to rural Bhils.

It did not take long before I became associated personally with this process, and began to be approached by individuals (usually women) for help in obtaining supplies or medicines. The extent to which I became associated in some eyes as part of the NGO community became apparent to me on one occasion when Bhatia came to Bagrunda on a monthly visit. As was our practice, when we were both in Bagrunda at the same time, we would meet and talk together in the UVM field office. During one such meeting, a group of men and women from the village gathered in the courtyard and on the steps leading up to the room where we sat, waiting to speak to him, individually or in small groups, with requests for aid or advice.

Simultaneously some women gathered whom I knew, and in a similar manner began approaching me with a respectful greeting and quiet requests. Bhatia observed this, and speaking to me in English as he usually did, said, "So you have your own clients here now?" I asked him what he meant by that, and he replied with references to the "old days" and how the pattern of petition to the thakurs was being reenacted by both of us in the NGO office. When I asked him his explanation of this, he replied, "We come here regularly. Compared with them, they know how much we have. They have to come to us and ask. Where else will they go? At least we keep coming back. And we listen. Who else does?"

When the Patronage Model Doesn't Apply

The suggestion that NGO beneficiaries conceptualize the NGOs as replacement patrons, and behave accordingly, does not apply in all circumstances or interactions. Some people in the Scheduled Caste communities living within the city of Udaipur seem to have a very different relationship with the NGO people with whom they work.

I observed several women's groups organized by Sewa Mandir within the *Harijan Basti* or SC neighborhood, in the city of Udaipur, and had extensive opportunity to discuss these programs with Sewa Mandir's director of women's programs. A highly experienced social worker and administrator, she has traveled abroad frequently and was able to draw some comparisons between social work in Rajasthan and in the United States. She said that the women in the Harijan Basti were far more aware of their legal rights, and far more likely to demand them, than were the rural ST or SC women, and she added that in this respect they were comparable to better-educated American minority women. Political organization, awareness, and literacy among those who participate in NGO activities in the city are also much higher than in the rural communities.

I found her observation to be accurate; some of the women I met through Sewa Mandir's programs in Udaipur were far more outgoing and comfortable with me than were the rural women in the programs of this or any other organization. Perhaps this is due in part to their experiences with the constant stream of foreign visitors to this organization; these visitors, who rarely have the time for an overnight trip to the rural areas, seem to always make time for an auto-rickshaw (motorized three-wheeler) ride across town to see a women's nonformal education program or sewing center.

In one instance the outgoing nature of two of the SC women with whom I was acquainted took on confrontational, albeit comic, overtones. I had met them on several occasions during my visits to their centers to observe Sewa Mandir's programs, before encountering them later at a *mela* (gathering) for International Women's Day, sponsored by Sewa Mandir and attended by over 200 women and several representatives of different Udaipur district NGOs.

When I arrived at this mela these two women greeted me loudly and for the next two days they seemed to follow me wherever I went, commenting to me and anyone else within range about my strange behavior. On one of the mornings of the two-day session when I attempted to slip off unnoticed to take care of bodily functions, I spotted them up on a hill staring down at me, observing and commenting on every step of my morning ablutions. My "secret" use of toilet paper, contrary to local practice of wiping oneself clean with a small amount of water, and subsequent efforts to bury it unnoticed, brought howls of scorn and derision from these two observers from their strategic position. They later commented to one of my social worker friends that I must be truly crazy to do what they had observed, which struck them as an abhorrent act with polluting and ritual implications.

Later that evening, after the formal presentations and discussions, a spirited dance began, with the assembled women dancing joyously in circles, banging sticks, and having a wonderful time, myself included. Off to the side I spotted my two friends, who approached me and pulled me out of the circle, telling me that I was dancing incorrectly. Somewhat chastised, I sat down on the side, joining in with other women who were clapping in time to the rhythmic drumbeats. My two friends appeared again, told me that I was clapping incorrectly, and showed me how to clap in the proper way. I could not help laughing at their escalating levels of instruction, but in retrospect I realized that it was also the only time during my entire field stay that I was directly confronted and told in no uncertain terms that I was doing something incorrectly or erroneously, especially in front of others. No Bhil woman even spoke to me directly until I had been in the field for over two months. Nor did any observe my behavior so closely, let alone comment on it or criticize it in such a public manner.

"Sisterhood is Powerful"--until Teatime

In the summer of 1988 while conducting preliminary field research in Rajasthan, I attended a meeting (previously described from another perspective in Chapter 4) that was held in the western section of the state and focused around gender-specific issue identification and consciousness-raising. Designed for women villagers, the meeting was organized by and led by city-based, college-educated social workers, many of whom were fluent in English as well as Hindi and the local dialect.

About 50 village women attended, and after almost three hours of discussion, speech making, singing, and dancing the meeting broke for tea. I left the large meeting room and went out onto the long verandah around the building with one of the social workers who was a close friend of the other American anthropologist present, with whom I was traveling at the time. We--social workers, meeting organizers, and visitors--sat on mats on the verandah and the village women scattered in small groups off the verandah, sitting on the bare ground. Our group formed a circle, drank tea and engaged in intense discussion among ourselves. The few village women who approached this closed circle did so tentatively and shyly. None of the social workers or organizers engaged them in informal discussion, and the closed circle stayed seated on the verandah, facing inward and talking exclusively to each other until the next session began.

I repeatedly observed this general pattern whenever large meetings and gatherings of village and NGO women took place over several days and nights. The content of the meetings was controlled by and administered by the social workers. During breaks and meals there were varying degrees of interaction, but overnight sleeping arrangements invariably expressed a spatial segregation--with meeting organizers having their own better- furnished and better-supplied spaces in which to congregate and sleep.

This narrative encapsulates the difficulties of breaking down social barriers, even when the intentions and commitments to social change are at their highest. These particular events and their implications become even more problematical when viewed as a development strategy from the perspective of feminist ideology, placed within the framework of a social hierarchical society.

During my fieldwork, I discussed these events, and my observations of them, with several NGO directors and workers. One remarked that the government seems to be supporting programs with a feminist ideology as a way of diverting attention from the more explosive issues of caste-based and class-based exploitation. From the perspective of the social and political establishment, this person observed, organizing women around a feminist rhetoric gives them a rallying point that, politically, does not challenge the power of the state and is thought to be "safe" without directly confronting more potentially explosive issues of caste, class and religious exploitation. Although I cannot assert with any confidence that this is the intention, either overt or unconscious, of government strategy, some of my observations of state-supported women's programs bear out the observation that gender-specific rhetoric may obscure other aspects of social exploitation.

Chapter Summary

Random unrelated events and circumstances served to reinforce and provide evidence for the hypothesis that I formed early on during fieldwork: that the NGOs are acting as replacement patrons. The territoriality of the organizations echoed the descriptions of jajmani-based historically informed social relationships. The alleged breach of this relationship on the part of villagers who sought out another source of patronage was, it seemed to me, so basic to the social fabric of the community that few participants were actually able to articulate what exactly was wrong with the villagers' actions. People with whom I discussed this incident generally expressed the same view as one social worker who said, "They just should not have done it," without providing further explanation. These norms, however, like any other ideas, are changeable and changing. Increasing competition among NGOs has resulted in a more client-oriented, demand-driven strategy; villagers are now selecting, both individually and in groups, from among NGO sources, for advice and counsel on specific services. But embedded within the organizational structures and strategies are aspects of hierarchy and patronage relationships that are reinforced by the symbols of ritual behavior, and the multiple, often conflicting, interpretations of intentions and cultural norms.

Chapter 11

Some Conclusions

This book analyzes the relatively recent phenomenon of a new structural entity--the nongovernmental development organization--operating as a new patron in the rural village. What has happened to the "old" patrons? Why has their position been replaced by these new groups? Since Independence and the incorporation of the erstwhile princely states into Rajasthan and the nation of India, the Maharanas have been stripped of some of their land holdings and some of their assets. The local thakurs have likewise lost much of their lands because of a number of factors, including land reform policies designed to break up hereditary estates, the escalating costs of maintaining their pre-Independence economic and social lifestyles, and the increasing profitability potential of industrial or other entrepreneurial activities (especially tourist related) rather than agriculture. Based on some family histories and anecdotal evidence, it appears that in some families alcoholism and gambling have also contributed to loss of land and other resources that might have enabled them to act as influence-brokers in the new state setting.

The Maharanas have retained some significant real estate holdings in the city of Udaipur--particularly the two former palaces that are now luxurious five-star hotels. They and their family members also hold considerable sway over the political arena, and are important figures of influence there. Nevertheless, the local Rajput thakur families have lost most of their influence and assets; in the rural countryside, while the Rajputs retain their social status, their ability to dispense and control economic resources there has greatly diminished. And the state has not replaced the Rajputs as a powerful, reliable, or consistent source of linkage or benefits to the rural poor. The vacuum of services and resources has been filled by the NGOs. They have a continuous

Chapter 11 Some Conclusions

presence in the countryside, a growing infrastructure of staff, offices, and networks, and a clearly asserted commitment of presence and service to the rural poor. They have access to financial resources and political influence, and can theoretically serve as the link between rural communities and state services.

Other forces, however, influence the potential stability and effectiveness of this relationship between NGOs and the rural poor. As illustrated here, the NGO relationship with the state government is rife with pitfalls and potential conflict. Political change in the central government may eventually impact on local NGOs; the growing influence of conservative Hindu political parties may affect the relationship between the government and NGOs--particularly those with links to overseas funding organizations.

As has also been demonstrated, NGOs are by nature volatile and changeable. They are generally small in size, formed and led by a highly visible organizer, and are often staffed by a small group of people with an extremely strong commitment to self-sacrifice and dedication to living under very difficult conditions. Recruitment of like-minded people into this community of workers is very difficult. Most college and university graduates who enter the field are pursuing upwardly mobile careers, which the NGO sector often does not provide. Those who are interested in running their own organizations often spin off from larger, better established organizations, creating a fragmented, decentralized situation in which development benefits are dispensed very locally, without a unified philosophy or policy approach.

From the perspective of the Bhils and other NGO participants, the continued long-term reliance on these new patrons for economic and social support does not represent a sound development strategy in terms of their future voice in the economic and political spheres. For the present, however, until literacy and economic stability can be achieved, this survival strategy of dependence-based relationships remains a viable alternative as a route towards the goal of economic stability and a fuller political voice. These are development goals shared by both the NGOs and the rural poor. Although actualizing these goals has proven to be far more difficult than was originally envisioned in the post-Independence period throughout India generally and in Rajasthan in particular, political participation and a community-wide quest for literacy will no doubt aid in this process.

The economic future of marginal agriculturalists in drought-prone areas is questionable. For the rural poor of the district, small plots of land, which are becoming increasingly depleted by erosion and deforestation-related ecological degradation, are often their only productive assets. Despite laws designed to prevent the alienation of land from Adivasis by barring sale to other caste groups, transfer of property is eroding the resource base of the Bhils. A study conducted by the Tribal Research Institute in Udaipur concluded that in three villages in Banswara district, half of the land owned by Adivasis there had subsequently changed hands (Gupta 1977).

One possible solution to the economic constraints of the Bhils is to increase the value of their agricultural production by planting commodity crops like ginger, or multiuse crops like sugar cane, which can be converted into a variety of products with low capital requirements and high cash value; the introduction of sericulture (silkworm) technology may also represent potential income-generating possibilities for rural households.

These enterprises are not, however, risk-free. They increase dependence on and linkages with national and global economic demand. Replacement products that are produced more cheaply or more effectively in other parts of India closer to the city, or in other countries around the world, may dramatically impact on local prices. At present, illiteracy and other social factors place Bhil and other rural agriculturalists at a distinct disadvantage when they attempt to negotiate for terms and conditions. Despite these potential pitfalls, some NGOs and development workers regard increased household income through income-generating programs as a critical component in the economic and social development of this area.

Not all NGOs concur with this strategy. While the NGO sector in the area generally shares the goals of environmental protection and literacy, the various organizations are not all fully committed to pursuing a program of income-generation as an immediate priority. Poor, marginalized agriculturalists cannot undertake income-generating programs entirely on their own. They need some linkages--either through an individual or an organization--that will provide them with the necessary capital and training as well as expediting connections to the markets. Pursuing this strategy through multiple sources, including multiple NGOs, may put local villagers into conflict with these organizations. The necessity to forge alliances with patrons may also create conflict with followers or beneficiaries of other patrons, beneficiaries who are also invariably affines or cousins.

Even when the NGO workers and beneficiary groups are from the same geographic location, local development work invariably creates many different forms of cultural conflict. Despite the fact that many of the villagers and the social workers from "outside" share the same language, and in many cases were from the same district, they represent groups with different cultural norms and interpretations, interacting closely with one other. The educated, urbanized development worker brings his or her own social, political, economic, and organizational agenda to the interaction, as does the rural villager.

Neither of these two groups is entirely homogeneous. Different experiences, education levels and areas of origin are just some of the variables among members of both groups. Further, men and women of both groups bring entirely different perspectives to this complicated arena. And differences in language use often reinforce the existing social barriers in a rural village; most village women speak only Mewari and are therefore excluded from active public participation because of this and other social constraints.

A local villager who, by virtue of being hired by an organization, takes on many of the characteristics of the NGO "culture." The consequent changes in behavior, status, and income invariably influence subsequent social and political dynamics of the community, and introduce a form of individual mobility not always valued by either the NGO or local community members.

Such a male NGO worker has the possibility of emerging as a local leader of sorts, obtaining this status and position by virtue of association with the NGO. Although all of the NGOs in the area addressed the problems of women with various gender-specific programs, far fewer women than men were hired and paid wages by the NGOs to represent the organizations on the village level. An attempt to organize women and train them in various aspects of social and educational change is invariably undertaken, but women "leaders" were not always paid workers, and their status generally is not elevated by their association with NGOs. While women were urged to participate in organizing volunteer groups to address the social problems of women and children in the community, these types of activities did not lead the women to positions of power equal with males in the community. In addition, traditional patterns of behavior, particularly the public behavior of women in the company of men, still present a critical obstacle that restricts the public activities of rural women.

The interaction between the NGO and local villagers involves many instances of misunderstanding or unexpressed assumptions on the part of each, and requires a continuous process of negotiation and renegotiation. Only rarely do the two reach consensus on major theoretical issues and approaches. NGO presence in a village is therefore a creative and dynamic factor in alliance formation; often, conflict over an NGO issue emerges along the factional patterns of other types of disputes, including existing family-based feuds and property disputes of long standing.

At this time, the NGO sector serves critical village-level functions, but by its very nature of fragmentation and alliance-generation, has not fostered broad-based alliances among the rural poor. Although the rhetoric of alliance, based on shared poverty and low status, is present, the structural relationships of the NGOs with their beneficiary communities represent impediments to significant class-based unification or action. Regional alliance formation, spanning across villages, continues to be articulated through jati categories; the

Meghwal and Bhil social reform movements described previously are two such examples, that strengthen jati identity and mobilization.

What Can NGOs Accomplish?

Theoretically at least, the most successful outcome of NGO-based community mobilization and self-action would be the eventual obsolescence of their own services and presence in rural villages. Members of some of the NGOs with whom I spoke expressed the view that in theory they should be planning for their departure from these communities. But in practice, this long-term goal becomes a secondary one, replaced at least for the moment by organizational continuity.

In the areas of literacy and social reform, measuring the results of NGO activities is very difficult. There is no question that exposure to the concept of literacy and its importance, particularly to children, is becoming part of the local consciousness. Adults and children throughout the area talk about it, desire it, and despite social constraints will, I believe, eventually actualize their demands for literacy.

NGOs cannot work in a total vacuum, for literacy or any other form of social development. Without the support of the state and national governments, they cannot bring about dramatic and widespread change. For example, without the infrastructural support of schools, schoolteachers and continuity of educational programs, local literacy programs will flounder.

Local NGOs, almost by their nature, practice an intensive form of development, intensive in terms of the "person hours" expended. The number of people they reach is limited by their small staffs and difficult living conditions. The commitment on the part of the organization and its workers to concentrate time and effort at the village level requires long-term work in each and every community.

The effect NGOs have on individuals in these communities is considerable. One only had to observe the flurry of activity and excitement around election time, due in part to the training sessions sponsored by the local NGOs. Both men and women experienced the power of knowledge and political participation, many for the first time; their enthusiasm and optimism was palpable, and contagious. Their commitment to fighting for their own betterment is especially vivid when one sees them--adults and children--struggle by candlelight over barely visible multiplication tables and alphabet letters, late into the night at informal educational centers.

Women standing up in a group and saying their own names for the first time; fighting back against domestic abuse and demanding their right to participate equally in ritual events--these are small steps that provide evidence that social change is taking place, nurtured and supported by the NGO infrastructure. Yet these organizations are themselves fragile; they are small, and are subject to internal strife and conflict. Recruitment of new personnel who share the driving commitment and often dangerous, always difficult, living conditions that are part of sustaining ongoing programs in rural communities also presents a continuous challenge.

On the national scale, government support of NGOs is subject to the vagaries of political agenda. As was demonstrated with the inquiry convened under the comparatively liberal and secular Congress (I) government of Indira Gandhi, the national government can exert its pressure on NGOs at any moment. The more conservative BJP, in addition to stating its position on rural literacy programs, has expressed negative opinions about externally funded development programs. "Many of the party's leaders believe that India is being recolonized by the World Bank and the International Monetary Fund, agencies that are trying to assist India in restructuring its crippled economy" (*New York Times* January 24, 1993). This nationalistic rhetoric has been interpreted by some in the local NGO community as potentially threatening their overseas sources of funding.

The deeply committed individuals who work in the smaller organizations formed around specific rural communities such as UVM, have demonstrated that change can take place in the quality of the lives of individuals affected by their presence. Household income can increase with training and access to capital inputs. Political participation will grow with awareness and understanding. Literacy can be achieved with effort and commitment on the part of the teacher and learner. But despite the efforts and intentions of these smaller organizations, long-term continuity backed up by an intergenerational presence is difficult to maintain when an organizational strategy and development initiative is dependent upon one or two individuals. Their own life circumstances or personal priorities may change over the years, threatening the delivery of ongoing and consistent programs to a community that depends on those programs.

A larger organization like Sewa Mandir brings additional resources and institutional stability to bear in this local process. Its programs illustrate the potential of an organization with a large geographical reach as well as the advantages of a long-term community commitment supported by an equally long-term donor commitment. The ability to recruit professionals from other parts of the country and to attract volunteers and interns from around the world creates a highly cosmopolitan, as well as professionalized, development environment that impacts on its local programs. This is particularly apparent in the organization's ability not only to execute programs throughout the district, but to devote an increasingly significant amount of time and effort to research and analysis that candidly and critically assess the effectiveness of those programs.

I believe it is appropriate at the closing of this book to reassert a statement made at the beginning of Chapter One: the story of the NGO sector and its activities in rural communities in Udaipur district is an evolutionary history that is ongoing and multifaceted. There is no frozen moment in time that encapsulates this history, nor can it be reduced to development paradigms or theoretical perspective. It is a textured and complex human arena within which all the participants, despite their differences in strategy and interpretation, are grappling with the same goals: to understand, define, and ultimately, change conditions around them.

Appendices and Tables

Figure 4

Ford Foundation Delhi Office Grants and Projects by Type of Organization and Programs
(Four Sample Years)

Year	Central or state govt. ministries or programs	Semi-autonomous govt. institutions and programs	Universities research, mgt. institutions	Non-governmental private agencies, and programs
1960	81.5%	4.6%	13.2%	0.7%
1970	16.1%	22.2%	46.1%	15.6%
1980	21.6%	7.3%	21.5%	49.6%
1990	15.8%	1.1%	40.8%	42.3%

Source: Staples 1992: 79

Appendix 1

List of Scheduled Tribes--Rajasthan

1. Bhil, Bhil Garasia, Dholi Bhil, Dungri Bhil, Dungri Garasia, Mewasi Bhil, Rawal Bhil, Tadvi Bhil, Bhilalia, Bhalalia, Pawra, Varsava, Vasave.
2. Bhil Mina
3. Damor, Damaria
4. Dhanka, Tadvi, Tetaria, Valvi
5. Garasia (excluding Rajput Garasia)
6. Kathodi, Katkari, Dhor Kathodi, Dhor Katkari, Son Kathodi
7. Kokna, Kokni, Kukna
8. Koli Dhor, Tokre Koli, Kolcha, Kolgha
9. Mina
10. Naika, Nayaka, Chgolivala Nayaka, Kapadia Nayaka, Mota, Nayaka, Nana Nayaka
11. Patelia
12. Seharia, Saharia

Source: ICI 1988: 3.

Appendix 2: Population Tables

Table 1
Population 1991

Rajasthan		% of Total	% Growth 1981/1991	India	% of Total	% Growth 1981/91
Total	43,880,640	100.00%	28.07%	844,324,222	100.00%	23.56%
Rural	33,840,522	77.12%	25.10%	627,146,597	74.28%	19.71%
Urban	10,040,118	22.88%	39.24%	217,177,625	25.72%	36.19%

Table 2
Rajasthan Population by Residence and Sex 1991

	Persons	Male	Female	Rajasthan Sex Ratio (Females/ 1,000 Males)	India Sex Ratio (Females/ 1,000 Males)
Total	43,880,640	22,935,895	20,944,745	913	929
Rural	33,840,522	17,599,080	16,241,442	923	941
Urban	10,040,118	5,336,815	4,703,303	881	893

Source: ICI 1991:ix

Interpreting Development: Local Histories, Local Strategies

Table 3
Udaipur District Population by Residence and Sex 1991

Total	2,885,039	1,467,161	1,467,878
Rural	2,391,974	1,206,467	1,185,507
Urban	493,065	260,694	232,372

Gogunda Tehsil Population by Residence and Sex 1991

Total	122,502	61,996	60,506
Rural	122,502	61,996	60,506
Urban	---	---	---

Table 4
All-India Literacy by Residence and Sex 1991

	Literate Persons	Literacy Rate*	Literate Males	Male Literacy Rate*	Literate Females	Female Literacy Rate*
India:						
Total	362,174,360	52.11%	230,406,841	63.86%	131,767,519	39.42%
Rural	228,009,191		151,594,125		76,415,066	
Urban	134,165,169		78,812,716		55,352,453	

*Estimated and provisional figures

Appendices and Tables

Table 5
Rajasthan Literacy 1991

	Literate Persons	Literacy Rate*	Literate Males	Male Literacy Rate*	Literate Females	Female Literacy Rate*
Rajasthan:		38.81%		55.07%		20.84%
Total	13,618,272		10,143,275		3,474,997	
Rural	8,189,562		6,689,540		1,500,022	
Urban	5,428,710		5,428,710		1,974,975	
Udaipur District:		n.a.				
Total	806,862		589,969		216,893	
Rural	500,253		400,788		99,465	
Urban	306,609		189,181		117,428	
Gogunda Tehsil:		n.a.				
Total	23,034		18,679		4,355	
Rural	23,034		18,679		4,355	
Urban	---		---		---	

Source: ICI 1991: 32

Interpreting Development: Local Histories, Local Strategies

Table 6
Literacy Rate in Rajasthan in 1981

	Rajasthan Literacy Rate %	Udaipur District Literacy Rate %	Gogunda Tehsil Literacy Rate %
I. Total			
(a) Persons	24.05	22.01	15.17
(b) Males	35.82	33.02	25.54
(c) Females	11.31	10.76	4.69
II. Rural			
(a) Persons	17.71	15.79	15.17
(b) Males	29.24	26.31	25.54
(c) Females	5.41	5.21	4.69
III. Urban			
(a) Persons	47.92	57.11	–
(b) Males	60.02	68.74	–
(c) Females	34.24	43.97	–

Source: ICI 1983a: lxvii.

Table 7
Scheduled Tribe Population, Udaipur District 1981

Rural/urban	Males	Females	Total	% of Total
All Scheduled Tribes				
Rural	397,618	395,304	792,922	
Urban	9,016	7,213	16,234	
Total		809,156	100.00	
Bhil, Bhil Garasia, Dholi Bhil				
Rural	192,602	189,166	381,768	
Urban	5,707	5,234	10,941	
Total			392,709	48.53
Garasia				
Rural	19,336	18,921	38,257	
Urban	52	16	68	
Total			38,325	4.73
Mina				
Rural	182,273	183,757	366,030	
Urban	2,845	1,644	4,489	
Total			370,519	45.79

Source: ICI 1988: 1078.

Table 8
Educational Level of All Scheduled Tribes in Rural Areas--Udaipur District 1981

Educational Level	Number of Persons	
	Male	Female
1. Literate, without educational level indicated, non-formal	1,370	130
2. Literate, without educational level indicated, formal	23,060	1,387
3. Educational level: Primary	13,148	629
4. Educational level: Middle	3,873	179
5. Educational level: Matriculation/Secondary	889	46
6. Higher secondary/intermediate/pre-university	462	32
7. Non-technical diploma or certificate not equal to degree	6	--
8. Technical diploma or certificate not equal to degree	6	--
9. Graduate and above	156	10

Source: ICI 1988: 1078-9.

Table 9
Literacy Level of All Scheduled Tribes in Rural Areas--Udaipur District 1981.

All Scheduled	Total Population		Illiterate	
Tribes--Total	Male	Female	Male	Female
792,922	397,618	395,304	354,649	392,892
100%	50.15%	49.85%	89.1%	99.39%

Source: ICI 1988:1078-9.

Appendix 3

Scheduled Tribe Mukhi/Patel's Meeting
Tribal (Bhil-Gameti) Rules for Social Reform:

For the past many months the tribal people of Jhadol region have been discussing among themselves the problems and rituals dominant in their society and about common rules and regulations for all. From the 24 panchayats 9 panchayat Mukhis-Patels [headmen] organised a meeting in which about 70 Mukhiyas, Patels, wardpanch and 30 other socially aware persons from 60 villages participated. This meeting was conducted to decide upon the areas to be undertaken for social reform or change and to form new social rules and regulations. After two days of deep and serious discussions they unitedly decided upon the following rules and regulations and everyone present took an oath to follow them. It was also decided that everyone at this level will communicate these results to people in all villages.

The rules formed:

a. Rules regarding marriage
  1. It was decided that the boy's parents will not give more than Rs. 701 to the girls' parents out of which Mukhiyas expenditure will be 30 Rs. In engagement and marriage ceremonies use of beef is prohibited. Use of only 2 quintal food stuff has been agreed upon.
  2. [It was agreed that] the bride will receive at most 50 gms. of silver jewelry.
  3. When the bridegroom's party (barat) reaches the bride's house at that time killing of goats is prohibited. Instead [the bride's villagers] can prepare a maximum of 20 kgs. sweet wheat porridge (prepared without milk).
  4. A widow can remarry or can go to live with someone if she wishes and for that the expenditure should not be more than Rs. 200; jaggery [concentrated sugar cane] should be distributed.
  5. If someone takes a married woman to live with him he will pay Rs. 500 fine and he will also be an outcaste.
  6. If a wife has no children then her husband can remarry, but in such a case the woman has to be first checked by a doctor [to verify that she is incapable of bearing children].
  7. It is compulsory to marry within 3 months of engagement.
  8. After engagement if the boy refuses to marry then he will have to pay a fine of Rs. 700; if the girl refuses she will have to pay a fine of Rs. 1,500.

9. In marriage and engagement ceremonies use of liquor should be stopped. Instead, jaggery should be distributed.

10. If the parents get their daughter married to an already-married man they will have to pay a fine of Rs. 501 and also bring back their daughter.

b. Rules regarding the funeral feast:

1. The turban will be given only to the eldest son, and from that day on he will be the family head and representative. The eldest son in law will bring jaggery for distribution.

2. Use of beef and liquor is strictly prohibited.

c. Penalty:

1. If a woman (wife) is murdered by forcing her to commit suicide the murderer will have to pay a Rs. 5,000 penalty.

2. No one will give their daughter in marriage to the murderer.

d. Animosity:

1. If a person kills any man or woman then he will have to pay Rs. 20,000 as punishment. He will not harass any villagers because of this.

2. Killing, beating and looting of villagers, panchayat people and brothers of the murderer is forbidden.

3. If the murderer disappears or does not pay the punishment fine then the fine will be taken from his property.

e. Songs

1. During marriages, fairs, festivals, singing vulgar, unseemly songs is prohibited.

2. Everyone together will strictly stop this.

f. Robbery

1. On robbing any item the robber will have to pay six times the original price of the item as fine.

g. Others

1. Butchering of male buffalo as offering is not permitted. If one does so he will have to pay Rs. 501 as fine.

2. On molestation of women the person will have to pay Rs. 1,000 as fine.

3. A fine of Rs. 1.26 will be made against scoundrels and urchins.

4. Giving of daughters in marriage out of the caste in exchange for money is banned.

5. The poor and helpless will be aided by society.

Decisions to be followed henceforth:

1. In any type of problem it will be only the people of the community who will take decisions and enforce them.

2. In settlement of small disputes the Panch will be paid Rs. 200 as fee and on large disputes Rs. 500.

At the conclusion of the meetings all the Panchs promised each other that they will follow the above rules and will propagate them. At the end of the meeting it was also decided that after a few days a meeting will be called in which tribal people from Gujarat, Sirohi and Udaipur will decided upon common rules and regulations.

References

Annis, Sheldon. 1988. Can Small-Scale Development Be Large-Scale Policy? *In* Direct to the Poor: Grassroots Development in Latin America, edited by Sheldon Annis and Peter Hakim, pp. 209-218. Boulder: Lynn Rienner Publishers.

Attwood, D. W. 1974. Patrons and Mobilizers: Political Entrepreneurs in an Agrarian State. Journal of Anthropological Research. 30(4): 225-241.

Baden-Powell, B. H. 1957(1896). The Indian Village Community. New Haven: Human Relations Area Files.

Berreman, Gerald D. 1993. Sanskritization as Female Oppression in India. *In* Sex and Gender Hierarchies, edited by Barbara Diane Miller, pp. 366-392. Cambridge: Cambridge University Press.

Beteille, Andre. 1965. Caste, Class and Power: Changing Patterns of Stratification in a Tanjore Village. Berkeley: University of California Press.

———. 1987. Essays in Comparative Sociology. New Delhi: Oxford University Press.

Billig, Michael S. 1991. The Marriage Squeeze on High-Caste Rajasthani Women. The Journal of Asian Studies 50(2): 341-360.

Boserup, Ester. 1970. Woman's Role in Economic Development. New York: St. Martin's Press.

Bremen, Jan. 1974. Patronage and Exploitation: Changing Agrarian Relations in South Gujarat, India. Berkeley: University of California Press.

———. 1989. The Disintegration of the *Hali* System. *In* Sociology of "Developing Societies" of South Asia, edited by Hamza Alavi and John Harriss, pp. 149-159. New York: Monthly Review Press.

Bumiller, Elisabeth. 1990. May You Be The Mother of A Hundred Sons. New York: Fawcett Columbine.

Campaign for People's Action and Rural Technology (CAPART). 1986. CAPART and Voluntary Organizations, Guidelines. New Delhi: CAPART.

Carmen, Raff. 1996. Autonomous Development: Humanizing the Landscape. London: Zed Books.

Carstairs, Morris. 1954. The Bhils of Kotra Bhomat. The Eastern Anthropologist VII(3&4): 169-181.
_____. 1960. Bhil Villages of Udaipur. *In* India's Villages, edited by M. N. Srinivas, pp. 68-76. Bombay: Asia Publishing House.
_____. 1961. The Twice-Born: A Study of a community of High-Caste Hindus. Bloomington: Indiana University Press.
_____. 1983. Death of a Witch: A Village in North India 1950-1981. London: Hutchinson Co.
Cernea, Michael. 1988. Nongovernmental Organizations and Local Development. Washington, D.C.: The World Bank.
Chauhan, B. R. 1963. Gauri--A Bhil Festival. Bulletin of the Tribal Research Institute Chindwara. 3(2): 30-37.
_____. 1967. A Rajasthani Village. New Delhi: Vir Publishing House.
Chauhan, B. R. and D. S. Chelawat. 1966. Bhil Gauri. Tribe vol. 3: 5-25.
Chowdhary, A. N. 1989. Let Grassroots Speak: People's Participation, Self-Help Groups, and NGOs in Bangladesh. Dhaka: University Press Limited.
Coyer, Brian W. 1975. the Political Distribution of Public Policy Goods in Rural India: Rajasthan, 1961-1971. Ph.D. dissertation, Political Science Department, Michigan State University.
Crooke, William. 1920. Introduction to Annals and Antiquities of Rajasthan by James Tod. London: Oxford University Press.
Deegan, Chris. 1990. Village Study on Water Use and Perceptions, and Statistical Profile on Treated/Reported Guineaworm Patients and Villages. UNICEF: Udaipur, Rajasthan.
deKadt, Emanuel. 1976. Tourism--Passport to Development? Oxford: Oxford University Press.
Deliege, Robert. 1985. the Bhils of Western India: Some Empirical and Theoretical Issues in Anthropology in India. New Delhi: National Publishing House.
Doshi, J. K. 1969. Social Structure and Cultural Change in a Bhil Village. New Delhi: New Heights Publishers.
Doshi, S. L. 1971. Bhils: Between Societal Self-Awareness and Cultural Synthesis. New Delhi: Sterling Publishers.
Dubey, Suman. 1992. The Middle Class. *In* India Briefing, 1992, edited by Leonard A. Gordon and Philip Oldenburg, pp. 137-164. Boulder, Colorado: Westview Press.
Economic and Political Weekly. June 1-8, 1991. "The Story of Hadmatiya: Adivasi Struggles in South Rajasthan."
Elder, Joseph. 1970. Ranjpur: Change in the Jajmani System of an Uttar Pradesh Village. *In* Change and Continuity in India's Villages, edited by K. Ishwaran, pp. 102-127. New York: Columbia University Press.
Enthoven, R. E. 1920. The Tribes and Castes of Bombay. New Delhi: Cosmo Publications.
Erskine, K. D. 1908. Rajputana Gazetteers. Volume II-A The Mewar Residency. Ajmer: Scottish Mission Industries Co. Inc.

Escobar, Arturo. 1991. Anthropology and the Development Encounter: The Making and Marketing of Development Anthropology. American Ethnologist 18(4): 16-40.

_____. 1995. Encountering Development: The Making and Unmaking of the Third World. Princeton: Princeton University Press.

Fernandes, Walter and Geeta Menon. 1987. Tribal Women and Forest Economy: Deforestation, Exploitation, and Status Change. New Delhi: Indian Social Institute.

Fernandes, Walter, Geeta Menon and Philip Viegas. 1988. Forests, Environment and Tribal Economy: Deforestation, Impoverishment and Marginalisation in Orissa. New Delhi: Indian Social Institute.

Fisher, William F. 1995. Development and Resistance. In Toward Sustainable Development?: Struggling Over India's Narmada River, edited by William F. Fisher, pp. 3-46. Armonk, N.Y.: M. E. Sharpe.

Franda, Marcus. 1983. Voluntary Associations and Local Development in India: The Janata Phase. New Delhi: Young Asia Publications.

Fried, Morton H. 1966. On the Concept of "Tribe" and "Tribal Society." Transactions of The New York Academy of Sciences Series II 29(4): 527-540.

Fuchs, Stephen. 1965. Rebellious Prophets: A Study of Messianic Movements in Indian Religion. Bombay: Asia Publishing House.

_____. 1973. The Aboriginal Tribes of India. New Delhi: McMillan India.

Fuller, C. J. 1989. Misconceiving the Grain Heap: A Critique of the Indian Jajmani System. In Money and the Morality of Exchange, edited by J. Parry and M. Bloch, pp. 33-63. Cambridge: Cambridge University Press.

Galanter, Marc. 1984. Competing Equalities: Law and the Backward Classes in India. Berkeley: University of California Press.

Gender and Poverty in India. 1991. Washington, D.C.: The World Bank.

Ghurye, G. S. 1963. The Scheduled Tribes. Third Edition. Bombay: The Popular Prakashan.

Gold, Ann G. 1988. Fruitful Journeys: The Ways of Rajasthani Pilgrims. Berkeley: University of California Press.

Gold, Anne G. and Bhoju Ram Gujar. 1989. Of Gods, Trees and Boundaries: Divine Conservation in Rajasthan. Asian Folklore Studies Vol. 48: 211-229.

Gould, Harold A. 1964. A Jajmani System of North India: Its Structure, Magnitude and Meaning. Ethnology III: 12-41.

Government of India Planning Commission. 1985. Seventh Five Year Plan 1985-90. New Delhi.

Gupta, L. C. 1977. Rajasthan. In Land, Alienation and Reforestation in Tribal Communities in India, edited by S. N. Dubey and Ratna Murdia. Bombay: Himalaya Publishing House.

Hadden, Susan G. 1974. Rural Electrification and Decentralized Decision-Making in Rajasthan, India. Ithaca: Center for International Studies, Cornell University.

Hall, Andrew. 1990. India After the Elections. Asian Affairs Vol. 21 (Old Series 77) Part III: 312-323.

Hardiman, David. 1987. The Coming of the Devi: Adivasi Assertion in Western India. New Delhi: Oxford University Press.

―――. 1989. Adivasi Assertion in South Gujarat: The Devi Movement of 1922-3. *In* Subaltern Studies III: Writings on South Asian History and Society., edited by R. Guha, pp. 196-230. Oxford: Oxford University Press.

Harlan, Lindsey. 1992. Religion and Rajput Women: The Ethic of Protection in Contemporary Narratives. Berkeley: University of California Press.

Harris, Marvin. 1966. The Cultural Ecology of India's Sacred Cattle. Current Anthropology 7(1): 51-66.

Henderson, Carol. 1993. Famine Relief Policy and the Environment in India: The Case of Rajasthan. Unpublished paper.

―――. Forthcoming. The Great Cow Explosion in Rajasthan, India: Institutions, Landscape, and Livestock in Historical Ecological Perspective. *In* Advances in Historical Anthropology, edited by William Balee. New York: Columbia University Press.

Hitchcock, John T. 1958. The Idea of the Martial Rajput. Journal of American Folklore 71(281): 216-223.

Imperial Gazetteer of India. 1908. The Bhil Tribes. Vol. 8. New Edition. Oxford: Clarendon Press.

Inden, Ronald. 1990. Imagining India. Cambridge: Blackwell.

India. Census of India, 1981 (ICI). 1983a. Series 18, Rajasthan, Parts 13 A&B District Census Handbook, Udaipur District.

―――. 1983b. Series 18, Rajasthan, Part 2-A, General Population Tables.

―――. 1988 Series 18, Rajasthan, Part 9, Special Tables for Scheduled Tribes.

―――. 1991. Series 21 Rajasthan Provisional Population Totals.

India Today. October 15, 1987. "A Pagan Sacrifice."

―――. October 31, 1987. "Militant Defiance."

Indian Express. October 19, 1989. "The Royalty Factor in Rajasthan."

Jain, P. C. 1991. Social Movements Among Tribals: A Sociological Analysis of Bhils of Rajasthan. Jaipur: Rawat Publications.

Jones, Gregory. 1991. Peaceful Revolutionaries. Sewa Mandir: Udaipur.

Jones, J. Howard. 1991. Jain Shopkeepers and Moneylenders: Rural Informal Credit Networks in South Rajasthan. *In* The Assembly of Listeners: Jains in Society, edited by Michael Carrithers and Caroline Humphrey, pp. 109-138. Cambridge: Cambridge University Press.

Joshi, P. 1991. Herbal Drugs Used in Guinea Worm Disease by the Tribals of Southern Rajasthan. International Journal of Pharmacognosy 29(1): 33-38.

Klass, Morton. 1978. From Field to Factory: Community Structure and Industrialization in West Bengal. Philadelphia: Institute for the Study of Human Issues.

Kolenda, Pauline Mahar. 1963. Toward a Model of the Hindu Jajmani System. Human Organization 22(1): 11-31.

Koppers, W. and L. Jungblut. 1976. Bowmen of Mid-India. Wien: Acta Ethnologica et Linguistica.

Kothari, Rajni. 1986 NGOs, the State and World Capitalism. Economic and Political Weekly. 21(50).
Kottak, Conrad P. 1994. Cultural Anthropology. Sixth Edition. New York: McGraw-Hill, Inc.
Law, B. C. 1973. Tribes in Ancient India. Poona: Bhandarkar Oriental Research Institute.
Leach, E. R. editor. 1971. Aspects of Caste in South Asia, Ceylon and North-West Pakistan. Cambridge: Cambridge University Press.
Lynch, Owen M. 1969. The Politics of Untouchability. New York: Columbia University Press.
Mahar, Michael J. editor. 1972. The Untouchables in Contemporary India. Tucson: University of Arizona Press.
Malcolm, Sir John. 1970(1823) A Memoir of Central India. New Delhi: Sagar Publications.
_____. 1827 Essay on the Bhills. Transactions of the Royal Asiatic Society of Great Britain and Ireland. Vol. I.
Mandelbaum, David G. 1970. Society in India. Berkeley: University of California Press.
Mann, R. S. 1983. Structure and Role Dynamics Among the Bhils of Rajasthan: A Case of the Bhagats. *In* Tribal Movements of India, edited by K. S. Singh, Vol. 2, pp. 309-323. New Delhi: Manohar.
Masters, Brian. 1990. Maharana: the Story of the Rulers of Udaipur. Ahmedabad: Mapin Publishing Ltd.
Mathur, U. B. 1986. Folkways in Rajasthan. Jaipur: The Folklorists.
McCrindle, J. W. 1973(1882) Ancient India as Described by Ktesias the Knidian. New Delhi: Manohar Reprints.
McCurdy, David W. 1964. A Bhil Village of Rajasthan. Ph.D. dissertation. Department of Anthropology, Cornell University.
_____. 1971. The Changing Economy of an Indian Village. *In* Conformity and Conflict: Readings in Cultural Anthropology, edited by David McCurdy and James Spradley, pp. 219-228. Boston: Little, Brown and Company.
Mehta, Ajay. 1988. The Role of NGOs in Change: Their Relationship to Politics. Unpublished paper.
Mencher, Joan. 1974. The Caste System Upside Down, or The Not-So-Mysterious East. Current Anthropology 15(4): 469-492.
Michie, Barry H. 1978. Baniyas in the Indian Agrarian Economy: A Case of Stagnant Entrepreneurship. Journal of Asian Studies 37(4): 637-652.
_____. 1981. The Transformation of Agrarian Patron-Client Relations: Illustrations from India. American Ethnologist 8(1): 21-40.
Miller, Barbara D. 1981. The Endangered Sex: Neglect of Female Children in Rural North India. Ithaca: Cornell University Press.
Naik, T. B. 1956. The Bhils: A Study. Delhi: Bharatiya Adimjati Sevak Singh.
Nath, Y. V. S. 1960. Bhils of Ratanmal: An Analysis of the Social Structure of a Western Indian Community. Baroda: The Maharaja Sayajirao University of Baroda.
New York Times. March 24, 1967. "India To Conduct Inquiry on C.I.A."

_____. October 25, 1967. "Russians Say Ex-C.I.A. Man Who Spied in India Has Defected."
_____. August 22, 1990. "Affirmative Action Has India's Students Astir."
_____. January 24, 1993. "Demands Growing for an India That's Truly Hindu."
Oldenburg, Philip, editor. 1995. India Briefing: Staying the Course. Armonk, N.Y.: M. E. Sharpe.
Omvedt, Gail. 1989. Classes and Popular Struggles. *In* Sociology of "Developing Societies" South Asia, edited by Hamza Alavi and John Harriss, pp. 288-296. New York: Monthly Review Press.
_____. Reinventing Revolution: New Social Movements and the Socialist Tradition in India. Armonk, N.Y.: M. E. Sharpe.
Quanungo, K. L. 1969. Studies in Rajput History. New Delhi: S. Chand & Company
Raghuvanshi, Kalpana. 1983. Rural Women in Rajasthan. Jaipur: Kanchenjunga Publications.
Raheja, Gloria G. 1988. India: Caste, Kingship, and Dominance Reconsidered. Annual Review of Anthropology 17: 497-522.
Rahnema, Majid. 1992. Participation. *In* The Development Dictionary, edited by Wolfgang Sachs, pp. 116-132. London: Zed Books.
Rajasthan District Gazetteer. 1979. Jaipur: Directorate of District Gazetteers, Government of Rajasthan.
Rajasthan Election Atlas. 1990. Jaipur: Election Department Rajasthan.
Rajora, S. C. 1987. Social Structure and Tribal Elites. Udaipur: Himanshu Publications.
Rao, A. 1988. Tribal Social Stratification. Udaipur: Himanshu Publications.
Risley, H. H. 1969(1915) The People of India. Delhi: Oriental Books Reprint Corporation.
Rizvi, S. H. M. 1987. Mina, The Ruling Tribe of Rajasthan. New Delhi: B. R. Publishing Corp.
Rudolph, Lloyd I. 1993. Tod's Influence on Shymaldass's Historiography in *Vir Vinod*. Paper presented at 22nd Annual Conference on South Asia, Madison, Wisconsin, November 1993.
Rudolph, Susanne H. and Lloyd Rudolph. 1984. Essays on Rajputana: Reflections on History, Culture and Administration. New Delhi: Concept Publishing Co.
Sachs, Wolfgang. 1992. Introduction to The Development Dictionary. London: Zed Books.
Saint, Kishore. 1988. Drought in the Aravallis. Social Action Vol. 38: 129-37.
_____. 1989. Aravalli Bhils Show the Way. Indian Express September 29, 1989.
Saxena, H. S. 1989. Changing Agrarian Labour System in Rural Rajasthan. Journal of Rural Development 8(2): 147-165.
Schuurman, Frans J. 1993. Modernity, Post-Modernity and the New Social Movements. *In* Beyond the Impasses: New Directions in Development

References

Theory, edited by Frans J. Schuurman, pp. 187-206. London: Zed Books.
Sen, G. and C. Grown. 1987. Development, Crises and Alternative Visions: Third World Women's Perspectives. New York: Monthly Review Press.
Sharma, B. K. 1990. Peasant Movements in Rajasthan (1920-1949). Jaipur: Pointer Publishers.
Sharma, G. N. 1992. Kaviraj Shymaldas. *In* The Historians and Sources of History of Rajasthan, edited by G. N. Sharma and B. S Bhatnagar, pp. 57-70. Jaipur: Center for Rajasthan Studies, University of Rajasthan.
Sharma, H. S. 1986. Social and Political Awakening Among the Bhils of Mewar State During 1938-48. *In* Social and Political Awakening Among the Tribals of Rajasthan, edited by G. N. Sharma. Jaipur: Center for Rajasthan Studies, University of Rajasthan.
Shiva, Vandana. 1988. Staying Alive: Women, Ecology and Survival in India. New Delhi: Kali for Women.
Shymaldas, Kaviraj. 1985. Vir Vinod. Edited by M. Sharma and B. Gupta Jodhpur: Rajasthani Granthagar.
SIDA: SWACH Evaluation Rajasthan: India Final Report. 1994. Center for Development Studies: University of Wales.
Singh, J. P., N. N. Vyas and R. S. Mann. 1985. Tribal Women and Development. Udaipur: MLV Tribal Research and Training Institute.
Srinivas, M. N. 1952. Religion and Society Among the Coorgs of South India. Oxford: Clarenden Press.
_____. 1962. Caste in Modern India and Other Essays. Bombay: MMP Ltd.
_____. 1966. Social Change in Modern India. Berkeley: University of California Press.
Tandon, Rajesh. Growing Stateism. *In* Seminar 348: The Voluntary Option. August 1988 pp. 16-20.
The Hindu. August 8, 1989. "A Commission to the Rescue."
Thomas, Christopher. 1993. Perceptions of India in the Foreign Press. India International Quarterly Vol. 2: 1-2.
Times of India. August 9, 1989. "Digging With Kudal."
Tod, James. 1983(1829). Annals and Antiquities of Rajasthan. New Delhi: Oriental Books Reprint Company.
_____. 1839. Travels in Western India. New Delhi: Oriental Books Reprint Company.
Ubeshwar Vikas Mandal. 1992. Living Traditions: Local Water and Land Management Systems in the Bagdunda Region of the Mewar Aravallis. Udaipur: Chowdhary Printers.
Unia, Pramod. 1991. Social Action Group Strategies in the Indian Sub-Continent. Development in Practice 1(2): 84-96.
UNICEF. 1990. The Integrated Sanitation, Water, Guineaworm Control and Community Health Project-Rajasthan (SWACH) Third progress Report Covering the Period July 1988 to June 1989. Unpublished paper.
Unnithan, Maya. 1991. Caste, 'Tribe,' and Gender in South Rajasthan. Cambridge Anthropology 15:1: 27-45.

Unnithan-Kumar, Maya. 1991. Gender and 'Tribal' Identity in Western India. Economic and Political Weekly April 27, 1991: WS36-38.

Vyas, N. N. 1980. Bondage and Exploitation in Tribal India. Jaipur: Rawat Publications.

Vyas, N. N. and N. D. Chaudhary. 1968. Sagri--An Economic Institution Among the Bhils of Rajasthan. Tribe 5(3): 14-36.

Wadley, Susan
  1989 the Village in 1984. *In* Behind Mud Walls 1930-1960, by William and Charlotte Wiser, pp. 276-312. Berkeley: University of California Press.

Webb, A. W. T. 1941. These Ten Years: A Short Account of the 1941 Census Operations in Rajputana and Ajmer-Merwara. Rajputana Census Volume 24--Part 1. Bombay: Census Department of India.

Weisgrau, Maxine K. 1993. The Social and Political Relations of Development: NGOs and Adivasi Bhils in Rural Rajasthan. Ph.D. dissertation, Department of Anthropology, Columbia University.

_____. Forthcoming. Gavri. *In* Encyclopedia of South Asian Folklore. New York: Garland Press.

Wiser, William H. 1988(1930). The Hindu Jajmani System. New Delhi: Munshiram Manoharlal Publishers.

Wood, John R. 1995. On the Periphery but in the Thick of It. *In* India Briefing: Staying the Course, edited by Philip Oldenburg, pp. 23-46. Armonk, N.Y.: M. E. Sharpe.

Woodcock, George. 1962. The Rajputs, Sons of Kings. History Today 12(10): 696-704.

Film and video:

Dorman, Joseph. 1992. Common Destinies: Deserts of Silk. International Commentary Service (ICS) Inc.

Index

Adivasi 10, 12
Adsi padsi 148
Agriculture 23-24, 118; and animal use 120; and deforestation 120, 136, 204; income 121; supplemental income 26
Annals and Antiquities of Rajasthan 32
Anthropology and development 5-6, 54
Aravallis 19, 28
Astha 87, 105

Bagdunda 49-50, 143, 153, elections in 174-189, 197
Bharatiya Janata Party (BJP) 70, 107, 175, 209
Bhatia, Mr. B. N. 53, 84, 140, 144
Bhil identity and terminology, construction of 11, 31, 58-68; self-identity terminology 12, 76-77; and tourism discourse 47
Bhil uprisings and social reform movements 38-41
Bhil-Rajput relations 61-65, 70-72, 77-78

Bhils:
British and 57-61; forced labor 63-65, 73-77; households 118-119; land holdings 24, 118; marriage patterns and exchanges 124; perspectives on poverty and economic mobility 23, 43-44, 75-76, 139-140, 160; politics and 70, 131, 145, 174-189; political institutions 131-133; religion 69-71; ritual expenditures 123, 130; social reform (contemporary) 77; widows and remarriage 128; women and gender issues 127-30, 157-168
Bhopas 70, 191, 194
Bigha 55fn
Birth control 171-172
British race theory in India 57-60; rule in Mewar 33, 34-43

Caste system 8-9, 29-30, 55fn; changes in 42; group mobility within

(Sanskritization) 29, 31,
55fn, and politics 8, 9, 11,
70
Census of India 67; British
period 66
Christian missionaries in
Mewar 35-37, in India 81
CIA involvement in India,
allegations of 106
Congress(I) Party 111, 176

Dalits 11
Debt (rural households) 26,
121-123
Deforestation 26-29, 119,
136-139; and NGO strategy
29, 190-192, 205;
perception of causes 28;
perceptions of solutions
Development 1, 2, 3, 4-5;
conflicting definitions of 5;
hierarchy in 14; local-global
linkages 2, 102-106; and
NGOs 79-82, 90-91
Deliege, Robert 57, 65
Dowry 46,
Drought 24, 26-27

Extended families 45, in urban
Udaipur 44-45

Fertilizer and manure 26
fieldwork 49-54
Ford Foundation 83
Forestry Department 134, 181-183
Fried, Morton 57
Funding of NGOs, foreign
sources 106, 189 Indian
domestic sources 107

Gandhi, Rajiv 110
Gameti 132
Gavri 53, 194
Gogunda 22

Guineaworm disease 150, 155

Hadmatiya 112-114
Hallam, Henry 32
Harijans 11
Health issues and medical care
49; 169-172

Imperial Gazetteer 59
Income-generating projects
105, state-based
implications 103-104
Indian National Congress 41

Jajmani 41-43
Jati 8, 76

Kothari, Rajni 103-4
Kudal Commission 110

Land holdings 24, 118
Literacy and education 22,
140, 166; rural-urban bias
22

Maharanas of Mewar 6, 31,
32, 33, 204
Meghwals 12, 30-31, 70
Mehta, Ajay 109
Mehta, Mohan Singh 15, 85-87
Mewar princely state 34-35;
British rule in 35-38
Mewar Bhil Corps 35-37, 39
Monsoons 27
Morwa 50, 72

Narmada River Valley Dam
Project, NGO opposition to
102-103
NGOs (Non-governmental
organizations 1, 3, 79-81
NGOs and government 15,
103-111
NGOs in India 81-84

NGOs in Rajasthan 47-49, 98-99
NGOs in Udaipur 12-15, 49-51, 84-9; funding of 89, gender programs 158-180, hierarchy in 16, 94, 96, 156, 186-203; history of 84-88 "NGO Row" 51; intercaste relationships and activities 92; patronage and 77-78, 198-200; politics and 70, 174-189; proliferation in 13, 79-80, 88-89, 188-189, 193; relationships between 93, 96, 152, 190-192; relations with government 15, 106; strategy 14-15, 16, 84, 88, 91, 94, 96, 100-101; 154-155; violence 111, 112; volunteer vs. paid labor 165-66

Panchayat Raj 133, 134-35
Patronage systems (rural) 41; 72, changes in 42, 70-79
People's participation 98-99, 100-101, 156, 186
Phala 24, 70-72

Rahat 24, 25
Rajasthan 7, 18-21; British rule in Rajputana 31-33, 56fn; historiography 31-32; underdevelopment in 17-19; women and underdevelopment 158
Rajputs 18, 19, 27, 29, 30, 33, 188; Bhil-Rajput relations 61- 65; 70-76; women and family 44
Rajputization 29, 31
Risley, Sir Herbert H. 59

Saint, Kishore 87, 105-106

Sati 18
Scheduled Castes and Scheduled Tribes (SCs and STs) 7, 10; in Udaipur District 7; and politics 176; reservation system, 67-68, 188
Sewa Mandir 51, 86-87, 127, 143, 174, 189, 193, 200, 209
Shymaldas, Kaviraj 32-33
Social movements 82
Social Action Groups 82
Solaria 24, 50-51, 74-76, 117-123, 131, 143
Srivastava, Om and Ginny Dobson 87
Stepwells 55fn, 151, 155
SWACH (Sanitation, Water and Community Health) project 149-156

Thakurs 27, 204
Thar Desert 28
Thikanas 34,
Tod, James 32
Tourism 6, 47-49
Tribe and race 57-58
"Tribe" and "Tribal" ambiguity in terminology 57
Trickle Up 53

Ubeshwar Vikas Mandal (UVM) 49, 84, 87, 144-149; 181-184, 190-193, 196-7
Udaipur District 7, 9, 22; agriculture 23; roads and transport 50; rural poverty 9; SC/STs in 7, 67
Udaipur city 6-7, 22; tourism in 47
UNICEF 149
"Untouchables" 11

Violence and NGO activity
113-115
Vir Vinod 32-33

Wells and water technology
23-25, 50, 135, 192-3
Witchcraft, accusations of 129-130
Women and gender issues: and agriculture 136-139; urban Udaipur 44-47, rural NGO programs 157-166, 201-202